CAPTAINS OF INDUSTRY

OR

MEN OF BUSINESS WHO DID SOMETHING BESIDES MAKING MONEY

A BOOK FOR YOUNG AMERICANS

BY

JAMES PARTON

Fredonia Books
Amsterdam, The Netherlands

Captains of Industry:
Men of Business who did Something Besides
Making Money

by
James Parton

ISBN: 1-4101-0062-6

Reprinted from the 1896 edition

Fredonia Books
Amsterdam, The Netherlands
http://www.fredoniabooks.com

In order to make original editions of historical works available to scholars at an economical price, this facsimile of the original edition of 1896 is reproduced from the best available copy and has been digitally enhanced to improve legibility, but the text remains unaltered to retain historical authenticity.

PREFACE.

In this volume are presented examples of men who shed lustre upon ordinary pursuits, either by the superior manner in which they exercised them or by the noble use they made of the leisure which success in them usually gives. Such men are the nobility of republics. The American people were fortunate in having at an early period an ideal man of this kind in Benjamin Franklin, who, at the age of forty-two, just mid-way in his life, deliberately relinquished the most profitable business of its kind in the colonies for the sole purpose of developing electrical science. In this, as in other respects, his example has had great influence with his countrymen.

A distinguished author, who lived some years at Newport, has expressed the opinion that the men who occupy the villas of that emerald isle exert very little power compared with that of an orator or a writer. To be, he adds, at the head of a normal school, or to be a professor in a college, is to

have a sway over the destinies of America which
reduces to nothingness the power of successful men
of business.

Being myself a member of the fraternity of writers, I suppose I ought to yield a joyful assent to
such remarks. It is flattering to the self-love of
those who drive along Bellevue Avenue in a shabby
hired vehicle to be told that they are personages of
much more consequence than the heavy capitalist
who swings by in a resplendent curricle, drawn by
two matched and matchless steeds, in a six-hun-
dred dollar harness. Perhaps they are. But I advise young men who aspire to serve their generation effectively not to undervalue the importance
of the gentleman in the curricle.

One of the individuals who has figured lately
in the society of Newport is the proprietor of an
important newspaper. He is not a writer, nor a
teacher in a normal school, but he wields a considerable power in this country. Fifty men write
for the journal which he conducts, some of whom
write to admiration, for they are animated by a
humane and patriotic spirit. The late lamented
Ivory Chamberlain was a writer whose leading edi-
torials were of national value. But, mark: a tele-
gram of ten words from that young man at Newport, written with perspiring hand in a pause of
the game of polo, determines without appeal the

course of the paper in any crisis of business or politics.

I do not complain of this arrangement of things. I think it is just; I know it is unalterable.

It is then of the greatest possible importance that the men who control during their lifetime, and create endowments when they are dead, should share the best civilization of their age and country. It is also of the greatest importance that young men whom nature has fitted to be leaders should, at the beginning of life, take to the steep and thorny path which leads at length to mastership.

Most of these chapters were published originally in "The Ledger" of New York, and a few of them in "The Youths' Companion" of Boston, the largest two circulations in the country. I have occasionally had reason to think that they were of some service to young readers, and I may add that they represent more labor and research than would be naturally supposed from their brevity. Perhaps in this new form they may reach and influence the minds of future leaders in the great and growing realm of business. I should pity any young man who could read the briefest account of what has been done in manufacturing towns by such men as John Smedley and Robert Owen without forming a secret resolve to do something similar if ever he should win the opportunity.

TABLE OF CONTENTS.

PORTRAITS.

——◆——

CAPTAINS OF INDUSTRY.

DAVID MAYDOLE,

HAMMER-MAKER.

WHEN a young man begins to think of making
his fortune, his first notion usually is to go away
from home to some very distant place. At present,
the favorite spot is Colorado; awhile ago it was
California; and old men remember when Buffalo
was about as far west as the most enterprising person thought of venturing.

It is not always a foolish thing to go out into
the world far beyond the parent nest, as the young
birds do in midsummer. But I can tell you, boys,
from actual inquiry, that a great number of the
most important and famous business men of the
United States struck down roots where they were
first planted, and where no one supposed there was
room or chance for any large thing to grow.

I will tell you a story of one of these men, as
I heard it from his own lips some time ago, in a
beautiful village where I lectured.

He was an old man then; and a curious thing about him was that, although he was too deaf to hear one word of a public address, even of the loudest speaker, he not only attended church every Sunday, but was rarely absent when a lecture was delivered.

While I was performing on that occasion, I saw him sitting just in front of the platform, sleeping the sleep of the just till the last word was uttered.

Upon being introduced to this old gentleman in his office, and learning that his business was to make hammers, I was at a loss for a subject of conversation, as it never occurred to me that there was anything to be said about hammers.

I have generally possessed a hammer, and frequently inflicted damage on my fingers therewith, but I had supposed that a hammer was simply a hammer, and that hammers were very much alike. At last I said,—

" And here you make hammers for mankind, Mr. Maydole ? "

You may have noticed the name of David Maydole upon hammers.   He is the man.

" Yes," said he, " I have made hammers here for twenty-eight years."

" Well, then," said I, shouting in his best ear, " by this time you ought to be able to make a pretty good hammer."

" No, I can't," was his reply.   " I can't make a pretty good hammer.   I make the best hammer that's made."

That was strong language. I thought, at first, he meant it as a joke; but I soon found it was no joke at all.

He had made hammers the study of his lifetime, and, after many years of thoughtful and laborious experiment, he had actually produced an article, to which, with all his knowledge and experience, he could suggest no improvement.

I was astonished to discover how many points there are about an instrument which I had always supposed a very simple thing. I was surprised to learn in how many ways a hammer can be bad.

But, first, let me tell you how he came to think of hammers.

There he was, forty years ago, in a small village of the State of New York; no railroad yet, and even the Erie Canal many miles distant. He was the village blacksmith, his establishment consisting of himself and a boy to blow the bellows.

He was a good deal troubled with his hammers. Sometimes the heads would fly off. If the metal was too soft, the hammer would spread out and wear away; if it was too hard, it would split.

At that time blacksmiths made their own hammers, and he knew very little about mixing ores so as to produce the toughest iron. But he was particularly troubled with the hammer getting off the handle, a mishap which could be dangerous as well as inconvenient.

At this point of his narrative the old gentleman

showed a number of old hammers, such as were in use before he began to improve the instrument; and it was plain that men had tried very hard before him to overcome this difficulty.

One hammer had an iron rod running down through the handle with a nut screwed on at the end. Another was wholly composed of iron, the head and handle being all of one piece. There were various other devices, some of which were exceedingly clumsy and awkward.

At last, he hit upon an improvement which led to his being able to put a hammer upon a handle in such a way that it would stay there. He made what is called an adze-handled hammer, the head being attached to the handle after the manner of an adze.

The improvement consists in merely making *a longer hole* for the handle to go into, by which device it has a much firmer hold of the head, and can easily be made extremely tight.

With this improvement, if the handle is well seasoned and well wedged, there is no danger of the head flying off. He made some other changes, all of them merely for his own convenience, without a thought of going into the manufacture of hammers.

The neighborhood in which he lived would have scarcely required half a dozen new hammers per annum. But one day there came to the village six carpenters to work upon a new church, and one of these men, having left his hammer at home, came to David Maydole's blacksmith's shop to get one made.

"Make me as good a hammer," said the carpenter, "as you know how."

That was touching David upon a tender place.

"As good a one as I know how?" said he. "But perhaps you don't want to pay for as good a one as I know how to make."

"Yes, I do," replied the man; "I want a good hammer."

The blacksmith made him one of his best. It was probably the best hammer that had ever been made in the world, since it contained two or three important improvements never before combined in the instrument.

The carpenter was delighted with it, and showed it, with a good deal of exultation, to his five companions; every man of whom came the next day to the shop and wanted one just like it. They did not understand all the blacksmith's notions about tempering and mixing the metals, but they saw at a glance that the head and the handle were so united that there never was likely to be any divorce between them.

To a carpenter building a wooden house, the mere removal of that one defect was a boon beyond price; he could hammer away with confidence, and without fear of seeing the head of his hammer leap into the next field, unless stopped by a comrade's head.

When all the six carpenters had been supplied with these improved hammers, the contractor came and ordered two more. He seemed to think, and, in fact, said as much, that the blacksmith ought to make *his* hammers a little better than those he had made for the men.

"I can't make any better ones," said honest David. "When I make a thing, I make it as well as I can, no matter who it's for."

Soon after, the store-keeper of the village, seeing what excellent hammers these were, gave the blacksmith a magnificent order for two dozen, which, in due time, were placed upon his counter for sale.

At this time something happened to David Maydole which may fairly be called good luck; and you will generally notice events of the kind in the lives of meritorious men. "Fortune favors the brave," is an old saying, and good luck in business is very apt to befall the man who could do very well without it.

It so happened that a New York dealer in tools, named Wood, whose store is still kept in Chatham Street, New York, happened to be in the village getting orders for tools. As soon as his eye fell upon those hammers, he saw their merits, and bought them all. He did more. He left a standing order for as many hammers of that kind as David Maydole could make.

That was the beginning. The young blacksmith

hired a man or two, then more men, and made
more hammers, and kept on making hammers during the whole of his active life, employing at last a
hundred and fifteen men.

During the first twenty years, he was frequently
experimenting with a view to improve the hammer.
He discovered just the best combination of ores to
make his hammers hard enough, without being too
hard.

He gradually found out precisely the best form
of every part. There is not a turn or curve about
either the handle or the head which has not been
patiently considered, and reconsidered, and considered again, until no further improvement seemed
possible. Every handle is seasoned three years, or
until there is no shrink left in it.

Perhaps the most important discovery which he
made was that a perfect tool cannot be made by
machinery.

Naturally, his first thought, when he found his
business increasing, was to apply machinery to the
manufacture, and for some years several parts of
the process were thus performed. Gradually, his
machines were discarded, and for many years before his retirement, every portion of the work was
done by hand.

Each hammer is hammered out from a piece of
iron, and is tempered over a slow charcoal fire,
under the inspection of an experienced man. He
looks as though he were cooking his hammers on a

charcoal furnace, and he watches them until the process is complete, as a cook watches mutton chops.

I heard some curious things about the management of this business. The founder never did anything to "push" it. He never advertised. He never reduced the price of his hammers because other manufacturers were doing so.

His only care, he said, had been to make a perfect hammer, to make just as many of them as people wanted, and *no more*, and to sell them at a fair price. If people did not want his hammers, he did not want to make them. If they did not want to pay what they were worth, they were welcome to buy cheaper ones of some one else.

For his own part, his wants were few, and he was ready at any time to go back to his blacksmith's shop.

The old gentleman concluded his interesting narration by making me a present of one of his hammers, which I now cherish among my treasures.

If it had been a picture, I should have had it framed and hung up over my desk, a perpetual admonition to me to do my work well; not too fast; not too much of it; not with any showy false polish; not letting anything go till I had done all I could to make it what it should be.

In telling this little story, I have told thousands of stories. Take the word *hammer* out of it, and put *glue* in its place, and you have the history of

Peter Cooper. By putting in other words, you can make the true history of every great business in the world which has lasted thirty years.

The true "protective system," of which we hear so much, is *to make the best article;* and he who does this need not buy a ticket for Colorado.

2

ICHABOD WASHBURN,

WIRE-MAKER

———◆———

OF all our manufactures few have had a more rapid development than wire-making. During the last thirty years the world has been girdled by telegraphic wires and cables, requiring an immense and continuous supply of the article. In New York alone two hundred pianos a week have been made, each containing miles of wire. There have been years during which a garment composed chiefly of wire was worn by nearly every woman in the land, even by the remotest and poorest.

Who has supplied all these millions of miles of wire? A large part of the answer to this question is given when we pronounce the name at the head of this article, Ichabod Washburn. In the last years of his life he had seven hundred men at Worcester making wire, the product of whose labor was increased a hundred fold by machinery which he had invented or adapted.

It is curious to note how he seemed to stumble into the business just in the nick of time. I say, *seemed ;* but, in truth, he had been prepared for success in it by a long course of experience and training. He was a poor widow's son, born on the coast of Massachusetts, a few miles from Plymouth Rock; his father having died in early manhood, when this boy and a twin brother were two months old. His mother, suddenly left with three little children, and having no property except the house in which she lived, supported her family by weaving, in which her children from a very early age could give her some help. She kept them at school, however, during part of the winter, and instilled into their minds good principles. When this boy was nine years of age she was obliged, as the saying was, " to put him out to live " to a master five miles from her house.

On his way to his new home he was made to feel the difference between a hard master and a kind mother. Having a quick intelligent mind, he questioned the man concerning the objects they passed. At length the boy saw a windmill, and he asked what that was.

"Don't ask me so many questions, boy," answered the man, in a harsh, rough voice.

The little fellow was silenced, and he vividly remembered the event, the tone, and the scene, to old age. His employer was a maker of harness, carriages, and trunks, and it was the boy's business to take care of a horse and two cows, light fires, chop wood, run errands, and work in the shop. He never forgot the cold winter mornings, and the loud voice of his master rousing him from sleep to make the fire, and go out to the barn and get the milking done before daylight. His sleeping-place was a loft above the shop reached by a ladder. Being always a timid boy, he suffered extremely from fear in the dark and lonely garret of a building where no one else slept, and to which he had to grope his way alone.

What would the dainty boys of the present time think of going to mill on a frosty morning astride of a bag of corn on the horse's back, without stockings or shoes and with trousers half way up to the knees? On one occasion the little Ichabod was so thoroughly chilled that he had to stop at a house to get warm, and the good woman took pity on him, made him put on a pair of long black stockings, and a pair of her own shoes. Thus equipped, with his long black legs extending far out of his short trousers, and the woman's shoes lashed to his feet, he presented a highly ludicrous appearance, and one which, he thought, might have conveyed a valuable hint to his master. In the daytime he was usually employed in the shop making harnesses, a business in which he became expert. He served this man five years, or until he was fourteen years of age, when he made a complete harness for one of his cousins, which rendered excellent service for many years, and a part of it lasted almost as long as the maker.

Thus, at fourteen, he had completed his first apprenticeship, and had learned his first trade. The War of 1812 having given a sudden start to manufactures in this country, he went to work in a cotton factory for a while, where, for the first time in his life, he saw complicated machinery. Like a true Yankee as he was, he was strongly attracted by it, and proposed to learn the machinist's trade. His guardian opposed the scheme strongly, on the ground that, in all probability, by the time he had learned the trade the country would be so full of factories that there would be no more machinery required.

Thus discouraged, he did the next best thing: he went apprentice to the blacksmith's trade, near Worcester, where he was destined to spend the rest of his life. He was sixteen years of age when he began this second apprenticeship; but he was still one of the most timid and bashful of lads. In a fragment of autobiography found among his papers after his death he says: —

"I arrived at Worcester about one o'clock, at Syke's tavern where we were to dine; but the sight of the long table in the dining-room so overpowered my bashful spirit that I left the room and went into the yard without dinner to wait till the stage was ready."

On reaching his new home, eighty miles from his mother's house, he was so overcome by homesickness that, the first night, he sobbed himself to sleep. Soon he became interested in his shop and in his work, made rapid progress, and approved him-self a skillful hand. Having been brought up to go to church every Sunday, he now hired a seat in the gallery of one of the churches at fifty cents a year, which he earned in over-time by forging pot-hooks. Every cent of his spending money was earned in similar ways. Once he made six toasting - irons, and carried them to Worcester, where he sold them for a dollar and a quarter each, taking a book in part payment. When his sister was married he made her a wedding present of a toasting - iron. Nor was it an easy matter for an apprentice then to do work in over-time, for he was expected to labor in his master's service from sunrise to sunset in the summer, and from sunrise to nine o'clock in the winter.

On a bright day in August, 1818, his twentieth birthday, he was out of his time, and, according to the custom of the period, he celebrated the joyful event by a game of ball! In a few months, having saved a little money, he went into business as a manufacturer of ploughs, in which he had some lit-tle success. But still yearning to know more of ma-chinery he entered upon what we may call his third apprenticeship, in an armory near Worcester, where he soon acquired skill enough to do the finer parts of the work. Then he engaged in the manufac-ture of lead pipe, in which he attained a moderate success.

At length, in 1831, being then thirty-three years

old, he began the business of making wire, in which
he continued during the remainder of his active
life. The making of wire, especially the finer and
better kinds, is a nice operation. Until Ichabod
Washburn entered into the business, wire of good
quality was not made in the United States; and
there was only one house in Great Britain that had
the secret of making the steel wire for pianos, and
they had had a monopoly of the manufacture for
about eighty years.

Wire is made by drawing a rod of soft, hot iron
through a hole which is too small for it. If a still
smaller sized wire is desired, it is drawn through
a smaller hole, and this process is repeated until
the required size is attained. Considerable power
is needed to draw the wire through, and the hole
through which it is drawn is soon worn larger.
The first wire machine that Washburn ever saw
was arranged with a pair of self-acting pincers
which drew a foot of wire and then had to let go
and take a fresh hold. By this machine a man
could make fifty pounds of coarse wire in a day.
He soon improved this machine so that the pincers
drew fifteen feet without letting go; and by this
improvement alone the product of one man's labor was increased about eleven times. A good
workman could make five or six hundred pounds a
day by it. By another improvement which Washburn adopted the product was increased to twenty-
five hundred pounds a day.

He was now in his element. He always had a partner to manage the counting-room part of the business, which he disliked.

" I never," said he, " had taste or inclination for it, always preferring to be among the machinery, doing the work and handling the tools I was used to, though oftentimes at the expense of a smutty face and greasy hands."

His masterpiece in the way of invention was his machinery for making steel wire for pianos, — a branch of the business which was urged upon him by the late Jonas Chickering, piano manufacturer, of Boston. The most careless glance at the strings of a piano shows us that the wire must be exquisitely tempered and most thoroughly wrought, in order to remain in tune, subjected as they are to a steady pull of many tons. Washburn experimented for years in perfecting his process, and he was never satisfied until he was able to produce a wire which he could honestly claim to be the best in the world. He had amazing success in his business. At one time he was making two hundred and fifty thousand yards of crinoline wire every day. His whole daily product was seven tons of iron wire, and five tons of steel wire.

This excellent man, in the midst of a success which would have dazzled and corrupted some men, retained all the simplicity, the modesty, and the generosity of his character. He felt, as he said, nowhere so much at home as among his own machinery, surrounded by thoughtful mechanics, dressed like them for work, and possibly with a black smudge upon his face. In his person, however, he was scrupulously clean and nice, a hater of tobacco and all other polluting things and lowering influences.

Rev. H. T. Cheever, the editor of his "Memorials," mentions also that he remained to the end of his life in the warmest sympathy with the natural desires of the workingman. He was a collector of facts concerning the condition of workingmen everywhere, and for many years cherished a project of making his own business a coöperative one.

"He believed," remarks Mr. Cheever, "that the skilled and faithful manual worker, as well as the employer, was entitled to a participation in the net proceeds of business, over and above his actual wages. He held that in this country the entire people are one great working class, working with brains, or hands, or both, who should therefore act in harmony — the brain-workers and the hand-workers — for the equal rights of all, without distinction of color, condition, or religion. Holding that capital is accumulated labor, and wealth the creation of capital and labor combined, he thought it to be the wise policy of the large capitalists and corporations to help in the process of elevating and advancing labor by a proffered interest."

These were the opinions of a man who had had long experience in all the grades, from half-frozen apprentice to millionaire manufacturer.

He died in 1868, aged seventy-one years, leaving an immense estate; which, however, chiefly consisted in his wire-manufactory. He had made it a principle not to accumulate money for the sake of money, and he gave away in his lifetime a large portion of his revenue every year. He bequeathed to charitable associations the sum of four hundred and twenty-four thousand dollars, which was distributed among twenty-one objects. His great bequests were to institutions of practical and homely benevolence: to the Home for Aged Women and Widows, one hundred thousand dollars; to found a hospital and free dispensary, the same amount; smaller sums to industrial schools and mission schools.

It was one of his fixed convictions that boys cannot be properly fitted for life without being both taught and required to use their hands, as well as their heads, and it was long his intention to found some kind of industrial college. Finding that something of the kind was already in existence at Worcester, he made a bequest to it of one hundred and ten thousand dollars. The institution is called the Worcester County Free Institute of Industrial Science.

ELIHU BURRITT,

THE LEARNED BLACKSMITH

ELIHU BURRITT, with whom we have all been familiar for many years as the Learned Blacksmith, was born in 1810 at the beautiful town of New Britain, in Connecticut, about ten miles from Hartford. He was the youngest son in an old-fashioned family of ten children. His father owned and cultivated a small farm; but spent the winters at the shoemaker's bench, according to the rational custom of Connecticut in that day. When Elihu was sixteen years of age, his father died and the lad soon after apprenticed himself to a blacksmith in his native village.

He was an ardent reader of books from childhood up; and he was enabled to gratify this taste by means of a small village library, which contained several books of history, of which he was naturally fond. This boy, however, was a shy, devoted student, brave to maintain what he thought right, but so bashful that he was known to hide in the cellar when his parents were going to have company.

As his father's long sickness had kept him out of

school for some time, he was the more earnest to learn during his apprenticeship; particularly mathematics, since he desired to become, among other things, a good surveyor. He was obliged to work from ten to twelve hours a day at the forge; but while he was blowing the bellows he employed his mind in doing sums in his head. His biographer gives a specimen of these calculations which he wrought out without making a single figure: —

" How many yards of cloth, three feet in width, cut into strips an inch wide, and allowing half an inch at each end for the lap, would it require to reach from the centre of the earth to the surface, and how much would it all cost at a shilling a yard ? "

He would go home at night with several of these sums done in his head, and report the results to an elder brother who had worked his way through Williams College. His brother would perform the calculations upon a slate, and usually found his answers correct.

When he was about half through his apprenticeship he suddenly took it into his head to learn Latin, and began at once through the assistance of the same elder brother. In the evenings of one winter he read the Æneid of Virgil; and, after going on for a while with Cicero and a few other Latin authors, he began Greek. During the winter months he was obliged to spend every hour of daylight at the forge, and even in the summer his leisure minutes were few and far between. But he carried his Greek grammar in his hat, and often found a chance, while he was waiting for a large piece of iron to get hot, to open his book with his black fingers, and go through a pronoun, an adjective or part of a verb, without being noticed by his fellow-apprentices.

So he worked his way until he was out of his time, when he treated himself to a whole quarter's schooling at his brother's school, where he studied mathematics, Latin and other languages. Then he went back to the forge, studying hard in the evenings at the same branches, until he had saved a little money; when he resolved to go to New Haven, and spend a winter in study. It was far from his thoughts, as it was from his means, to enter Yale College; but he seems to have had an idea that the very atmosphere of the college would assist him. He was still so timid that he determined to work his way without asking the least assistance from a professor or tutor.

He took lodgings at a cheap tavern in New Haven, and began the very next morning a course of heroic study. As soon as the fire was made in the sitting-room of the inn, which was at half-past four in the morning, he took possession, and studied German until breakfast-time, which was half-past seven. When the other boarders had gone to business, he sat down to Homer's Iliad, of which he knew nothing, and with only a dictionary to help him.

"The proudest moment of my life," he once wrote, "was when I had first gained the full meaning of the first fifteen lines of that noble work. I took a short triumphal walk in favor of that exploit."

Just before the boarders came back for their dinner, he put away all his Greek and Latin books, and took up a work in Italian, because it was less likely to attract the notice of the noisy crowd. After dinner he fell again upon his Greek, and in the evening read Spanish until bed-time. In this way he lived and labored for three months, a solitary student in the midst of a community of students; his mind imbued with the grandeurs and dignity of the past, while eating flapjacks and molasses at a poor tavern.

Returning to his home in New Britain, he obtained the mastership of an academy in a town near by: but he could not bear a life wholly sedentary; and, at the end of a year, abandoned his school and became what is called a "runner" for one of the manufacturers of New Britain. This business he pursued until he was about twenty-five years of age, when, tired of wandering, he came home again, and set up a grocery and provision store, in which he invested all the money he had saved. Soon came the commercial crash of 1837, and he was involved in the widespread ruin. He lost the whole of his capital, and had to begin the world anew.

He resolved to return to his studies in the lan-

guages of the East. Unable to buy or find the
necessary books, he tied up his effects in a small
handkerchief, and walked to Boston, one hundred
miles distant, hoping there to find a ship in which
he could work his passage across the ocean, and
collect oriental works from port to port. He could
not find a berth. He turned back, and walked as
far as Worcester, where he found work, and found
something else which he liked better. There is an
Antiquarian Society at Worcester, with a large
and peculiar library, containing a great number of
books in languages not usually studied, such as
the Icelandic, the Russian, the Celtic dialects, and
others. The directors of the Society placed all
their treasures at his command, and he now divided his time between hard study of languages
and hard labor at the forge. To show how he
passed his days, I will copy an entry or two from
a private diary he then kept : —

"Monday, June 18. Headache; 40 pages Cuvier's Theory of the Earth; 64 pages French; 11
hours forging.

"Tuesday, June 19. 60 lines Hebrew; 30 pages
French; 10 pages of Cuvier; 8 lines Syriac; 10
lines Danish; 10 lines Bohemian; 9 lines Polish;
15 names of stars; 10 hours forging.

"Wednesday, June 20. 25 lines Hebrew; 8
lines Syriac; 11 hours forging."

He spent five years at Worcester in such labors
as these. When work at his trade became slack.

or when he had earned a little more money than usual, he would spend more time in the library; but, on the other hand, when work in the shop was pressing, he could give less time to study. After a while, he began to think that he might perhaps earn his subsistence in part by his knowledge of languages, and thus save much waste of time and vitality at the forge. He wrote a letter to William Lincoln, of Worcester, who had aided and encouraged him; and in this letter he gave a short history of his life, and asked whether he could not find employment in translating some foreign work into English. Mr. Lincoln was so much struck with his letter that he sent it to Edward Everett, and he having occasion soon after to address a convention of teachers, read it to his audience as a wonderful instance of the pursuit of knowledge under difficulties. Mr. Everett prefaced it by saying that such a resolute purpose of improvement against such obstacles excited his admiration, and even his veneration.

"It is enough," he added, "to make one who has good opportunities for education hang his head in shame."

All this, including the whole of the letter, was published in the newspapers, with eulogistic comments, in which the student was spoken of as the Learned Blacksmith. The bashful scholar was overwhelmed with shame at finding himself suddenly famous. However, it led to his entering upon public life. Lecturing was then coming into vogue, and he was frequently invited to the platform. Accordingly, he wrote a lecture, entitled "Application and Genius," in which he endeavored to show that there is no such thing as genius, but that all extraordinary attainments are the results of application. After delivering this lecture sixty times in one season, he went back to his forge at Worcester, mingling study with labor in the old way.

On sitting down to write a new lecture for the following season, on the "Anatomy of the Earth," a certain impression was made upon his mind, which changed the current of his life. Studying the globe, he was impressed with the *need* that one nation has of other nations, and one zone of another zone ; the tropics producing what assuages life in the northern latitudes, and northern lands furnishing the means of mitigating tropical discomforts. He felt that the earth was made for friendliness and coöperation, not for fierce competition and bloody wars.

Under the influence of these feelings, his lecture became an eloquent plea for peace, and to this object his after life was chiefly devoted. The dispute with England upon the Oregon boundary induced him to go to England, with the design of traveling on foot from village to village, preaching peace, and exposing the horrors and folly of war. His addresses attracting attention, he was invited to speak to larger bodies, and, in short, he spent twenty years of his life as a lecturer upon peace, organizing Peace Congresses, advocating low uniform rates of ocean postage, and spreading abroad among the people of Europe the feeling which issued, at length, in the arbitration of the dispute between the United States and Great Britain; an event which posterity will, perhaps, consider the most important of this century. He heard Victor Hugo say at the Paris Congress of 1850: —

"A day will come when a cannon will be exhibited in public museums, just as an instrument of torture is now, and people will be amazed that such a thing could ever have been."

If he had sympathetic hearers, he produced upon them extraordinary effects. Nathaniel P. Rogers, one of the heroes of the Anti-slavery agitation, chanced to hear him in Boston in 1845 on his favorite subject of Peace. He wrote soon after: —

"I had been introduced to Elihu Burritt the day before, and was much interested in his original appearance, and desirous of knowing him further. I had not formed the highest opinion of his liberality. But on entering the hall my friends and I soon forgot everything but the speaker. The dim-lit hall, the handful audience, the contrast of both with the illuminated chapel and ocean multitude assembled overhead, bespeak painfully the estimation in which the great cause of peace is held in Christendom. I wish all Christendom could have

heard Elihu Burritt's speech. One unbroken, un-
abated stream it was of profound and lofty and
original eloquence. I felt riveted to my seat till
he finished it. There was no oratory about it, in
the ordinary sense of that word ; no graces of elo-
cution. It was mighty thoughts radiating off from
his heated mind like the sparkles from the glowing
steel on his own anvil, getting on as they come out
what clothing of language they might, and thus
having on the most appropriate and expressive
imaginable. Not a waste word, nor a wanting one.
And he stood and delivered himself in a simplicity
and earnestness of attitude and gesture belonging
to his manly and now honored and distinguished
trade. I admired the touch of rusticity in his ac-
cent, amid his truly splendid diction, which be-
tokened, as well as the vein of solid sense that ran
entirely through his speech, that he had not been
educated at the college. I thought of ploughman
Burns as I listened to blacksmith Burritt. Oh !
what a dignity and beauty labor imparts to learning."

Elihu Burritt spent the last years of his life
upon a little farm which he had contrived to buy
in his native town. He was never married, but
lived with his sister and her daughters. He was
not so very much richer in worldly goods than
when he had started for Boston with his property
wrapped in a small handkerchief. He died in
March, 1879, aged sixty-nine years.

MICHAEL REYNOLDS,

ENGINE–DRIVER.

———◆———

LITERATURE in these days throws light into many an out-of-the-way corner. It is rapidly making us all acquainted with one another. A locomotive engineer in England has recently written a book upon his art, in order, as he says, "to communicate that species of knowledge which it is necessary for an engine-driver to possess who aspires to take high rank on the footplate!" He magnifies his office, and evidently regards the position of an engineer as highly enviable.

"It is very *natural*," he remarks, "for those who are unacquainted with locomotive driving to admire the life of an engine-man, and to imagine how very pleasant it must be to travel on the engine. But they do not think of the gradations by which alone the higher positions are reached; they see only on the express engine the picturesque side of the result of many years of patient observation and toil."

This passage was to me a revelation; for I had looked upon an engineer and his assistant with some compassion as well as admiration, and have often thought how extremely disagreeable it must be to travel on the engine as they do. Not so Michael Reynolds, the author of this book, who has risen from the rank of fireman to that of locomotive inspector on the London and Brighton railroad. He tells us that a model engineer "is possessed by a master passion — a passion for the monarch of speed." Such an engineer is distinguished, also, for his minute knowledge of the engine, and nothing makes him happier than to get some new light upon one of its numberless parts. So familiar is he with it that his ear detects the slightest variation in the beats of the machinery, and can tell the shocks and shakes which are caused by a defective road from those which are due to a defective engine. Even his nose acquires a peculiar sensitiveness. In the midst of so much heat, he can detect that which arises from friction before any mischief has been done. At every rate of speed he knows just how his engine ought to sound, shake, and smell.

Let us see how life passes on a locomotive, and what is the secret of success in the business of an engineer. The art of arts in engine-driving is the management of the fire. Every reader is aware that taking care of a fire is something in which few persons become expert. Most of us think that we ourselves possess the knack of it, but not another individual of our household agrees with us. Now, a man born with a genius for managing a locomotive is one who has a high degree of the fire-making instinct. Mr. Reynolds distinctly says that a man may be a good mechanic, may have even built locomotives, and yet, if he is not a good " shovel-man," if he does not know how to manage his fire, he will never rise to distinction in his profession. The great secret is to build the fire so that the whole mass of fuel will ignite and burn freely without the use of the blower, and so bring the engine to the train with a fire that will last. When we see an engine blowing off steam furiously at the beginning of the trip, we must not be surprised if the train reaches the first station behind time, since it indicates a fierce, thin fire, that has been rapidly ignited by the blower. An accomplished engineer backs his engine to the train without any sign of steam or smoke, but with a fire so strong and sound that he can make a run of fifty miles in an hour without touching it.

The engineer, it appears, if he has an important run to make, comes to his engine an hour before starting. His first business, on an English railroad, is to read the notices, posted up in the engine house, of any change in the condition of the road requiring special care. His next duty is to inspect his engine in every part: first, to see if there is water enough in the boiler, and that the fire is proceeding properly; then, that he has the necessary quantity of water and coal in the tender. He next gets into the pit under his engine, with the proper tools, and inspects every portion of it, trying every nut and pin within his reach from below. Then he walks around the engine, and particularly notices if the oiling apparatus is exactly adjusted. Some parts require, for example, four drops of oil every minute, and he must see that the apparatus is set so as to yield just that quantity. He is also to look into his tool-box, and see if every article is in its place. Mr. Reynolds enumerates twenty-two objects which a good engineer will always have within his reach, such as fire implements of various kinds, machinist tools, lamps of several sorts, oiling vessels, a quantity of flax and yarn, copper wire, a copy of the rules and his time-table; all of which are to be in the exact place designed for them, so that they can be snatched in a moment.

One of the chief virtues of the engineer and his companion, the fireman, is one which we are not accustomed to associate with their profession; and that is cleanliness. On this point our author grows eloquent, and he declares that a clean engineer is almost certain to be an excellent one in every particular. The men upon a locomotive cannot, it is true, avoid getting black smudge upon their faces. The point is that both the men and their engines should be clean in all the essential particulars, so that all the faculties of the men and all the devices of the engine shall work with ease and certainty.

"There is something," he remarks, "so very

degrading about dirt, that even a poor beast highly appreciates clean straw. Cleanliness hath a charm that hideth a multitude of faults, and it is not difficult to trace a connection between habitual cleanliness and a respect for general order, for punctuality, for truthfulness, for all placed in authority."

Do you mark that sentence, reader? The spirit of the Saxon race speaks in those lines. You observe that this author ranks among the virtues "a respect for all placed in authority." That, of course, may be carried too far; nevertheless, the strong races, and the worthy men of all races, do cherish a respect for lawful authority. A good soldier is *proud* to salute his officer.

On some English railroads both engineers and engines are put to tests much severer than upon roads elsewhere. Between Holyhead and Chester, a distance of ninety-seven miles, the express trains run without stopping, and they do this with so little strain that an engine performed the duty every day for several years. A day's work of some crack engineers is to run from London to Crewe and back again in ten hours, a distance of three hundred and thirty miles, stopping only at Rugby for three minutes on each trip. There are men who perform this service every working day the whole year through, without a single delay. This is a very great achievement, and can only be done by engineers of the greatest skill and steadiness. It was long, indeed, before any man could do it, and even now there are engineers who dare not take the risk. On the Hudson River road some of the trains run from New York to Poughkeepsie, eighty miles, without stopping, but not every engineer could do it at first, and very often a train stopped at Peekskill to take in water. The water is the difficulty, and the good engineer is one who wastes no water and no coal.

Mr. Reynolds enumerates all the causes of accidents from the engine, many of which cannot be understood by the uninitiated. As we read them over, and see in how many ways an engine can go wrong, we wonder that a train ever arrives at its journey's end in safety. At the conclusion of this formidable list, the author confesses that it is incomplete, and notifies young engineers that *nobody* can teach them the innermost secrets of the engine. Some of these, he remarks, require "years of study," and even then they remain in some degree mysterious. Nevertheless, he holds out to ambition the possibility of final success, and calls upon young men to concentrate all their energies upon the work.

"Self-reliance," he says, "is a grand element of character: it has won Olympic crowns and Isthmian laurels; it confers kinship with men who have vindicated their divine right to be held in the world's memory. Let the master passion of the soul evoke undaunted energy in pursuit of the attainment of one end, aiming for the highest in the spirit of the lowest, prompted by the burning thought of reward, which sooner or later will come."

We perceive that Michael Reynolds possesses one of the prime requisites of success: he believes in the worth and dignity of his vocation; and in writing this little book he has done something to elevate it in the regard of others. To judge from some of his directions, I should suppose that engineers in England are not, as a class, as well educated or as intelligent as ours. Locomotive engineers in the United States rank very high in intelligence and respectability of character.

MAJOR ROBERT PIKE,

FARMER.

I ADVISE people who desire, above all things, to have a comfortable time in the world to be good conservatives. Do as other people do, think as other people think, swim with the current — that is the way to glide pleasantly down the stream of life. But mark, O you lovers of inglorious ease, the men who are remembered with honor after they are dead do not do so! They sometimes *breast* the current, and often have a hard time of it, with the water splashing back in their faces, and the easy-going crowd jeering at them as they pant against the tide.

This valiant, stalwart Puritan, Major Robert Pike, of Salisbury, Massachusetts, who was born in 1616, the year in which Shakespeare died, is a case in point. Salisbury, in the early day, was one of the frontier towns of Massachusetts, lying north of the Merrimac River, and close to the Atlantic Ocean. For fifty years it was a kind of outpost of that part of the State. It lay right in the path by which the Indians of Maine and Canada were accustomed to

slink down along the coast, often traveling on the
sands of the beaches, and burst upon the settlements.   During a long lifetime Major Pike was a
magistrate and personage in that town, one of the
leading spirits, upon whom the defense of the frontier chiefly devolved.

Others were as brave as he in fighting Indians.
Many a man could acquit himself valiantly in battle
who would not have the courage to differ from the
public opinion of his community.   But on several
occasions, when Massachusetts was wrong, Major
Pike was right; and he had the courage sometimes
to resist the current of opinion when it was swollen
into a raging torrent.   He opposed, for example,
the persecution of the Quakers, which is such a blot
upon the records both of New England and old
England.   We can imagine what it must have cost
to go against this policy by a single incident, which
occurred in the year 1659 in Robert Pike's own
town of Salisbury.

On a certain day in August, Thomas Macy was
caught in a violent storm of rain, and hurried home
drenched to the skin.   He found in his house four
wayfarers, who had also come in for shelter.   His
wife being sick in bed, no one had seen or spoken
to them.   They asked him how far it was to Casco
Bay.   From their dress and demeanor he thought
they might be Quakers, and, as it was unlawful to
harbor persons of that sect, he asked them to go on
their way, since he feared to give offense in enter-

taining them. As soon as the worst of the storm was over, they left, and he never saw them again. They were in his house about three quarters of an hour, during which he said very little to them, having himself come home wet, and found his wife sick.

He was summoned to Boston, forty miles distant, to answer for this offense. Being unable to walk, and not rich enough to buy a horse, he wrote to the General Court, relating the circumstances, and explaining his non-appearance. He was fined thirty shillings, and ordered to be admonished by the governor. He paid his fine, received his reprimand, and removed to the island of Nantucket, of which he was the first settler, and for some time the only white inhabitant.

During this period of Quaker persecution, Major Pike led the opposition to it in Salisbury, until, at length, William Penn prevailed upon Charles II. to put an end to it in all his dominions. If the history of that period had not been so carefully recorded in official documents, we could scarcely believe to what a point the principle of authority was then carried. One of the laws which Robert Pike dared openly to oppose made it a misdemeanor for any one to exhort on Sunday who had not been regularly ordained. He declared that the men who voted for that law had broken their oaths, for they had sworn on taking their seats to enact nothing against the just liberty of Englishmen.

For saying this he was pronounced guilty of " de-faming " the legislature, and he was sentenced to be disfranchised, disabled from holding any public office, bound to good behavior, and fined twenty marks, equal to about two hundred dollars in our present currency.

Petitions were presented to the legislature asking the remission of the severe sentence. But even this was regarded as a criminal offense, and pro-ceedings were instituted against every signer. A few acknowledged that the signing was an offense, and asked the forgiveness of the court, but all the rest were required to give bonds for their appear-ance to answer.

Another curious incident shows the rigor of the government of that day. According to the Puritan law, Sunday began at sunset on Saturday evening, and ended at sunset on Sunday evening. During the March thaw of 1680, Major Pike had occasion to go to Boston, then a journey of two days. Fear-ing that the roads were about to break up, he deter-mined to start on Sunday evening, get across the Merrimac, which was then a matter of difficulty during the melting of the ice, and make an early start from the other side of the river on Monday morning. The gallant major being, of course, a member of the church, and very religious, went to church twice that Sunday. Now, as to what fol-lowed, I will quote the testimony of an eye-witness, his traveling companion : —

"I do further testify that, though it was pretty late ere Mr. Burrows (the clergyman) ended his afternoon's exercise, yet did the major stay in his daughter's house till repetition of both forenoon and afternoon sermons was over, and the duties of the day concluded with prayer; and, after a little stay, to be sure the sun was down, then we mounted, and not till then. The sun did indeed set in a cloud, and after we were mounted, I do remember the major spake of lightening up where the sun set; but I saw no sun."

A personal enemy of the major's brought a charge against him of violating the holy day by starting on his journey *before* the setting of the sun. The case was brought for trial, and several witnesses were examined. The accuser testified that "he did see Major Robert Pike ride by his house toward the ferry upon the Lord's day when the sun was about half an hour high." Another witness confirmed this. Another testified: —

"The sun did indeed set in a cloud, and, a little after the major was mounted, there appeared a light where the sun went down, which soon vanished again, possibly half a quarter of an hour."

Nevertheless, there were two witnesses who declared that the sun was not down when the major mounted, and so this worthy gentleman, then sixty-four years of age, a man of honorable renown in the commonwealth, was convicted of "profaning the Sabbath," fined ten shillings, and condemned to pay costs and fees, which were eight shillings more. He paid his fine, and was probably more careful during the rest of his life to mount on Sunday evenings by the almanac.

The special glory of this man's life was his steadfast and brave opposition to the witchcraft mania of 1692. This deplorable madness was in New England a mere transitory panic, from which the people quickly recovered; but while it lasted it almost silenced opposition, and it required genuine heroism to lift a voice against it. No country of Europe was free from the delusion during that century, and some of its wisest men were carried away by it. The eminent judge, Sir William Blackstone, in his "Commentaries," published in 1765, used this language: —

" To deny the existence of witchcraft is to flatly contradict the revealed word of God, and the thing itself is a truth to which every nation has in its turn borne testimony."

This was the conviction of that age, and hundreds of persons were executed for practicing witchcraft. In Massachusetts, while the mania lasted, fear blanched every face and haunted every house.

It was the more perilous to oppose the trials because there was a mingling of personal malevolence in the fell business, and an individual who objected was in danger of being himself accused. No station, no age, no merit, was a sufficient protection. Mary Bradbury, seventy-five years of age, the wife of one of the leading men of Salisbury, a woman of singular excellence and dignity of character, was among the convicted. She was a neighbor of Major Pike's, and a life-long friend.

In the height of the panic he addressed to one of the judges an argument against the trials for witchcraft which is one of the most ingenious pieces of writing to be found among the documents of that age. The peculiarity of it is that the author argues on purely Biblical grounds; for he accepted the whole Bible as authoritative, and all its parts as equally authoritative, from Genesis to Revelation. His main point was that witchcraft, whatever it may be, cannot be certainly proved against any one. The eye, he said, may be deceived; the ear may be; and all the senses. The devil himself may take the shape and likeness of a person or thing, when it is not that person or thing. The truth on the subject, he held, lay out of the range of mortal ken.

"And therefore," he adds, "I humbly conceive that, in such a difficulty, it may be more safe, for the present, to let a guilty person live till further discovery than to put an innocent person to death."

Happily this mania speedily passed, and troubled New England no more. Robert Pike lived many years longer, and died in 1706, when he was nearly ninety-one years of age. He was a farmer, and gained a considerable estate, the whole of which he gave away to his heirs before his death. The house in which he lived is still standing in the town of

Salisbury, and belongs to his descendants; for on that healthy coast men, families, and houses decay very slowly.   James S. Pike, one of his descendants, the well-remembered " J. S. P." of the " Tribune's " earlier day, and now an honored citizen of Maine, has recently written a little book about this ancient hero who assisted to set his fellow-citizens right when they were going wrong.

GEORGE GRAHAM,

CLOCK-MAKER, BURIED IN WESTMINSTER ABBEY.

It is supposed that the oldest clock in existence
is one in the ancient castle of Dover, on the southern coast of England, bearing the date, 1348. It
has been running, therefore, five hundred and thirty-six years. Other clocks of the same century
exist in various parts of Europe, the works of which
have but one hand, which points the hour, and require winding every twenty-four hours. From the
fact of so many large clocks of that period having
been preserved in whole or in part, it is highly
probable that the clock was then an old invention.

But how did people measure time during the
countless ages that rolled away before the invention
of the clock? The first time-measurer was probably a post stuck in the ground, the shadow of
which, varying in length and direction, indicated
the time of day, whenever the sun was not obscured
by clouds. The sun-dial, which was an improvement upon this, was known to the ancient Jews and
Greeks. The ancient Chinese and Egyptians possessed an instrument called the Clepsydra (water-

stealer), which was merely a vessel full of water with a small hole in the bottom by which the water slowly escaped. There were marks in the inside of the vessel which showed the hour. An improvement upon this was made about two hundred and thirty-five years before Christ by an Egyptian, who caused the escaping water to turn a system of wheels; and the motion was communicated to a rod which pointed to the hours upon a circle resembling a clock-face. Similar clocks were made in which sand was used instead of water. The hourglass was a time-measurer for many centuries in Europe, and all the ancient literatures abound in allusions to the rapid, unobserved, running away of its sands.

The next advance was the invention of the wheel-and-weight-clock, such as has been in use ever since. The first instrument of this kind may have been made by the ancients; but no clear allusion to its existence has been discovered earlier than 996, when Pope Sylvester II. is known to have had one constructed. It was Christian Huygens, the famous Dutch philosopher, who applied, in 1658, the pendulum to the clock, and thus led directly to those more refined and subtle improvements, which render our present clocks and watches among the least imperfect of all human contrivances.

George Graham, the great London clock-maker of Queen Anne's and George the First's time, and one of the most noted improvers of the clock, was

born in 1675. After spending the first thirteen
years of his life in a village in the North of England, he made his way to London, an intelligent
and well-bred Quaker boy; and there he was so
fortunate as to be taken as an apprentice by Tompion, then the most celebrated clock-maker in England, whose name is still to be seen upon ancient
watches and clocks. Tompion was a most exquisite mechanic, proud of his work and jealous of his
name. He is the Tompion who figured in Far-
quhar's play of "The Inconstant;" and Prior mentions him in his "Essay on Learning," where he
says that Tompion on a watch or clock was proof
positive of its excellence. A person once brought
him a watch to repair, upon which his name had
been fraudulently engraved. He took up a hammer and smashed it, and then selecting one of his
own watches, gave it to the astonished customer,
saying: "Sir, here is a watch of my making."

Graham was worthy to be the apprentice of such
a master, for he not only showed intelligence, skill,
and fidelity, but a happy turn for invention. Tompion became warmly attached to him, treated him
as a son, gave him the full benefit of his skill and
knowledge, took him into partnership, and finally
left him sole possessor of the business. For nearly
half a century George Graham, Clock-maker, was
one of the best known signs in Fleet Street, and
the instruments made in his shop were valued in all
the principal countries of Europe. The great clock

at Greenwich Observatory, made by him one hundred and fifty years ago, is still in use and could hardly now be surpassed in substantial excellence. The mural arch in the same establishment, used for the testing of quadrants and other marine instruments, was also his work. When the French government sent Maupertuis within the polar circle, to ascertain the exact figure of the earth, it was George Graham, Clock-maker of Fleet Street, who supplied the requisite instruments.

But it was not his excellence as a mechanic that causes his name to be remembered at the present time. He made two capital inventions in clock-machinery which are still universally used, and will probably never be superseded. It was a common complaint among clock - makers, when he was a young man, that the pendulum varied in length according to the temperature, and consequently caused the clock to go too slowly in hot weather, and too fast in cold. Thus, if a clock went correctly at a temperature of sixty degrees, it would lose three seconds a day if the temperature rose to seventy, and three more seconds a day for every additional ten degrees of heat. Graham first endeavored to rectify this inconvenience by making the pendulum of several different kinds of metal, which was a partial remedy. But the invention by which he overcame the difficulty completely, consisted in employing a column of mercury as the "bob" of the pendulum. The hot weather, which lengthened the steel rods, raised the column of mercury, and so brought the centre of oscillation higher. If the column of mercury was of the right length, the lengthening or the shortening of the pendulum was exactly counterbalanced, and the variation of the clock, through changes of the temperature, almost annihilated.

This was a truly exquisite invention. The clock he himself made on this plan for Greenwich, after being in use a century and a half, requires attention not oftener than once in fifteen months. Some important discoveries in astronomy are due to the exactness with which Graham's clock measures time. He also invented what is called the "dead escapement," still used, I believe, in all clocks and watches, from the commonest five-dollar watch to the most elaborate and costly regulator. Another pretty invention of his was a machine for showing the position and motions of the heavenly bodies, which was exceedingly admired by our grandfathers. Lord Orrery having amused himself by copying this machine, a French traveler who saw it complimented the maker by naming it an Orrery, which has led many to suppose it to have been an invention of that lord. It now appears, however, that the true inventor was the Fleet Street clock-maker.

The merits of this admirable mechanic procured for him, while he was still little more than a young man, the honor of being elected a member of the Royal Society, the most illustrious scientific body in the world. And a very worthy member he proved. If the reader will turn to the Transactions of that learned society, he may find in them twenty-one papers contributed by George Graham. He was, however, far from regarding himself as a philosopher, but to the end of his days always styled himself a clock-maker.

They still relate an anecdote showing the confidence he had in his work. A gentleman who bought a watch of him just before departing for India, asked him how far he could depend on its keeping the correct time.

"Sir," replied Graham, "it is a watch which I have made and regulated myself; take it with you wherever you please. If after seven years you come back to see me, and can tell me there has been a difference of five minutes, I will return you your money."

Seven years passed, and the gentleman returned.

"Sir," said he, "I bring you back your watch."

"I remember," said Graham, "our conditions. Let me see the watch. Well, what do you complain of?"

"Why," was the reply, "I have had it seven years, and there is a difference of more than five minutes."

"Indeed!" said Graham. "In that case I return you your money."

"I would not part with my watch," said the gentleman, "for ten times the sum I paid for it."

"And I," rejoined Graham, "would not break my word for any consideration."

He insisted on taking back the watch, which ever after he used as a regulator.

This is a very good story, and is doubtless substantially true; but no watch was ever yet made which has varied as little as five minutes in seven years. Readers may remember that the British government once offered a reward of twenty thousand pounds sterling for the best chronometer, and the prize was awarded to Harrison for a chronometer which varied two minutes in a sailing voyage from England to Jamaica and back.

George Graham died in 1751, aged seventy-six years, universally esteemed as an ornament of his age and country. In Westminster Abbey, among the tombs of poets, philosophers, and statesmen, may be seen the graves of the two clock-makers, master and apprentice, Tompion and Graham.

JOHN HARRISON,

EXQUISITE WATCH-MAKER.

———◆———

HE was first a carpenter, and the son of a carpenter, born and reared in English Yorkshire, in a village too insignificant to appear on any but a county map. Faulby is about twenty miles from York, and there John Harrison was born in 1693, when William and Mary reigned in England. He was thirty-five years of age before he was known beyond his own neighborhood. He was noted there, however, for being a most skillful workman. There is, perhaps, no trade in which the degrees of skill are so far apart as that of carpenter. The difference is great indeed between the clumsy-fisted fellow who knocks together a farmer's pig-pen, and the almost artist who makes a dining-room floor equal to a piece of mosaic. Dr. Franklin speaks with peculiar relish of one of his young comrades in Philadelphia, as "the most exquisite joiner" he had ever known.

It was not only in carpentry that John Harrison reached extraordinary skill and delicacy of stroke. He became an excellent machinist, and was par-

ticularly devoted from an early age to clock-work.
He was a student also in the science of the day. A
contemporary of Newton, he made himself capable
of understanding the discoveries of that great man,
and of following the Transactions of the Royal Society in mathematics, astronomy, and natural philosophy.

Clock-work, however, was his ruling taste as a
workman, for many years, and he appears to have
set before him as a task the making of a clock that
should surpass all others. He says in one of his
pamphlets that, in the year 1726, when he was
thirty-three years of age, he finished two large pendulum clocks which, being placed in different houses
some distance apart, differed from each other only
one second in a month. He also says that one of
his clocks, which he kept for his own use, the going
of which he compared with a fixed star, varied from
the true time only one minute in ten years.

Modern clock-makers are disposed to deride these
extraordinary claims, particularly those of Paris and
Switzerland. We know, however, that John Harrison was one of the most perfect workmen that
ever lived, and I find it difficult to believe that a
man whose works were so true could be false in his
words.

In perfecting these amateur clocks he made a
beautiful invention, the principle of which is still
employed in other machines besides clock-work.
Like George Graham, he observed that the chief

cause of irregularity in a well-made clock was the varying length of the pendulum, which in warm weather expanded and became a little longer, and in cold weather became shorter. He remedied this by the invention of what is often called the gridiron pendulum, made of several bars of steel and brass, and so arranged as to neutralize and correct the tendency of the pendulum to vary in length. Brass is very sensitive to changes of temperature, steel much less so; and hence it is not difficult to arrange the pendulum so that the long exterior bars of steel shall very nearly curb the expansion and contraction of the shorter brass ones.

While he was thus perfecting himself in obscurity, the great world was in movement also, and it was even stimulating his labors, as well as giving them their direction.

The navigation of the ocean was increasing every year in importance, chiefly through the growth of the American colonies and the taste for the rich products of India. The art of navigation was still imperfect. In order that the captain of a ship at sea may know precisely where he is, he must know two things: how far he is from the equator, and how far he is from a certain known place, say Greenwich, Paris, Washington. Being sure of those two things, he can take his chart and mark upon it the precise spot where his ship is at a given moment. Then he knows how to steer, and all else that he needs to know in order to pursue his course with confidence.

When John Harrison was a young man, the art of navigation had so far advanced that the distance from the equator, or the latitude, could be ascertained with certainty by observation of the heavenly bodies. One great difficulty remained to be overcome — the finding of the longitude. This was done imperfectly by means of a watch which kept Greenwich time as near as possible. Every fine day the captain could ascertain by an observation of the sun just when it was twelve o'clock. If, on looking at this chronometer, he found that by Greenwich time it was quarter past two, he could at once ascertain his distance from Greenwich, or in other words, his longitude.

But the terrible question was, how near right is the chronometer? A variation of a very few minutes would make a difference of more than a hundred miles.

To this day, no perfect time-keeper has ever been made. From an early period, the governments of commercial nations were solicitous to find a way of determining the longitude that would be sufficiently correct. Thus, the King of Spain, in 1598, offered a reward of a thousand crowns to any one who should discover an approximately correct method. Soon after, the government of Holland offered ten thousand florins. In 1714 the English government took hold of the matter, and offered a series of

dazzling prizes: Five thousand pounds for a chronometer that would enable a ship six months from
home to get her longitude within sixty miles; seven
thousand five hundred pounds, if within forty
miles; ten thousand pounds if within thirty miles.
Another clause of the bill offered a premium of
twenty thousand pounds for the invention of any
method whatever, by means of which the longitude
could be determined within thirty miles. The bill
appears to have been drawn somewhat carelessly;
but the substance of it was sufficiently plain, namely, that the British Government was ready to make
the fortune of any man who should enable navi-
gators to make their way across the ocean in a
straight line to their desired port.

Two years after, the Regent of France offered a
prize of a hundred thousand francs for the same
object.

All the world went to watch-making. John Harrison, stimulated by these offers to increased exertion, in the year 1736 presented himself at Greenwich with one of his wonderful clocks, provided
with the gridiron pendulum, which he exhibited
and explained to the commissioners. Perceiving
the merit and beauty of his invention, they placed
the clock on board a ship bound for Lisbon. This
was subjecting a pendulum clock to a very unfair
trial; but it corrected the ship's reckoning several
miles. The commissioners now urged him to com-
pete for the chronometer prize, and in order to

enable him to do so they supplied him with money, from time to time, for twenty-four years. At length he produced his chronometer, about four inches in diameter, and so mounted as not to share the motion of the vessel.

In 1761, when he was sixty-eight years of age, he wrote to the commissioners that he had completed a chronometer for trial, and requested them to test it on a voyage to the West Indies, under the care of his son William. His requests were granted. The success of the chronometer was wonderful. On arriving at Jamaica, the chronometer varied but four seconds from Greenwich time, and on returning to England the entire variation was a little short of two minutes; which was equivalent to a longitudinal variation of eighteen miles. The ship had been absent from Portsmouth one hundred and forty-seven days.

This signal triumph was won after forty years of labor and experiment. The commissioners demanding another trial, the watch was taken to Barbadoes, and, after an absence of a hundred and fifty-six days, showed a variation of only fifteen seconds. After other and very exacting tests, it was decided that John Harrison had fulfilled all the prescribed conditions, and he received accordingly the whole sum of twenty thousand pounds sterling.

It is now asserted by experts that he owed the success of his watch, not so much to originality of invention, as to the exquisite skill and precision of his workmanship. ·He had one of the most perfect mechanical hands that ever existed. It was the touch of a Raphael applied to mechanism.

John Harrison lived to the good old age of eighty-three years. He died in London in 1776, about the time when General Washington was getting ready to drive the English troops and their Tory friends out of Boston. It is not uncommon now-a-days for a ship to be out four or five months, and to hit her port so exactly as to sail straight into it without altering her course more than a point or two.

PETER FANEUIL,

AND THE GREAT HALL HE BUILT.

———•———

A STORY is told of the late Ralph Waldo Emerson's first lecture in Cincinnati, forty years ago. A worthy pork-packer, who was observed to listen with close attention to the enigmatic utterances of the sage, was asked by one of his friends what he thought of the performance.

"I liked it very well," said he, "and I'm glad I went, because I learned from it how the Boston people pronounce Faneuil Hall."

He was perhaps mistaken, for it is hardly probable that Mr. Emerson gave the name in the old-fashioned Boston style, which was a good deal like the word *funnel*. The story, however, may serve to show what a wide-spread and intense reputation the building has. Of all the objects in Boston it is probably the one best known to the people of the United States, and the one surest to be visited by the stranger. The Hall is a curious, quaint little interior, with its high galleries, and its collection of busts and pictures of Revolutionary heroes. Peter Faneuil little thought what he was doing

5

when he built it, though he appears to have been a man of liberal and enlightened mind.

The Faneuils were prosperous merchants in the French city of Rochelle in 1685, when Louis XIV. revoked the Edict of Nantes. The great-grandfather of John Jay was also in large business there at that time, and so were the ancestors of our Delanceys, Badeaus, Pells, Secors, Allaires, and other families familiar to the ears of New Yorkers, many of them having distinguished living representatives among us. They were of the religion "called Reformed," as the king of France contemptuously styled it. Reformed or not, they were among the most intelligent, enterprising, and wealthy of the merchants of Rochelle.

How little we can conceive the effect upon their minds of the order which came from Paris in October, 1685, which was intended to put an end for-ever to the Protestant religion in France. The king meant to make thorough work of it. He ordered all the Huguenot churches in the kingdom to be instantly demolished. He forbade the dissenters to assemble either in a building or out of doors, on pain of death and confiscation of all their goods. Their clergymen were required to leave the kingdom within fifteen days. Their schools were interdicted, and all children hereafter born of Protestant parents were to be baptized by the Catholic clergymen, and reared as Catholics.

These orders were enforced with reckless ferocity, particularly in the remoter provinces and cities of the kingdom. The Faneuils, the Jays, and the Delanceys of that renowned city saw their house of worship leveled with the ground. Dragoons were quartered in their houses, whom they were obliged to maintain, and to whose insolence they were obliged to submit, for the troops were given to understand that they were the king's enemies and had no rights which royal soldiers were bound to respect. At the same time, the edict forbade them to depart from the kingdom, and particular precautions were taken to prevent men of capital from doing so.

John Jay records that the ancestor of his family made his escape by artifice, and succeeded in taking with him a portion of his property. Such was also the good fortune of the brothers Faneuil, who were part of the numerous company from old Rochelle who emigrated to New York about 1690, and formed a settlement upon Long Island Sound, twelve miles from New York, which they named, and which is still called, New Rochelle. The old names can still be read in that region, both in the churchyards and upon the door plates, and the village of Pelham recalls the name of the Pell family who fled from Rochelle about the same time, and obtained a grant of six thousand acres of land near by. The newcomers were warmly welcomed, as their friends and relations were in England.

The Faneuil brothers did not remain long in New Rochelle. but removed to Boston in 1691. Benjamin and Andrew were their names. There are many traces of them in the early records, indicating that they were merchants of large capital and extensive business for that day. There are evidences also that they were men of intelligence and public spirit. They appear to have been members of the Church of England in Boston, which of itself placed them somewhat apart from the majority of their fellow-citizens.

Peter Faneuil, the builder of the famous Hall, who was born in Boston about 1701, the oldest of eleven children, succeeded to the business founded by his uncle Andrew, and while still a young man had greatly increased it, and was reckoned one of the leading citizens.

A curious controversy had agitated the people of Boston for many years. The town had existed for nearly a century without having a public market of any kind, the country people bringing in their produce and selling it from door to door. In February, 1717, occurred the Great Snow, which destroyed great numbers of domestic and wild animals, and caused provisions for some weeks to be scarce and dear. The inhabitants laid the blame of the dearness to the rapacity of the hucksters, and the subject being brought up in town meeting, a committee reported that the true remedy was to build a market, to appoint market days, and establish rules. The farmers opposed the scheme, as did also many of the citizens. The project being defeated, it was revived year after year, but the country people always contrived to defeat it. An old chronicler has a quaint passage on the subject.

"The country people," he says, "always opposed the market, so that the question could not be settled. The reason they give for it is, that if market days were appointed, all the country people coming in at the same time would glut it, and the towns-people would buy their provisions for what they pleased; so rather choose to send them as they think fit. And sometimes a tall fellow brings in a turkey or goose to sell, and will travel through the whole town to see who will give most for it, and it is at last sold for three and six pence or four shillings; and if he had stayed at home, he could have earned a crown by his labor, which is the customary price for a day's work. So any one may judge of the stupidity of the country people."

In Boston libraries, pamphlets are still preserved on this burning question of a market, which required seventeen years of discussion before a town meeting was brought to vote for the erection of market houses. In 1734, seven hundred pounds were appropriated for the purpose. The market hours were fixed from sunrise to 1 P. M., and a bell was ordered to be rung to announce the time of opening. The country people, however, had their way, notwithstanding. They so resolutely refrained from attending the markets that in less than four years the houses fell into complete disuse. One of the buildings was taken down, and the timber used in constructing a workhouse; one was turned into stores, and the third was torn to pieces by a mob, who carried off the material for their own use.

Nevertheless, the market question could not be allayed, for the respectable inhabitants of the town were still convinced of the need of a market as a defense against exorbitant charges. For some years the subject was brought up in town meetings; but as often as it came to the point of appropriating money the motion was lost. At length Mr. Peter Faneuil came forward to end the dissension in a truly magnificent manner. He offered to build a market house at his own expense, and make a present of it to the town.

Even this liberal offer did not silence opposition. A petition was presented to the town meeting, signed by three hundred and forty inhabitants, asking the acceptance of Peter Faneuil's proposal. The opposition to it, however, was strong. At length it was agreed that, if a market house were built, the country people should be at liberty to sell their produce from door to door if they pleased. Even with this concession, only 367 citizens voted for the market and 360 voted against it. Thus, by a majority of seven, the people of Boston voted to accept the most munificent gift the town had received since it was founded.

Peter Faneuil went beyond his promise. Besides building an ample market place, he added a second story for a town hall, and other offices for public use. The building originally measured one hundred feet by forty, and was finished in so elegant a style as to be reckoned the chief ornament of the town. It was completed in 1742, after two years had been spent in building it. It had scarcely been opened for public use when Peter Faneuil died, aged a little less than forty-three years. The grateful citizens gave him a public funeral, and the Selectmen appointed Mr. John Lovell, schoolmaster, to deliver his funeral oration in the Hall bearing his name. The oration was entered at length upon the records of the town, and has been frequently published.

In 1761 the Hall was destroyed by fire. It was immediately rebuilt, and this second structure was the Faneuil Hall in which were held the meetings preceding and during the war for Independence, which have given it such universal celebrity. Here Samuel Adams spoke. Here the feeling was created which made Massachusetts the centre and source of the revolutionary movement.

Let me not omit to state that those obstinate country people, who knew what they wanted, were proof against the attractions of Faneuil Hall market. They availed themselves of their privilege of selling their produce from door to door, as they had done from the beginning of the colony. Fewer and fewer hucksters kept stalls in the market, and in a few years the lower room was closed altogether.

The building served, however, as Town Hall until it was superseded by structures more in harmony with modern needs and tastes.

What thrilling scenes the Hall has witnessed! That is a pleasing touch in one of the letters of John Adams to Thomas Jefferson, where he alludes to what was probably his last visit to the scene of his youthful glory, Faneuil Hall. Mr. Adams was eighty-three years old at the time, and it was the artist Trumbull, also an old man, who prevailed upon him to go to the Hall.

"Trumbull," he wrote, "with a band of associates, drew me by the cords of old friendship to see his picture, on Saturday, where I got a great cold. The air of Faneuil is changed. *I have not been used to catch cold there.*"

No, indeed. If the process of storing electricity had been applied to the interior of this electric edifice, enough of the fluid could have been saved to illuminate Boston every Fourth of July. It is hard to conceive of a tranquil or commonplace meeting there, so associated is it in our minds with outbursts of passionate feeling.

Speaking of John Adams calls to mind an anecdote related recently by a venerable clergyman of New York, Rev. William Hague. Mr. Hague officiated as chaplain at the celebration of the Fourth of July in Boston, in 1843, when Charles Francis Adams delivered the oration in Faneuil Hall, which was his first appearance on a public platform.

While the procession was forming to march to the Hall, ex-President John Quincy Adams entered into conversation with the chaplain, during which he spoke as follows : —

" This is one of the happiest days of my whole life. Fifty years expire to-day since I performed in Boston my first public service, which was the delivery of an oration to celebrate our national independence. After half a century of active life, I am spared by a benign Providence to witness my son's performance of his first public service, to deliver an oration in honor of the same great event."

The chaplain replied to Mr. Adams : —

" President, I am well aware of the notable connection of events to which you refer ; and having committed and declaimed a part of your own great oration when a schoolboy in New York, I could without effort repeat it to you now."

The aged statesman was surprised and gratified at this statement. The procession was formed and the oration successfully delivered. Since that time, I believe, an Adams of the fourth generation has spoken in the same place, and probably some readers will live to hear one of the fifth and sixth.

The venerable John Adams might well say that he had not been used to catch cold in the air of Faneuil Hall, for as far as I know there has never been held there a meeting which has not something of extraordinary warmth in its character. I have mentioned above that the first public meeting ever

held in it after its completion in 1742 was to commemorate the premature death of the donor of the
edifice ; on which occasion Mr. John Lovell delivered a glowing eulogium.

" Let this stately edifice which bears his name,"
cried the orator, " witness for him what sums he
expended in public munificence.   This building,
erected by him, at his own immense charge, for the
convenience and ornament of the town, is incomparably the greatest benefaction ever yet known to
our western shore."

Towards the close of his speech, the eloquent
schoolmaster gave utterance to a sentiment which
has often since been repeated within those walls."

" May this hall be ever sacred to the interests of
truth, of justice, of loyalty, of honor, of liberty.
May no private views nor party broils ever enter
these walls."

Whether this wish has been fulfilled or not is a
matter of opinion.   General Gage doubtless thought
that it had not been.

Scenes of peculiar interest took place in the Hall
about the beginning of the year 1761, when the
news was received in Boston that King George II.
had fallen dead in his palace at Kensington, and
that George III., his grandson, had been proclaimed king.   It required just two months for
this intelligence to cross the ocean.   The first thing
in order, it seems, was to celebrate the accession of
the young king.   He was proclaimed from the bal·

cony of the town house ; guns were fired from all
the forts in the harbor ; and in the afternoon a
grand dinner was given in Faneuil Hall. These
events occurred on the last day but one of the year
1760.

The first day of the new year, 1761, was ushered
in by the solemn tolling of the church bells in the
town, and the firing of minute guns on Castle Island. These mournful sounds were heard all day,
even to the setting of the sun. However dole-
ful the day may have seemed, there was more ap-
propriateness in these signs of mourning than any
man of that generation could have known ; for with
George II. died the indolent but salutary let-them-
alone policy under which the colonies enjoyed prosperity and peace. With the accession of the new
king the troubles began which ended in the disrup-
tion of the empire. George III. was the last king
whose accession received official recognition in the
thirteen colonies.

I have hunted in vain through my books to find
some record of the dinner given in Faneuil Hall to
celebrate the beginning of the new reign. It would
be interesting to know how the sedate people of
Boston comported themselves on a festive occasion
of that character. John Adams was a young bar-
rister then. If the after-dinner speeches were as
outspoken as the political comments he entered in
his Diary, the proceedings could not have been very
acceptable to the royal governor. Mr. Adams was

far from thinking that England had issued victorious from the late campaigns, and he thought that
France was then by far the most brilliant and powerful nation in Europe.

A few days after these loyal ceremonies, Boston
experienced what is now known there as a " cold
snap," and it was so severe as almost to close the
harbor with ice. One evening, in the midst of it, a
fire broke out opposite Faneuil Hall. Such was the
extremity of cold that the water forced from the
engines fell upon the ground in particles of ice. The
fire swept across the street and caught Faneuil Hall,
the interior of which was entirely consumed, nothing remaining but the solid brick walls. It was rebuilt in just two years, and reopened in the midst of
another remarkably cold time, which was signalized
by another bad fire. There was so much distress
among the poor that winter that a meeting was
held in Faneuil Hall for their relief, Rev. Samuel
Mather preaching a sermon on the occasion, and
this was the first discourse delivered in it after it
was rebuilt.

Seven years later the Hall was put to a very different use. A powerful fleet of twelve men-of-war,
filled with troops, was coming across the ocean to
apply military pressure to the friends of liberty.
A convention was held in Faneuil Hall, attended
by delegates from the surrounding towns, as well as
by the citizens of Boston. The people were in con-
sternation, for they feared that any attempt to land

the troops would lead to violent resistance. The convention indeed requested the inhabitants to "provide themselves with firearms, that they may be prepared in case of sudden danger."

The atmosphere was extremely electric in Boston just then. The governor sent word to the convention assembled in Faneuil Hall that their meeting was "a very high offense" which only their ignorance of the law could excuse; but the plea of ignorance could no longer avail them, and he commanded them to disperse. The convention sent a reply to the governor, which he refused to receive, and they continued in session until the fleet entered the harbor.

October 2, 1768, the twelve British men-of-war were anchored in a semicircle opposite the town, with cannon loaded, and cleared for action, as though Boston were a hostile stronghold, instead of a defenseless country town of loyal and innocent fellow-citizens. Two regiments landed; one of which encamped on the Common, and the other marched to Faneuil Hall, where they were quartered for four or five weeks. With one accord the merchants and property-owners refused to let any building for the use of the troops.

Boston people to this day chuckle over the mishap of the sheriff who tried to get possession of a large warehouse through a secret aperture in the cellar wall. He did succeed in effecting an entrance, with several of his deputies. But as soon as they were inside the building, the patriots out-side closed the hole ; and thus, instead of getting possession of the building, the loyal officers found themselves prisoners in a dark cellar.

They were there for several hours before they could get word to the commanding officer, who re-leased them.

The joke was consolatory to the inhabitants. It was on this occasion that Rev. Mather Byles height-ened the general merriment by his celebrated jest on the British soldiers :

" The people," said he, " sent over to England to obtain a redress of grievances. The grievances have returned *red-dressed.*"

The Hall is still used for public meetings, and the region roundabout is still an important public market.

Chauncey Jerome

CHAUNCEY JEROME,

YANKEE CLOCK-MAKER.

———————

Poor boys had a hard time of it in New England
eighty years ago. Observe, now, how it fared with
Chauncey Jerome, — he who founded a celebrated
clock business in Connecticut, that turned out six
hundred clocks a day, and sent them to foreign
countries by the ship-load.

But do not run away with the idea that it was
the hardship and loneliness of his boyhood that
"made a man of him." On the contrary, they
injured, narrowed, and saddened him. He would
have been twice the man he was, and happier all
his days, if he had passed an easier and a more
cheerful childhood. It is not good for boys to live
as he lived, and work as he worked, during the
period of growth, and I am glad that fewer boys
are now compelled to bear such a lot as his.

His father was a blacksmith and nailmaker, of
Plymouth, Connecticut, with a houseful of hungry
boys and girls; and, consequently, as soon as
Chauncey could handle a hoe or tie up a bundle of
grain he was kept at work on the farm; for, in

those days, almost all mechanics in New England cultivated land in the summer time. The boy went to school during the three winter months, until he was ten years old; then his school-days and play-days were over forever, and his father took him into the shop to help make nails.

Even as a child he showed that power of keeping on, to which he owed his after-success. There was a great lazy boy at the district school he attended who had a load of wood to chop, which he hated to do, and this small Chauncey, eight or nine years of age, chopped the whole of it for him for *one cent!* Often he would chop wood for the neighbors in moonlight evenings for a few cents a load. It is evident that the quality which made him a successful man of business was not developed by hardship, for he performed these labors voluntarily. He was naturally industrious and persevering.

When he was eleven years of age his father suddenly died, and he found himself obliged to leave his happy home and find farm work as a poor hireling boy. There were few farmers then in Connecticut — nay, there were few people anywhere in the world — who knew how to treat an orphan obliged to work for his subsistence among strangers. On a Monday morning, with his little bundle of clothes in his hand, and an almost bursting heart, he bade his mother and his brothers and sisters good-by, and walked to the place which he had found for himself, on a farm a few miles from home.

He was most willing to work; but his affectionate heart was starved at his new place; and scarcely a day passed during his first year when he did not burst into tears as he worked alone in the fields, thinking of the father he had lost, and of the happy family broken up never to live together again. It was a lonely farm, and the people with whom he lived took no interest in him as a human being, but regarded him with little more consideration than one of their other working animals. They took care, however, to keep him steadily at work, early and late, hot and cold, rain and shine. Often he worked all day in the woods chopping down trees with his shoes full of snow; he never had a pair of boots till he was nearly twenty-one years of age.

Once in two weeks he had a great joy; for his master let him go to church every other Sunday. After working two weeks without seeing more than half a dozen people, it gave him a peculiar and intense delight just to sit in the church gallery and look down upon so many human beings. It was the only alleviation of his dismal lot.

Poor little lonely wretch! One day, when he was thirteen years of age, there occurred a total eclipse of the sun, a phenomenon of which he had scarcely heard, and he had not the least idea what it could be. He was hoeing corn that day in a solitary place. When the darkness and the chill of the eclipse fell upon the earth, feeling sure the day of

6

judgment had come, he was terrified beyond description. He watched the sun disappearing with the deepest apprehension, and felt no relief until it shone out bright and warm as before.

It seems strange that people in a Christian country could have had a good steady boy like this in their house and yet do nothing to cheer or comfort his life. Old men tell me it was a very common case in New England seventy years ago.

This hard experience on the farm lasted until he was old enough to be apprenticed. At fourteen he was bound to a carpenter for seven years, during which he was to receive for his services his board and his clothes. Already he had done almost the work of a man on the farm, being a stout, handy fellow, and in the course of two or three years he did the work of a full-grown carpenter; nevertheless, he received no wages except the necessaries of life. Fortunately the carpenter's family were human beings, and he had a pleasant, friendly home during his apprenticeship.

Even under the gentlest masters apprentices, in old times, were kept most strictly to their duty. They were lucky if they got the whole of Thanksgiving and the Fourth of July for holidays.

Now, this apprentice, when he was sixteen, was so homesick on a certain occasion that he felt he *must* go and see his mother, who lived near her old home, twenty miles from where he was working on a job. He walked the distance in the night, in order not to rob his master of any of the time due to him.

It was a terrible night's work. He was sorry he had undertaken it; but having started he could not bear to give it up. Half the way was through the woods, and every noise he heard he thought was a wild beast coming to kill him, and even the piercing notes of the whippoorwill made his hair stand on end. When he passed a house the dogs were after him in full cry, and he spent the whole night in terror. Let us hope the caresses of his mother compensated him for this suffering.

The next year when his master had a job thirty miles distant, he frequently walked the distance on a hot summer's day, with his carpenter's tools upon his back. At that time light vehicles, or any kind of one-horse carriage, were very rarely kept in country places, and mechanics generally had to trudge to their place of work, carrying their tools with them. So passed the first years of his apprenticeship.

All this time he was thinking of quite another business, — that of clock-making, — which had been developed during his childhood near his father's house, by Eli Terry, the founder of the Yankee wooden-clock manufacture.

This ingenious Mr. Terry, with a small saw and a jack-knife, would cut out the wheels and works for twenty-five clocks during the winter, and, when the spring opened, he would sling three or four of them across the back of a horse, and keep going till he sold them, for about twenty-five dollars apiece. This was for the works only. When a farmer had bought the machinery of a clock for twenty-five dollars, he employed the village carpenter to make a case for it, which might cost ten or fifteen dollars more.

It was in this simple way that the country was supplied with those tall, old-fashioned clocks, of which almost every ancient farm-house still contains a specimen. The clock-case was sometimes built into the house like a pillar, and helped to support the upper story. Some of them were made by very clumsy workmen, out of the commonest timber, just planed in the roughest way, and contained wood enough for a pretty good-sized organ.

The clock business had fascinated Chauncey Jerome from his childhood, and he longed to work at it. His guardian dissuaded him. So many clocks were then making, he said, that in two or three years the whole country would be supplied, and then there would be no more business for a clock-maker. This was the general opinion. At a training, one day, the boy overheard a group talking of Eli Terry's *folly* in undertaking to make two hundred clocks all at once.

"He'll never live long enough to finish them," said one.

"If he should," said another, "he could not possibly sell so many. The very idea is ridiculous."

The boy was not convinced by these wise men of the East, and he lived to make and to sell two hundred thousand clocks in one year!

When his apprenticeship was a little more than half over, he told his master that if he would give him four months in the winter of each year, when business was dull, he would buy his own clothes. His master consenting, he went to Waterbury, Connecticut, and began to work making clock dials, and very soon got an insight into the art and mystery of clock-making.

The clock-makers of that day, who carried round their clock-movements upon a horse's back, often found it difficult to sell them in remote country places, because there was no carpenter near by competent to make a case. Two smart Yankees hired our apprentice to go with them to the distant State of New Jersey, for the express purpose of making cases for the clocks they sold. On this journey he first saw the city of New York. He was perfectly astonished at the bustle and confusion. He stood on the corner of Chatham and Pearl Streets for more than an hour, wondering why so many people were hurrying about so in every direction.

"What is going on?" said he, to a passer-by. "What's the excitement about?"

The man hurried on without noticing him; which led him to conclude that city people were not over polite.

The workmen were just finishing the interior of the City Hall, and he was greatly puzzled to understand how those winding stone stairs could be fixed without any visible means of support. In New Jersey he found another wonder. The people there kept Christmas more strictly than Sunday; a thing very strange to a child of the Puritans, who hardly knew what Christmas was.

Every winter added something to his knowledge of clock-making, and, soon after he was out of his apprenticeship, he bought some portions of clocks, a little mahogany, and began to put clocks together on his own account, with encouraging success from the beginning.

It was a great day with him when he received his first magnificent order from a Southern merchant for twelve wooden clocks at twelve dollars apiece! When they were done, he delivered them himself to his customer, and found it impossible to believe that he should actually receive so vast a sum as a hundred and forty-four dollars. He took the money with a trembling hand, and buttoned it up in his pocket. Then he felt an awful apprehension that some robbers might have heard of his expecting to receive this enormous amount, and would waylay him on the road home.

He worked but too steadily. He used to say that he loved to work as well as he did to eat, and that sometimes he would not go outside of his gate from one Sunday to the next. He soon began to make inventions and improvements. His business rapidly increased, though occasionally he had heavy losses and misfortunes.

His most important contribution to the business of clock-making was his substitution of brass for wood in the cheap clocks. He found that his wooden clocks, when they were transported by sea, were often spoiled by the swelling of the wooden wheels. One night, in a moment of extreme depression during the panic of 1837, the thought darted into his mind, —

" A cheap clock can be made of brass as well as wood ! "

It kept him awake nearly all night. He began at once to carry out the idea. It gave an immense development to the business, because brass clocks could be exported to all parts of the world, and the cost of making them was greatly lessened by new machinery. It was Chauncey Jerome who learned how to make a pretty good brass clock for forty cents, and a good one for two dollars ; and it was he who began their exportation to foreign lands. Clocks of his making ticked during his lifetime at Jerusalem, Saint Helena, Calcutta, Honolulu, and most of the other ends of the earth.

After making millions of clocks, and acquiring a large fortune, he retired from active business, leaving his splendid manufactory at New Haven to the management of others. They thought they knew more than the old man; they mismanaged the business terribly, and involved him in their own ruin. He was obliged to leave his beautiful home at seventy years of age, and seek employment at weekly wages — he who had given employment to three hundred men at once.

He scorned to be dependent. I saw and talked long with this good old man when he was working upon a salary, at the age of seventy-three, as superintendent of a large clock factory in Chicago. He did not pretend to be indifferent to the change in his position. He felt it acutely. He was proud of the splendid business he had created, and he lamented its destruction. He said it was one of his consolations to know that, in the course of his long life, he had never brought upon others the pains he was then enduring. He bore his misfortunes as a man should, and enjoyed the confidence and esteem of his new associates.

CAPTAIN PIERRE LACLEDE LIGUEST,
PIONEER

CAPTAIN PIERRE LACLEDE LIGUEST,

PIONEER

THE bridge which springs so lightly and so gracefully over the Mississippi at St. Louis is a truly wonderful structure. It often happens in this world that the work which is done best conceals the merit of the worker. All is finished so thoroughly and smoothly, and fulfills its purpose with so little jar and friction, that the difficulties overcome by the engineer become almost incredible. No one would suppose, while looking down upon the three steel arches of this exquisite bridge, that its foundations are one hundred and twenty feet below the surface of the water, and that its construction cost nine millions of dollars and six years of time. Its great height above the river is also completely concealed by the breadth of its span. The largest steamboat on the river passes under it at the highest stage of water, and yet the curve of the arches appears to have been selected merely for its pictorial effect.

It is indeed a noble and admirable work, an honor to the city and country, and, above all, to

Captain James B. Eads, who designed and constructed it. The spectator who sees for the first time St. Louis, now covering as far as the eye can reach the great bend of the river on which it is built, the shore fringed with steamboats puffing black smoke, and the city glittering in the morning sun, beholds one of the most striking and animating spectacles which this continent affords.

Go back one hundred and twenty years. That bend was then covered with the primeval forest, and the only object upon it which betrayed the hand of man was a huge green mound, a hundred feet high, that had been thrown up ages before by some tribe which inhabited the spot before our Indians had appeared. All that region swarmed with fur-bearing animals, deer, bear, buffalo, and beaver. It is difficult to see how this continent ever could have been settled but for the fur trade. It was beaver skin which enabled the Pilgrim Fathers of New England to hold their own during the first fifty years of their settlement. It was in quest of furs that the pioneers pushed westward, and it was by the sale of furs that the frontier settlers were at first supplied with arms, ammunition, tools, and salt.

The fur trade also led to the founding of St. Louis. In the year 1763 a great fleet of heavy batteaux, loaded with the rude merchandise needed by trappers and Indians, approached the spot on which St. Louis stands. This fleet had made its way up the Mississippi with enormous difficulty and toil from New Orleans, and only reached the mouth of the Missouri at the end of the fourth month. It was commanded by Pierre Laclede Liguest, the chief partner in a company chartered to trade with the Indians of the Missouri River. He was a Frenchman, a man of great energy and executive force, and his company of hunters, trappers, mechanics, and farmers, were also French.

On his way up the river Captain Liguest had noticed this superb bend of land, high enough above the water to avoid the floods, and its surface only undulating enough for the purposes of a settlement. Having reached the mouth of the Muddy River (as they called the Missouri) in the month of December, and finding no place there well suited to his purpose, he dropped down the stream seventeen miles, and drove the prows of his boats into what is now the Levee of St. Louis. It was too late in the season to begin a settlement. But he "blazed" the trees to mark the spot, and he said to a young man of his company, Auguste Chouteau: —

"You will come here as soon as the river is free from ice, and will cause this place to be cleared, and form a settlement according to the plan I shall give you."

The fleet fell down the river to the nearest French settlement, Fort de Chartres. Captain Liguest said to the commander of this fort on arriving: —

" I have found a situation where I intend to establish a settlement which in the future will become one of the most beautiful cities in America."

These are not imaginary words. Auguste Chouteau, who was selected to form the settlement, kept a diary, part of which is now preserved in the Mercantile Library at St. Louis, and in it this saying of Captain Liguest is recorded. So, the next spring he dispatched young Chouteau with a select body of thirty mechanics and hunters to the site of the proposed settlement.

"You will go," said he, "and disembark at the place where we marked the trees. You will begin to clear the place and build a large shed to contain the provisions and tools and some little cabins to lodge the men."

On the fifteenth of February, 1764, the party arrived, and the next morning began to build their shed. Liguest named the settlement St. Louis, in honor of the patron saint of the royal house of France — Louis XV. being then upon the throne. All went well with the settlement, and it soon became the seat of the fur trade for an immense region of country, extending gradually from the Mississippi to the Rocky Mountains.

The French lived more peacefully with the Indians than any other people who assisted to settle this continent, and the reason appears to have been that they became almost Indian themselves. They built their huts in the wigwam fashion, with poles stuck in the ground. They imitated the ways and customs of the Indians, both in living and in hunting. They went on hunting expeditions with Indians, wore the same garments, and learned to live on meat only, as Indian hunting parties generally did. But the circumstance which most endeared the French to the Indians was their marrying the daughters of the chiefs, which made the Indians regard them as belonging to their tribe. Besides this, they accommodated themselves to the Indian character, and learned how to please them. A St. Louis fur trader, who was living a few years ago in the ninetieth year of his age, used to speak of the ease with which an influential chief could be conciliated.

"I could always," said he, "make the principal chief of a tribe my friend by a piece of vermilion, a pocket looking-glass, some flashy-looking beads, and a knife. These things made him a puppet in my hands."

Even if a valuable horse had been stolen, a chief, whose friendship had been won in this manner, would continue to scold the tribe until the horse was brought back. The Indians, too, were delighted with the Frenchman's fiddle, his dancing, his gayety of manner, and even with the bright pageantry of his religion. It was when the settlement was six years old that the inhabitants of St. Louis, a very few hundreds in number, gathered to take part in the consecration of a little church,

made very much like the great council wigwam of
the Indians, the logs being placed upright, and the
interstices filled with mortar. This church stood
near the river, almost on the very site of the present cathedral. Mass was said, and the Te Deum
was chanted. At the first laying out of the village,
Captain Liguest set apart the whole block as a site
for the church, and it remains church property to
this day.

It is evident from Chouteau's diary that Pierre
Laclede Liguest, though he had able and energetic
assistants, was the soul of the enterprise, and the
real founder of St. Louis. He was one of that
stock of Frenchmen who put the imprint of their
nation, never to be effaced, upon the map of North
America — a kind of Frenchman unspeakably different from those who figured in the comic opera
and the masquerade ball of the late corrupt and
effeminating empire. He was a genial and generous man, who rewarded his followers bountifully,
and took the lead in every service of difficulty and
danger. While on a visit to New Orleans he died
of one of the diseases of the country, and was buried
on the shore near the mouth of the Arkansas River.

His executor and chief assistant, Auguste Chouteau, born at New Orleans in 1739, lived one hundred years, not dying till 1839. There are many
people in St. Louis who remember him. A very
remarkable coincidence was, that his brother, Pierre
Chouteau, born in New Orleans in 1749, died in

St. Louis in 1849, having also lived just one hundred years. Both of these brothers were identified with St. Louis from the beginning, where they lived in affluence and honor for seventy years, and where their descendants still reside.

The growth of St. Louis was long retarded by the narrowness and tyranny of the Spanish government, to which the French ceded the country about the time when St. Louis was settled. But in 1804 it was transferred to the United States, and from that time its progress has been rapid and almost uninterrupted. When President Jefferson's agent took possession, there was no post-office, no ferry over the river, no newspaper, no hotel, no Protestant church, and no school. Nor could any one hold land who was not a Catholic. Instantly, and as a matter of course, all restricting laws were swept away; and before two years had passed there was a ferry, a post-office, a newspaper, a Protestant church, a hotel, and two schools, one French and one English.

ISRAEL PUTNAM.

IT is strange that so straightforward and trans-
parent a character as " Old Put " should have become the subject of controversy. Too much is
claimed for him by some disputants, and much too
little is conceded to him by others. He was certainly as far from being a rustic booby as he was
from being a great general.

Conceive him, first, as a thriving, vigorous, enterprising Connecticut farmer, thirty years of age,
cultivating with great success his own farm of five
hundred and fourteen acres, all paid for. Himself
one of a family of twelve children, and belonging to
a prolific race which has scattered Putnams all over
the United States, besides leaving an extraordinary
number in New England, he had married young at
his native Salem, and established himself soon after
in the northeastern corner of Connecticut. At that
period, 1740, Connecticut was to Massachusetts what
Colorado is to New York at present ; and thither,
accordingly, this vigorous young man and his young
wife early removed, and hewed out a farm from the
primeval woods.

He was just the man for a pioneer. His strength of body was extraordinary, and he had a power of sustained exertion more valuable even than great strength. Nothing is more certain than that he was an enterprising and successful farmer, who introduced new fruits, better breeds of cattle, and improved implements.

There is still to be seen on his farm a long avenue of ancient apple trees, which, the old men of the neighborhood affirm, were set out by Israel Putnam one hundred and forty years ago. The well which he dug is still used. Coming to the place with considerable property inherited from his father (for the Putnams were a thriving race from the beginning), it is not surprising that he should have become one of the leading farmers in a county of farmers.

At the same time he was not a studious man, and had no taste for intellectual enjoyments. He was not then a member of the church. He never served upon the school committee. There was a Library Association at the next village, but he did not belong to it. For bold riding, skillful hunting, woodchopping, hay-tossing, ploughing, it was hard to find his equal; but, in the matter of learning, he could write legibly, read well enough, spell in an independent manner, and not much more.

With regard to the wolf story, which rests upon tradition only, it is not improbable, and there is no good reason to doubt it. Similar deeds have been

7

done by brave backwoodsmen from the beginning, and are still done within the boundaries of the United States every year. The story goes, that when he had been about two years on his new farm, the report was brought in one morning that a noted she-wolf of the neighborhood had killed seventy of his sheep and goats, besides wounding many lambs and kids. This wolf, the last of her race in that region, had long eluded the skill of every hunter. Upon seeing the slaughter of his flock, the young farmer, it appears, entered into a compact with five of his neighbors to hunt the pernicious creature by turns until they had killed her. The animal was at length tracked to her den, a cave extending deep into a rocky hill. The tradition is, that Putnam, with a rope around his body, a torch in one hand, and rifle in the other, went twice into the cave, and the second time shot the wolf dead, and was drawn out by the people, wolf and all. An exploit of this nature gave great celebrity in an outlying county in the year 1742. Meanwhile he continued to thrive, and one of the old-fashioned New England families of ten children gathered about him. As they grew towards maturity, he bought a share in the Library Association, built a pew for his family in the church, and comported himself in all ways as became a prosperous farmer and father of a numerous family.

So passed his life until he reached the age of thirty-seven, when he already had a boy fifteen years of age, and was rich in all the wealth which Connecticut then possessed. The French war broke out — the war which decided the question whether the French or the English race should possess North America. His reputation was such that the legislature of Connecticut appointed him at once a captain, and he had no difficulty in enlisting a company of the young men of his county, young farmers or the sons of farmers. He gained great note as a scouter and ranger, rendering such important service in this way to the army that the legislature made him a special grant of "fifty Spanish milled dollars" as an honorable gift. He was famous also for Yankee ingenuity. A colonial newspaper relates an anecdote illustrative of this. The British general was sorely perplexed by the presence of a French man-of-war commanding a piece of water which it was necessary for him to cross.

" General," said Putnam, "that ship must be taken."

" Aye," replied the general, " I would give the world if she was taken."

" I will take her," said Putnam.

" How ? " asked the general.

" Give me some wedges, a beetle, and a few men of my own choice."

When night came, Putnam rowed under the vessel's stern, and drove the wedges between the rudder and the ship. In the morning she was seen with her sails flapping helplessly in the middle of the lake, and she was soon after blown ashore and captured.

Among other adventures, Putnam was taken prisoner by the Indians, and carried to his grave great scars of the wounds inflicted by the savages. He served to the very end of the war, pursuing the enemy even into the tropics, and assisting at the capture of Havana. He returned home, after nine years of almost continuous service, with the rank of colonel, and such a reputation as made him the hero of Connecticut, as Washington was the hero of Virginia at the close of the same war. At any time of public danger requiring a resort to arms, he would be naturally looked to by the people of Connecticut to take the command.

Eleven peaceful years he now spent at home. His wife died, leaving an infant a year old. He joined the church; he married again; he cultivated his farm; he told his war stories. The Stamp Act excitement occurred in 1765, when Putnam joined the Sons of Liberty, and called upon the governor of the colony as a deputy from them.

" What shall I do," asked the governor, " if the stamped paper should be sent to me by the king's authority?"

" Lock it up," said Putnam, " until we visit you again."

" And what will you do with it?"

" We shall expect you to give us the key of the room where it is deposited; and if you think fit, in order to screen yourself from blame, you may forewarn us upon our peril not to enter the room."

"And what will you do afterwards?"

"Send it safely back again."

"But if I should refuse you admission?"

"Your house will be level with the dust in five minutes."

Fortunately, the stamped paper never reached Connecticut, and the act was repealed soon after.

The eventful year, 1774, arrived. Putnam was fifty-six years of age, a somewhat portly personage, weighing two hundred pounds, with a round, full countenance, adorned by curly locks, now turning gray — the very picture of a hale, hearty, good-humored, upright and downright country gentleman. News came that the port of Boston was closed, its business suspended, its people likely to be in want of food. The farmers of the neighborhood contributed a hundred and twenty-five sheep, which Putnam himself drove to Boston, sixty miles off, where he had a cordial reception by the people, and was visited by great numbers of them at the house of Dr. Warren, where he lived. The polite people of Boston were delighted with the scarred old hero, and were pleased to tell anecdotes of his homely ways and fervent, honest zeal. He mingled freely, too, with the British officers, who *chaffed* him, as the modern saying is, about his coming down to Boston to fight. They told him that twenty great ships and twenty regiments would come unless the people submitted.

"If they come," said Putnam, "I am ready to treat them as enemies."

One day in the following spring, April twentieth, while he was ploughing in one of his fields with a yoke of oxen driven by his son, Daniel, a boy of fifteen, an express reached him giving him the news of the battle of Lexington, which had occurred the day before. Daniel Putnam has left a record of what his father did on this occasion.

"He loitered not," wrote Daniel, "but left me, the driver of his team, to unyoke it in the furrow, and not many days after to follow him to camp."

Colonel Putnam mounted a horse, and set off instantly to alarm the officers of militia in the neighboring towns. Returning home a few hours after, he found hundreds of minute-men assembled, armed and equipped, who had chosen him for their commander. He accepted the command, and, giving them orders to follow, he pushed on without dismounting, rode the same horse all night, and reached Cambridge next morning at sunrise, still wearing the checked shirt which he had had on when ploughing in his field. As Mr. Bancroft remarks, he brought to his country's service an undaunted courage and a devoted heart. His services during the Revolution are known to almost every reader. Every one seems to have liked him, for he had a very happy turn for humor, sang a good song, and was a very cheerful old gentleman.

In 1789, after four years of vigorous and useful

service, too arduous for his age, he suffered a paralytic stroke, which obliged him to leave the army. He lived, however, to see his country free and prosperous, surviving to the year 1790, when he died, aged seventy-three. I saw his commission as major-general hanging in the house of one of his grandsons, Colonel A. P. Putnam, at Nashville, some years ago. He has descendants in every State.

GEORGE FLOWER.

PIONEER.

<hr>

TRAVELERS from old Europe are surprised to find in Chicago such an institution as an Historical Society. What can a city of yesterday, they ask, find to place in its archives, beyond the names of the first settlers, and the erection of the first elevator? They forget that the newest settlement of civilized men inherits and possesses the whole past of our race, and that no community has so much need to be instructed by History as one which has little of its own. Nor is it amiss for a new commonwealth to record its history as it makes it, and store away the records of its vigorous infancy for the entertainment of its mature age.

The first volume issued by the Chicago Historical Society contains an account of what is still called the "English Settlement," in Edwards County, Illinois, founded in 1817 by two wealthy English farmers, Morris Birkbeck and George Flower. These gentlemen sold out all their possessions in England, and set out in search of the prairies of the Great West, of which they had heard in the old country. They were not quite sure there were any prairies, for all the settled parts of the United States, they knew, had been covered with the dense primeval forest. The existence of the prairies rested upon the tales of travelers. So George Flower, in the spring of 1816, set out in advance to verify the story, bearing valuable letters of introduction, one from General La Fayette to ex-President Jefferson.

With plenty of money in his pocket and enjoying every other advantage, he was nearly two years in merely *finding* the prairies. First, he was fifty days in crossing the ocean, and he spent six weeks in Philadelphia, enjoying the hospitality of friends. The fourth month of his journey had nearly elapsed before he had fairly mounted his horse and started on his westward way.

It is a pity there is not another new continent to be explored and settled, because the experience gained in America would so much facilitate the work. Upon looking over such records as that of George Flower's History we frequently meet with devices and expedients of great value in their time and place, but which are destined soon to be numbered among the Lost Arts. For example, take the mode of saddling and loading a horse for a ride of fifteen hundred miles, say, from the Atlantic to the Far West, or back again. It was a matter of infinite importance to the rider, for every part of the load was subjected to desperate pulls and wrenches, and the breaking of a strap, at a critical moment in crossing a river or climbing a steep, might precipitate both horse and rider to destruction.

On the back of the horse was laid, first of all, a soft and thin blanket, which protected the animal in some degree against the venomous insects that abounded on the prairies, the attacks of which could sometimes madden the gentlest horse. Upon this was placed the saddle, which was large, and provided in front with a high pommel, and behind with a pad to receive part of the lading. The saddle was a matter of great importance, as well as its girths and crupper strap, all of which an experienced traveler subjected to most careful examination. Every stitch was looked at, and the strength of all the parts repeatedly tested.

Over the saddle — folded twice, if not three times — was a large, thick, and fine blanket, as good a one as the rider could afford, which was kept in its place by a broad surcingle. On the pad behind the saddle were securely fastened a cloak and umbrella, rolled together as tight as possible and bound with two straps. Next we have to consider the saddle bags, stuffed as full as they could hold, each bag being exactly of the same weight and size as the other. As the horseman put into them the few articles of necessity which they would hold he would balance them frequently, to see that one did not outweigh the other even by half a pound. If this were neglected, the bags would slip from one side to the other, graze the horse's leg, and start him off in a " furious kicking gallop." The saddle-bags were slung across the saddle under the blanket, and kept in their place by two loops through which the stirrup leathers passed.

So much for the horse. The next thing was for the rider to put on his leggings, which were pieces of cloth about a yard square, folded round the leg from the knee to the ankle, and fastened with pins and bands of tape. These leggings received the mud and water splashed up by the horse, and kept the trousers dry. Thus prepared, the rider proceeded to mount, which was by no means an easy matter, considering what was already upon the horse's back. The horse was placed as near as possible to a stump, from which, with a " pretty wide stride and fling of the leg," the rider would spring into his seat. It was so difficult to mount and dismount, that experienced travelers would seldom get off until the party halted for noon, and not again until it was time to camp.

Women often made the journey on horseback, and bore the fatigue of it about as well as men. Instead of a riding-habit, they wore over their ordinary dress a long skirt of dark-colored material, and tied their bonnets on with a large handkerchief over the top, which served to protect the face and ears from the weather.

The packing of the saddle made the seat more

comfortable, and even safer, for both men and women. The rider, in fact, was seldom thrown unless the whole load came off at once. Thus mounted, a party of experienced horsemen and horsewomen would average their thirty miles a day for a month at a time, providing no accident befel them. They were, nevertheless, liable to many accidents and vexatious delays. A horse falling lame would delay the party. Occasionally there would be a stampede of all the horses, and days lost in finding them.

The greatest difficulty of all was the overflowing waters. No reader can have forgotten the floods in the western country in the spring of 1884, when every brook was a torrent and every river a deluge. Imagine a party of travelers making their westward way on horseback at such a time, before there was even a raft ferry on any river west of the Alleghanies, and when all the valleys would be covered with water. It was by no means unusual for a party to be detained a month waiting for the waters of a large river to subside, and it was a thing at some seasons of daily occurrence for all of them to be soused up to their necks in water.

Many of the important fords, too, could only be crossed by people who knew their secret. I received once myself directions for crossing a ford in South Carolina something like this: I was told to go straight in four lengths of the horse; then "turn square to the right" and go two lengths; and finally "strike for the shore, slanting a little down the stream." Luckily, I had some one with me more expert in fords than I was, and through his friendly guidance managed to flounder through.

Between New York and Baltimore, in 1775, there were more than twenty streams to be forded, and six wide rivers or inlets to be ferried over. We little think, as we glide over these streams now, that the smallest of them, in some seasons, presented difficulties to our grandfathers going southward on horseback.

The art of camping out was wonderfully well understood by the early pioneers. Women were a great help in making the camp comfortable. As the Pilgrim Fathers may be said to have discovered the true method of settling the sea-shore, so the Western pioneer found the best way of traversing and subduing the interior wilderness. The secret in both cases was to get *the aid of women and children!* They supplied men with motive, did a full half of the labor, and made it next to impossible to turn back. Mr. Flower makes a remark in connection with this subject, the truth of which will be attested by many.

"It is astonishing," he says, "how soon we are restored from fatigue caused by exercise in the open air. Debility is of much longer duration from labor in factories, stores, and in rooms warmed by stoves. Hail, snow, thunder storms, and drenching rains are all *restoratives* to health and spirits."

Often, when the company would be all but tired out by a long day's ride in hot weather, and the line stretched out three or four miles, a good soaking rain would restore their spirits at once. Nor did a plunge into the stream, which would wet every fibre of their clothing, do them any harm. They would ride on in the sun, and let their clothes dry in the natural way.

It must be owned, however, that some of the winter experiences of travelers in the prairie country were most severe. In the forest a fire can be made and some shelter can be found. But imagine a party on the prairie in the midst of a driving snow-storm, overtaken by night, the temperature at zero. Even in these circumstances knowledge was safety. Each man would place his saddle on the ground and sit upon it, covering his shoulders and head with his blanket, and holding his horse by the bridle. In this way the human travelers usually derived warmth and shelter enough from the horses to keep them from freezing to death. Another method was to tie their horses, spread a blanket on the ground, and sit upon it as close together as they could.

Sometimes, indeed, a whole party would freeze together in a mass; but commonly all escaped without serious injury, and in some instances invalids were restored to health by exposure which we should imagine would kill a healthy man.

When George Flower rode westward in 1816,

Lancaster, Pa., was the largest inland town of the
United States, and Dr. Priestley's beautiful abode
at Sunbury on the Susquehanna was still on the
outside of the "Far West." He had more trouble
in getting to Pittsburg than he would now have in
going round the world. In the Alleghany Mountains he lost his way, and was rescued by the chance
of finding a stray horse which he caught and mounted, and was carried by it to the only cabin in the
region. The owner of this cabin was "a poor Irish-
man with a coat so darned, patched, and tattered as
to be quite a curiosity."

"How I cherished him!" says the traveler.
"No angel's visit could have pleased me so well.
He pointed out to me the course and showed me
into a path."

Pittsburg was already a smoky town. Leaving
it soon, he rode on westward to Cincinnati, then a
place of five or six thousand inhabitants, but growing rapidly. Even so far west as Cincinnati he
could still learn nothing of the prairies.

"Not a person that I saw," he declares, "knew
anything about them. I shrank from the idea of
settling in the midst of a wood of heavy timber, to
hack and to hew my way to a little farm, ever
bounded by a wall of gloomy forest."

Then he rode across Kentucky, where he was
struck, as every one was and is, by the luxuriant
beauty of the blue-grass farms. He dwells upon
the difficulty and horror of fording the rivers at

that season of the year. Some of his narrow escapes made such a deep impression upon his mind that he used to dream of them fifty years after. He paid a visit to old Governor Shelby of warlike renown, one of the heroes of the frontier, and there at last he got some news of the prairies! He says:

"It was at Governor Shelby's house (in Lincoln County, Ky.) that I met the first person who confirmed me in the existence of the prairies."

This informant was the Governor's brother, who had just come from the Mississippi River across the glorious prairies of Illinois to the Ohio. The information was a great relief. He was sure now that he had left his native land on no fool's errand, the victim of a traveler's lying tale. Being thus satisfied that there *were* prairies which could be found whenever they were wanted, he suspended the pursuit.

He had been then seven months from home, and November being at hand, too late to explore an unknown country, he changed his course, and went off to visit Mr. Jefferson at his estate of Poplar Forest in Virginia, upon which the Natural Bridge is situated. Passing through Nashville on his way, he saw General Andrew Jackson at a horse race. He describes the hero of New Orleans as an elderly man, "lean and lank, bronzed in complexion, deep marked countenance, grisly-gray hair, and a restless, fiery eye." He adds: —

"Jackson had a horse on the course which was

beaten that day. The recklessness of his bets, his violent gesticulations and imprecations, outdid all competition. If I had been told that he was to be a future President of the United States, I should have thought it a very strange thing."

There are still a few old men, I believe, at Nashville who remember General Jackson's demeanor on the race ground, and they confirm the record of Mr. Flower. After a ride of a thousand miles or so, he presented his letter of introduction to Mr. Jefferson at Poplar Forest, and had a cordial reception. The traveler describes the house as resembling a French château, with octagon rooms, doors of polished oak, lofty ceilings, and large mirrors. The ex-President's form, he says, was of somewhat majestic proportions, more than six feet in height; his manners simple, kind, and polite; his dress a dark pepper-and-salt coat, cut in the old Quaker fashion, with one row of large metal buttons, knee-breeches, gray worsted stockings, and shoes fastened by large metal buckles, all quite in the old style. His two grand-daughters, Misses Randolph, were living with him then. Mr. Jefferson soon after returned to his usual abode, Monticello, and there Mr. Flower spent the greater part of the winter, enjoying most keenly the evening conversations of the ex-President, who delighted to talk of the historic scenes in which he was for fifty years a conspicuous actor.

George Flower and his party would have settled

8

near Monticello, perhaps, but for the system of slavery, which perpetuated a wasteful mode of farming, and disfigured the beautiful land with dilapidation.

He had, meanwhile, sent home word that prairies existed in America, and in the spring of 1817 his partner in the enterprise, Morris Birkbeck, and his family of nine, came out from England, and they all started westward in search of the prairies. They went by stage to Pittsburg, where they bought horses, mounted them and continued their journey, men, ladies, and boys, a dozen people in all. The journey was not unpleasant, most of them being persons of education and refinement, with three agreeable young ladies among them, two of them being daughters of Mr. Birkbeck, and Miss Andrews, their friend and companion.

All went well and happily during the journey until Mr. Birkbeck, a widower of fifty-four with grown daughters, made an offer of marriage to Miss Andrews, aged twenty-five. It was an embarrassing situation. She was constrained to decline the offer, and as they were traveling in such close relations, the freedom and enjoyment of the journey were seriously impaired. Then Mr. Flower, who was a widower also, but in the prime of life, proposed to the young lady. She accepted him, and they were soon after married at Vincennes, the rejected Birkbeck officiating as father of the bride.

But this was not finding the prairies. At length,

toward the close of the second summer, they began
to meet with people who had seen prairies, and
finally their own eyes were greeted with the sight.
One day, after a ride of seven hours in extreme
heat, bruised and torn by the brushwood, exhausted
and almost in despair, suddenly a beautiful prairie
was disclosed to their view. It was an immense expanse stretching away in profound repose beneath
the light of an afternoon summer sun, surrounded
by forest and adorned with clumps of mighty oaks,
"the whole presenting a magnificence of park scen-
ery complete from the hand of nature." The writer
adds: "For once, the reality came up to the picture of the imagination."

If the reader supposes that their task was now
substantially accomplished, he is very much mistaken. After a good deal of laborious search, they
chose a site for their settlement in Edwards County,
Illinois, and bought a considerable tract; after
which Mr. Flower went to England to close up the
affairs of the two families, and raise the money to
pay for their land and build their houses. They
named their town Albion. It has enjoyed a safe
and steady prosperity ever since, and has been in
some respects a model town to that part of Illinois.

The art of founding a town must of course soon
cease to be practiced. It is curious to note how all
the institutions of civilized life were established in
their order. First was built a large log-cabin that
would answer as a tavern and blacksmith's shop,

the first requisites being to get the horses shod, and the riders supplied with whiskey. Then came other log-cabins, as they were needed, which pioneers would undertake to build for arriving emigrants for twenty-five dollars apiece. Very soon one of the people would try, for the first time in his life, to preach a sermon on Sundays, and as soon as there were children enough in the neighborhood, one of the settlers, unable to cope with the labors of agriculture, would undertake to teach them, and a log-cabin would be built or appropriated for the purpose.

Mr. Flower reports that, as soon as the school was established, civilization was safe. Some boys and some parents would hold out against it for a while, but all of them at last either join the movement or remove further into the wilderness.

"Occasionally," he says, "will be seen a boy, ten or twelve years old, leaning against a door-post intently gazing in upon the scholars at their lessons; after a time he slowly and moodily goes away. He feels his exclusion. He can no longer say: 'I am as good as you.' He must go to school or dive deeper into the forest."

All this is passing. Already it begins to read like ancient history.

George Flower survived until March, 1862, when he died at a good old age. Certainly the Historical Society of Chicago has done well to publish the record he left behind him.

EDWARD COLES,

NOBLEST OF THE PIONEERS, AND HIS GREAT SPEECH.

WHEN James Madison came to the presidency in 1809, he followed the example of his predecessor, Mr. Jefferson, in the selection of his private secretary. Mr. Jefferson chose Captain Meriwether Lewis, the son of one of his Virginia neighbors, whom he had known from his childhood. Mr. Madison gave the appointment to Edward Coles, the son of a family friend of Albermarle County, Va., who had recently died, leaving a large estate in land and slaves to his children.

Edward Coles, a graduate of William and Mary college, was twenty-three years of age when he entered the White House as a member of the President's family. He was a young man after James Madison's own heart, of gentle manners, handsome person, and singular firmness of character. In the correspondence both of Jefferson and Madison several letters can be found addressed to him which show the very high estimation in which he was held by those eminent men.

Among the many young men who have held the place of private secretary in the presidential mansion, Edward Coles was one of the most interesting. I know not which ought to rank highest in our esteem, the wise and gallant Lewis, who explored for us the Western wilderness, or Edward Coles, one of the rare men who know how to surrender, for conscience' sake, home, fortune, ease, and good repute.

While he was still in college he became deeply interested in the question, whether men could rightfully hold property in men. At that time the best of the educated class at the South were still abolitionists in a romantic or sentimental sense, just as Queen Marie Antoinette was a republican during the American Revolution. Here and there a young man like George Wythe had set free his slaves and gone into the profession of the law. With the great majority, however, their disapproval of slavery was only an affair of the intellect, which led to no practical results. It was not such with Edward Coles. The moment you look at the portrait given in the recent sketch of his life by Mr. E. B. Washburne, you perceive that he was a person who might be slow to make up his mind, but who, when he had once discovered the right course, could never again be at peace with himself until he had followed it.

While at college he read everything on the subject of slavery that fell in his way, and he studied it in the light of the Declaration of Independence, which assured him that men are born free and equal and endowed with certain natural rights which are inalienable. He made up his mind, while he was still a student, that it was wrong to hold slaves, and he resolved that he would neither hold them nor live in a State which permitted slaves to be held. He was determined, however, to do nothing rashly. One reason which induced him to accept the place offered him by Mr. Madison was his desire of getting a knowledge of the remoter parts of the Union, in order to choose the place where he could settle his slaves most advantageously.

While he was yet a member of the presidential household, he held that celebrated correspondence with Mr. Jefferson, in which he urged the ex-President to devote the rest of his life to promoting the abolition of slavery. Mr. Jefferson replied that the task was too arduous for a man who had passed his seventieth year. It was like bidding old Priam buckle on the armor of Hector.

"This enterprise," he added, "is for the young, for those who can follow it up and bear it through to its consummation. It shall have all my prayers and these are the only weapons of an old man. But, in the mean time, are you right in abandoning this property, and your country with it? I think not."

Mr. Jefferson endeavored to dissuade the young man from his project of removal. Mr. Coles, how-

ever, was not to be convinced. After serving for
six years as private secretary, and fulfilling a special diplomatic mission to Russia, he withdrew to his
ancestral home in Virginia, and prepared to lead
forth his slaves to the State of Illinois, then recently admitted into the Union, but still a scarcely
broken expanse of virgin prairie. He could not law-
fully emancipate his slaves in Virginia, and it was
far from his purpose to turn them loose in the wilderness. He was going with them, and to stay with
them until they were well rooted in the new soil.

All his friends and relations opposed his scheme ;
nor had he even the approval of the slaves themselves, for they knew nothing whatever of his intention. He had been a good master, and they followed him with blind faith, supposing that he was
merely going to remove, as they had seen other
planters remove, from an exhausted soil to virgin
lands. Placing his slaves in the charge of one of
their number, a mulatto man who had already made
the journey to Illinois with his master, he started
them in wagons on their long journey in April,
1819, over the Alleghany Mountains to a point
on the Monongahela River. There he bought two
large flat-bottomed boats, upon which he embarked
his whole company, with their horses, wagons, bag-
gage, and implements. His pilot proving a drunkard, he was obliged to take the command himself,
upon reaching Pittsburg.

The morning after he left Pittsburg, a lovely

April day, he called all the negroes together on the
deck of the boats, which were lashed together, and
explained what he was going to do with them. He
told them they were no longer slaves, but free people, free as he was, free to go on down the river
with him, and free to go ashore, just as they
pleased. He afterwards described the scene. "The
effect on them," he wrote, "was electrical. They
stared at me and at each other, as if doubting the
accuracy or reality of what they heard. In breath-
less silence they stood before me, unable to utter a
word, but with countenances beaming with expression which no words could convey, and which no
language can now describe. As they began to see
the truth of what they had heard, and to realize
their situation, there came on a kind of hysterical,
giggling laugh. After a pause of intense and un-
utterable emotion, bathed in tears, and with tremu-
lous voices, they gave vent to their gratitude, and
implored the blessings of God on me. When they
had in some degree recovered the command of
themselves, Ralph said he had long known I was
opposed to holding black people as slaves, and
thought it probable I would some time or other
give my people their freedom, but that he did not
expect me to do it so soon; and moreover, he
thought I ought not to do it till they had repaid
me the expense I had been at in removing them
from Virginia, and had improved my farm and
'gotten me well fixed in that new country.' To

this all simultaneously expressed their concurrence, and their desire to remain with me, as my servants, until they had comfortably fixed me at my new home.

"I told them, no. I had made up my mind to give to them immediate and unconditional freedom; that I had long been anxious to do it, but had been prevented by the delays, first in selling my property in Virginia, and then in collecting the money, and by other circumstances. That in consideration of this delay, and as a reward for their past services, as well as a stimulant to their future exertions, and with a hope it would add to their self-esteem and their standing in the estimation of others, I should give to each head of a family a quarter section, containing one hundred and sixty acres of land. To this all objected, saying I had done enough for them in giving them their freedom; and insisted on my keeping the land to supply my own wants, and added, in the kindest manner, the expression of their solicitude that I would not have the means of doing so after I had freed them. I told them I had thought much of my duty and of their rights, and that it was due alike to both that I should do what I had said I should do; and accordingly, soon after reaching Edwardsville, I executed and delivered to them deeds to the lands promised them.

"I stated to them that the lands I intended to give them were unimproved lands, and as they would not have the means of making the necessary improvements, of stocking their farms, and procuring the materials for at once living on them, they would have to hire themselves out till they could acquire by their labor the necessary means to commence cultivating and residing on their own lands. That I was willing to hire and employ on my farm a certain number of them (designating the individuals) ; the others I advised to seek employment in St. Louis, Edwardsville, and other·places, where smart, active young men and women could obtain much higher wages than they could on farms. At this some of them murmured, as it indicated a partiality, they said, on my part to those designated to live with me ; and contended they should all be equally dear to me, and that I ought not to keep a part and turn the others out on the world, to be badly treated, etc. I reminded them of what they seemed to have lost sight of, that they were free ; that no one had a right to beat or ill use them ; and if so treated they could at pleasure leave one place and seek a better ; that labor was much in demand in that new country, and highly paid for ; that there would be no difficulty in their obtaining good places, and being kindly treated ; but if not, I should be at hand, and would see they were well treated, and have justice done them.

" I availed myself of the deck scene to give the negroes some advice. I dwelt long and with much earnestness on their future conduct and success.

and my great anxiety that they should behave themselves and do well, not only for their own sakes, but for the sake of the black race held in bondage; many of whom were thus held because their masters believed they were incompetent to take care of themselves and that liberty would be to them a curse rather than a blessing. My anxious wish was that they should so conduct themselves as to show by their example that the descendants of Africa were competent to take care of and govern themselves, and enjoy all the blessings of liberty and all the other birthrights of man, and thus promote the universal emancipation of that unfortunate and outraged race of the human family." [1]

After floating six hundred miles down the Ohio, they had another land journey into Illinois, where the master performed his promises, and created a home for himself. A few years after, he was elected governor of the State. It was during his term of three years that a most determined effort was made to change the constitution of the State so as to legalize slavery in it. It was chiefly through the firmness and masterly management of Governor Coles that this attempt was frustrated.

When his purpose in moving to Illinois had been completely accomplished, he removed to Philadelphia, where he lived to the age of eighty-two.

[1] Sketch of Edward Coles. By E. B. Washburne. Chicago 1882.

Though not again in public life, he was always a public-spirited citizen. He corresponded with the venerable Madison to the close of that good man's life. Mr. Madison wrote two long letters to him on public topics in his eighty-fourth year. Governor Coles died at Philadelphia in 1868, having lived to see slavery abolished in every State of the Union.

I have been informed that few, if any, of his own slaves succeeded finally in farming prairie land, but that most of them gradually drifted to the towns, where they became waiters, barbers, porters, and domestic servants. My impression is that he over-estimated their capacity. But this does not diminish the moral sublimity of the experiment.

PETER H. BURNETT.

WHEN an aged bank president, who began life as a waiter in a backwoods tavern, tells the story of his life, we all like to gather close about him and listen to his tale. Peter H. Burnett, the first Governor of California, and now the President of the Pacific Bank in San Francisco, has recently related his history, or the "Recollections of an Old Pioneer;" and if I were asked by the "intelligent foreigner" we often read about to explain the United States of to-day, I would hand him that book, and say : —

"There! That is the stuff of which America is made."

He was born at Nashville, Tennessee, in 1807; his father a carpenter and farmer, an honest, strong-minded man, who built some of the first log-houses and frame-houses of what was then the frontier village of Nashville, now a beautiful and pleasant city. While he was still a child the family removed to Missouri, then on the outer edge of civilization, and they spent the first winter in a hovel with a dirt floor, boarded up at the sides, and with a hole in the middle of the roof for the escape of the smoke. All the family lived together in the same room. In a year or two, of course, they had a better house, and a farm under some cultivation.

Those pioneer settlements were good schools for the development of the pioneer virtues, courage, fortitude, handiness, directness of speech and conduct. Fancy a boy ten years old going on horseback to mill through the woods, and having to wait at the mill one or two days and nights for his turn, living chiefly on a little parched corn which he carried with him, and bringing back the flour all right.

"It often happened," says Governor Burnett, "that both bag and boy tumbled off, and then there was trouble; not so much because the boy was a little hurt (for he would soon recover), but because it was difficult to get the bag on again."

There was nothing for it but to wait until a man came along strong enough to shoulder three bushels of corn. Missouri was then, as it now is, a land of plenty; for besides the produce of the farms, the country was full of game, and a good deal of money was gained by the traffic in skins, honey, and beeswax. The simplicity of dress was such that a merchant attending church one day dressed in a suit of broadcloth, the aged preacher alluded to his "fine apparel," and condemned it as being contrary to the spirit of the Gospel. Fighting with fists was one of the chief amusements. At a training, some young bully would mount a stump, and after imitating the flapping and crowing of a cock, cry out : —

" I can whip any man in this crowd except my friends."

The challenge being accepted, the two combatants would fight until one of them cried, Enough ; whereupon they would wash their faces and take a friendly drink. Men would sometimes lose a part of an ear, the end of a nose, or the whole of an eye in these combats, for it was considered within the rules to bite and gouge.

In this wild country Peter Burnett grew to manhood, attending school occasionally in summer, and getting a pretty good rudimentary education. Coming of intelligent, honest, able ancestors, he used his opportunities well, and learned a great deal from books, but more from a close observation of the natural wonders by which he was surrounded. His acute and kindly remarks upon the wild animals and wild nature of this continent could be profitably studied by almost any naturalist. It is surprising that one who has almost all his life lived on the advanced wave of civilization in this country should have acquired, among his other possessions, an extensive knowledge of literature, as well as of life and nature. Nor is his case by any means uncommon.

When he was nineteen his father gave him a

horse three years old, a saddle and bridle, a new camlet cloak, and twenty-six dollars, and his mother furnished him with a good suit of jeans. Soon after, he mounted his young horse and rode back to his native State, and took charge of the tavern aforesaid in the town of Bolivar, Hardiman County, of which tavern he was waiter, clerk, and book-keeper. Here he had a pretty hard time. Being very young, gawky, and ill-dressed, he was subject to a good deal of jesting and ridicule. But he was fond of reading. Finding, by chance, at the house of an uncle, Pope's translation of the Iliad, he was perfectly entranced with it.

"Had it been gold or precious stones," he tells us, "the pleasure would not have equaled that which I enjoyed."

Nevertheless, he fancied that his ignorance, his country dress and uncouth manners caused him to be slighted even by his own relations.

"I was badly quizzed," he says, "and greatly mortified; but I worked on resolutely, said nothing, and was always at the post of duty."

Promotion is sure to come to a lad of that spirit, and accordingly we soon find him a clerk in a country store earning two hundred dollars a year and his board, besides being head over ears in love with a beautiful girl. At first he did not know that he was in love; but, one day, when he had been taking dinner with her family, and had talked with the young lady herself after dinner a good while,

9

he came out of the house, and was amazed to discover that the sun was gone from the sky.

"In a confused manner," he relates, "I inquired of her father what had become of the sun. He politely replied, 'It has gone down!' I knew then that I was in love. It was a plain case."

In those good old times marriage did not present the difficulties which it now does. He was soon married, obtained more lucrative employment, got into business for himself, failed, studied law, and found himself, at the age of thirty-six, the father of a family of six children, twenty-eight thousand dollars in debt, and, though in good practice at the bar, not able to reduce his indebtedness more than a thousand dollars a year. So he set his face toward Oregon, then containing only three or four hundred settlers. He mounted the stump and organized a wagon-train, the roll of which at the rendezvous contained two hundred and ninety-three names. With this party, whose effects were drawn by oxen and mules, he started in May, 1843, for a journey of seventeen hundred miles across a wilderness most of which had never been trodden by civilized men.

For six months they pursued their course westward. Six persons died on the way, five turned back, fifteen went to California, and those who held their course towards . Oregon endured hardships and privations which tasked their fortitude to the uttermost. Mr. Burnett surveyed the scenes of the wilderness with the eye of an intelligent and sympathetic observer. Many of his remarks upon the phenomena of those untrodden plains are of unusual interest, whether he is discoursing upon animate or inanimate nature.

Arrived in Oregon, an eight months' journey from Washington, the settlers were obliged to make a provisional government for themselves, to which the Tennessee lawyer lent an able hand. He relates an incident of the first collision between law and license. They selected for sheriff the famous Joseph L. Meek, a man of the best possible temper, but as brave as a lion. The first man who defied the new laws was one Dawson, a carpenter, scarcely less courageous than Meek himself. Dawson, who had been in a fight, disputed the right of the sheriff to arrest him. The sheriff simply replied: —

"Dawson, I came for you."

The carpenter raised his plane to defend himself. Meek wrested it from him. Dawson picked up his broad axe, but on rising found himself within a few inches of Meek's cocked revolver.

"Dawson," said the sheriff, laughing, "I came for you. Surrender or die."

Dawson surrendered, and from that hour to the present, Oregon has been ruled by law. In the course of five years the pioneer had brought under cultivation a good farm in Oregon, which supported his family in great abundance, but did not contribute much to the reduction of those Tennessee debts, which he was determined to pay if it took him all his life to do it.

The news of the gold discovery in California reached Oregon. He organized another wagon-train, and in a few months he and another lawyer were in the mining country, drawing deeds for town lots, from sunrise to sunset, at ten dollars a deed. They did their "level best," he says, and each made a hundred dollars a day at the business. Again he assisted in the formation of a government, and he was afterwards elected the first governor of the State of California. At present, at the age of seventy-five, his debts long ago paid, a good estate acquired, and his children all well settled in life, he amuses himself with discounting notes in the Pacific Bank of San Francisco. Every person concerned in the management of a bank would do well to consider his wise remarks on the business of banking. When a man brings him a note for discount, he says, he asks five questions : —

1. Is the supposed borrower an honest man? 2. Has he capital enough for his business? 3. Is his business reasonably safe? 4. Does he manage it well? 5. Does he live economically?

The first and last of these questions are the vital ones, he thinks, though the others are not to be slighted.

GERRIT SMITH.

----◆----

FOR many years we were in the habit of hearing, now and then, of a certain Gerrit Smith, a strange gentleman who lived near Lake Ontario, where he possessed whole townships of land, gave away vast quantities of money, and was pretty sure to be found on the unpopular side of all questions, beloved alike by those who agreed with him and those who differed from him. Every one that knew him spoke of the majestic beauty of his form and face, of his joyous demeanor, of the profuse hospitality of his village abode, where he lived like a jovial old German baron, but without a baron's battle-axe and hunting spear.

He was indeed an interesting character. Without his enormous wealth he would have been, perhaps, a benevolent, enterprising farmer, who would have lived beloved and died lamented by all who knew him. But his wealth made him remarkable; for the possession of wealth usually renders a man steady-going and conservative. It is like ballast to a ship. The slow and difficult process by which honest wealth is usually acquired is pretty sure to "take the nonsense out of a man," and give to all his enterprises a practicable character. But here was a man whose wealth was more like the gas to a balloon than ballast to a ship; and he flung it around with an ignorance of human nature most astonishing in a person so able and intelligent. There was room in the world for one Gerrit Smith, but not for two. If we had many such, benevolence itself would be brought into odium, and we should reserve all our admiration for the close-fisted.

His ancestors were Dutchmen, long settled in Rockland County, New York. Gerrit's father owned the farm upon which Major André was executed, and might even have witnessed the tragedy, since he was twelve years old at the time. Peter Smith was his name, and he had a touch of genius in his composition, just enough to disturb and injure his life. At sixteen this Peter Smith was a merchant's clerk in New York, with such a love of the stage that he performed minor parts at the old Park theatre, and it is said could have made a good actor. He was a sensitive youth, easily moved to tears, and exceedingly susceptible to religious impressions. While he was still a young man he went into the fur business with John Jacob Astor, and tramped all over western and northern New York, buying furs from the Indians, and becoming intimately acquainted with that magnificent domain. The country bordering upon Lake Ontario abounded in fur-bearing animals at that period, and both the partners foretold Rochester, Oswego, and the other lake ports, before any white man had built a log hut on their site.

Astor invested his profits in city lots, but Peter Smith bought great tracts of land in northern and western New York. He sometimes bought townships at a single purchase, and when he died he owned in the State not far from a million acres. His prosperity, however, was of little advantage to him, for as he advanced in life a kind of religious gloom gained possession of him. He went about distributing tracts, and became at length so much impaired in his disposition that his wife could not live with him; finally, he withdrew from business and active life, made over the bulk of his property to his son, Gerrit, and, settling in Schenectady, passed a lonely and melancholy old age.

Gerrit Smith, the son of this strong and perturbed spirit, was educated at Hamilton College, near Utica, where he figured in the character, very uncommon at colleges in those days, of rich man's son; a strikingly handsome, winning youth, with flowing hair and broad Byron collar, fond of all innocent pleasures, member of a card club, and by no means inattentive to his dress. It seems, too, that at college he was an enthusiastic reader of passing literature, although in after days he scarcely shared in the intellectual life of his time. At the age of twenty-two he was a married man. He fell in love at college with the president's daughter, who died after a married life of only seven months. Married happily a second time a year or two after, he settled at his well-known house in Peterboro, a village near Oswego, where he lived ever after. The profession of the law, for which he had prepared himself, he never practiced, since the care of his immense estate absorbed his time and ability; as much so as the most exacting profession. In all those operations which led to the development of Oswego from an outlying military post into a large and thriving city, Gerrit Smith was of necessity a leader or participant, — for the best of his property lay in that region.

And here was his first misfortune. Rich as he was, his estate was all undeveloped, and nothing but the personal labor of the owner could make it of value. For twenty years or more he was the slave of his estate. He could not travel abroad; he could not recreate his mind by pleasure. Albany, the nearest large town, was more than a hundred miles distant, a troublesome journey then; and consequently he had few opportunities of mingling with men of the world. He was a man of the frontier, an admirable leader of men engaged in the mighty work of subduing the wilderness and laying the foundations of empires. He, too, bought land, like his father before him, although his main interest lay in improving his estate and making it accessible.

In the midst of his business life, when he was

carrying a vast spread of sail (making canals, laying out towns, deep in all sorts of enterprises), the panic of 1837 struck him, laid him on his beam ends, and almost put him under water. He owed an immense sum of money — small, indeed, compared with his estate, but crushing at a time when no money could be raised upon the security of land. When he owned a million acres, as well as a great quantity of canal stock, plank-road stock, and wharf stock, and when fifteen hundred men owed him money, some in large amounts, he found it difficult to raise money enough to go to Philadelphia. In this extremity he had recourse to his father's friend and partner, John Jacob Astor, then the richest man in North America. Gerrit Smith described his situation in a letter, and asked for a large loan on land security.

Mr. Astor replied by inviting him to dinner. During the repast the old man was full of anecdote and reminiscence of the years when himself and Peter Smith camped out on the Oswego River, and went about with packs on their backs buying furs. When the cloth was removed the terrible topic was introduced, and the guest explained his situation once more.

" How much do you need ? " inquired Astor.

"In all, I must have two hundred and fifty thousand dollars."

"Do you want the whole of it at once ? " asked the millionaire.

" I do," was the reply.

Astor looked serious for a moment, and then said : —

" You shall have it."

The guest engaged to forward a mortgage on some lands along the Oswego River, and a few days after, before the mortgage was ready, the old man sent his check for the two hundred and fifty thousand dollars. Through the neglect of a clerk the mortgage papers were not sent for some weeks after, so that Mr. Astor had parted with this great sum upon no other security than a young man's word. But John Jacob Astor was a good judge of men, as well as of land.

Thus relieved, Gerrit Smith pursued his career without embarrassment, and in about twenty years paid off all his debts, and had then a revenue ranging from fifty to a hundred thousand dollars a year. He gave away money continuously, from thirty thousand to a hundred thousand dollars a year, in large sums and in small sums, to the deserving and the undeserving. Of course, he was inundated with begging letters. Every mail brought requests for help to redeem farms, to send children to school, to buy a piano, to buy an alpaca dress with the trimmings, to relieve sufferers by fire, and to pay election expenses.

" The small checks," Mr. Frothingham tells us, "flew about in all directions, carrying, in the aggregate, thousands of dollars, hundreds of which fell on sandy or gravelly soil, and produced nothing."

He gave, in fact, to every project which promised to relieve human distress, or promote human happiness. He used to have checks ready drawn to various amounts, only requiring to be signed and supplied with the name of the applicant. On one occasion he gave fifty dollars each to all the old maids and widows he could get knowledge of in the State of New York — six hundred of them in all. He gave away nearly three thousand small farms, from fifteen to seventy-five acres each, most of them to landless colored men.

"For years," said he, "I have indulged the thought that when I had sold enough land to pay my debts, I would give away the remainder to the poor. I am an Agrarian. I would that every man who desires a farm might have one, and no man covet the possession of more farms than one."

I need not say that these farms were of little benefit to those who received them, for our colored friends are by no means the men to go upon a patch of northern soil and wring an independent livelihood out of it. Gerrit Smith was a sort of blind, benevolent Samson, amazingly ignorant of human nature, of human life, and of the conditions upon which alone the welfare of our race is promoted. He died in 1874, aged seventy-seven, having lived one of the strangest lives ever recorded, and having exhibited a cast of character which excites equal admiration and regret.

PETER FORCE.

ONE of the interesting sights of the city of Washington used to be the library of " Old Peter Force," as he was familiarly called, — Colonel Peter Force, as he was more properly styled. He was one of the few colonels of that day who had actually held a colonel's command, having been regularly commissioned by the President of the United States as a colonel of artillery in the District of Columbia. He might, indeed, have been called major-general, for in his old age he held that rank in the militia of the district. And a very fine-looking soldier he must have been in his prime, judging from the portrait which used to hang in the library, representing a full-formed man, tall and erect, his handsome and benevolent countenance set off by an abundance of curly hair.

His library had about the roughest furniture ever seen in an apartment containing so much that was valuable. As I remember it, it was a long, low room, with streets and cross-streets of pine book-shelves, unpainted, all filled with books to their utmost capacity — a wilderness of books, in print and in manuscript, mostly old and dingy, and almost all of them relating in some way to American history. The place had a very musty smell; and as most of its treasures were in the original bindings, or without bindings, few persons would have suspected the priceless value of the collection. I am acquainted with a certain library in New York of several thousand volumes, most of which are bound resplendently in calf and gold, and the room in which they are kept is " as splendid as a steamboat," but old Peter Force could show you single alcoves of his library which, at a fair valuation, would buy out all that mass of sumptuosity.

It was not always easy to find the old gentleman in his dusty, dingy wilderness; but when you had discovered him in some remote recess he would take pleasure in exhibiting his treasures. He would take down his excellent copy of Eliot's Indian Bible, a book so faithfully made in every respect that I question if, as a mere piece of bookmaking, it could now be matched in the United States. He lived to see this rarity command in New York the price of fourteen hundred and fifty dollars. He would show you forty-one works, in the original editions, of Increase and Cotton Mather, the most recent of which was published in 1735. He possessed a large number of books printed and bound by Benjamin Franklin. He had two hundred volumes of the records of Colonial legislatures. He could show you a newspa-

per of almost every month — nay, almost every
week, since newspapers were first published in
America. He had in all nine hundred and fifty
bound volumes of newspapers, of which two hundred and forty-five volumes were published before
the year 1800. He would show you a collection of
more than thirty-nine thousand pamphlets, of which
eight thousand were printed before the year 1800.
His collection of maps relating to America was
truly wonderful. Besides all the early atlases
of any note, he had over a thousand detached
maps illustrative both of the geography and history of America; for many of them were maps
and plans drawn for military purposes. He would
show you, perhaps, a pen-drawing of date 1779,
by a British officer, upon which was written: "Plan
of the rebel works at West Point." He had also
several plans by British officers of "the rebel
works" around Boston during the revolution.

Besides such things (and he had over three
hundred plans and maps of which there was no
other copy in existence), he possessed a surprising
number of books printed in the infancy of the printer's art; among them specimens representing every
year from 1467 onward. He had more than two
hundred and fifty books printed before the year
1600, so arranged that a student could trace the
progress of the art of printing from the days of
Caxton. He had also a vast collection of manu-
scripts, numbering four hundred and twenty-nine

volumes, many of which were of particular interest. The whole number of volumes in the library was 22,529, and the number of pamphlets nearly 40,000.

The reader, perhaps, imagines that the collector of such a library must have been a very rich man, and that he traveled far and wide in search of these precious objects. Not at all. He never was a rich man, and I believe he rarely traveled beyond the sight of the dome of the Capitol. Indeed, the most wonderful thing about his collection was that he, who began life a journeyman printer, and was never in the receipt of a large income, should have been able to get together so vast an amount of valuable material. Part of the secret was that when he began to make his collection these things were not valued, and he obtained many of his most precious relics by merely taking the trouble to carry them away from the garrets in which they were mouldering into dust, unprized and unknown.

A wise old New York merchant, long ago himself mouldered into dust, used to say : —

"Men generally get in this world exactly what they *want.*"

"How can that be?" asked a youngster one day. "Almost everybody in New York wants to be rich, but very few of them ever will be. I *want* a million or so myself."

"Ah, boy," the old man replied, "you want a

million; but you don't want it enough. What you *want* at present is pleasure, and you want it so much that you are willing to spend all your surplus force, time, and revenue to get it. If you wanted your million as much as you *want pleasure*, by and by, when you have a bald head like mine, you would have your million."

Peter Force was a very good illustration of the old merchant's doctrine. He got all these precious things because he wanted them with a sustained passion of desire for half a century. There never was a time when he would not have gladly got up in the middle of the night and walked ten miles, in the face of a northeasterly storm, to get a rare pamphlet of four pages. He was a miser of such things. But, no; that word does not describe him; for one of the greatest pleasures of his life was to communicate his treasures to others; and he communicated to the whole American people the best of his collections in massive volumes of American Archives. He was a miser only in the strength of his desire.

"More than once," he said to Mr. George W. Greene, " did I hesitate between a barrel of flour and a rare book; but the book always got the upper hand."

To the same friend he made a remark which shows that his desire to communicate was quite as strong as his desire to obtain.

" Whenever," said he, " I found a little more

money in my purse than I absolutely needed, I published a volume of historical tracts."

It was interesting to hear the old man relate how this taste for the treasures of history was formed in his mind. His father, who served, during the revolution, in a New Jersey regiment, retired after the war to the city of New York, and at his house the Jersey veterans liked to meet and talk over the incidents of the campaigns they had made together. Peter, as a boy, loved to hear them tell their stories, and, as he listened, the thought occurred to him one evening, Why should all this be forgotten? Boy as he was, he began to write them down, under the title of "The Unwritten History of the War in New Jersey." He made considerable progress in it, but unfortunately the manuscript was lost. The taste then formed grew with his growth and strengthened with his strength. At ten he left school forever, and went into a printing office, which has proved an excellent school to more than one valuable American mind. He became an accomplished printer, and at twenty-two was elected president of the New York Typographical Society, an organization which still exists.

Then the war of 1812 began. Like his father before him, he served in the army, first as private, then as sergeant, then as sergeant-major, then as ensign, finally as lieutenant. The war ended. He went to Washington as foreman of a printing office, and at Washington, as printer, editor, publisher and collector, he lived the rest of his long and honorable life; never rich, as I have before remarked, though never without a share of reasonable prosperity. The most important work of his life was the publication of the American Archives, in which he was aided by Congress; he furnishing the documents and the labor, and Congress paying the cost of publication. Through the nine volumes of this work a great number of the most curious and interesting records and memorials of American history are not only preserved, but made accessible to all students who can get near a library. He had all the state-houses of the country ransacked for documents, and a room was assigned him in the Department of State in which his clerks could conveniently copy them.

All went well with the work until William Marcy became Secretary of State, whose duty it was to examine and approve each volume before it went to the printer. When Peter Force presented the manuscript of the tenth volume to Secretary Marcy he received a rebuff which threw a cloud over several years of his life.

" I don't believe in your work, sir," said the secretary. " It is of no use to anybody. I never read a page of it, and never expect to."

" But," said Mr. Force, "the work is published in virtue of a contract with the government. Here is the manuscript of the tenth volume. If there is anything there which you think ought not to be there, have the goodness to point it out to me."

" You may leave the papers, sir," said the secretary.

He left the papers; but neither Marcy nor his successors ever found time to examine that tenth volume, though on the first day of every official year the compiler called their attention to it. For seven years he was a suitor on behalf of his beloved tenth volume, and then the war occurred and all such matters were necessarily put aside. He was now seventy-one years of age, and his great desire was to dispose of his library in such a way that its treasures would not be scattered abroad, and perhaps lost forever to the country. At length, Congress having sanctioned the enlargement of their own library, their librarian, Mr. Spofford, induced them to purchase the whole mass, just as it stood, for one hundred thousand dollars, and the collection now forms part of the Congressional library.

Colonel Force lived to the year 1868, when he died at Washington, universally beloved and lamented, in the seventy-eighth year of his age, enjoying almost to the last two of the things he loved best — his books and his flowers.

JOHN BROMFIELD,

MERCHANT

JOHN BROMFIELD'S monument is more lasting
than brass. It was he who left to the city of Newburyport, in Massachusetts, ten thousand dollars
for planting and preserving trees in the streets,
and keeping the sidewalks in order. The income
of this bequest would not go far in any other sort
of monument, but it has embowered his native city
in beautiful trees. Every spring other trees are
planted, and, as long as that bequest is faithfully
administered, he cannot be forgotten.

Nothing brings a larger or surer return than
money judiciously spent in making towns and cities
pleasant. It not only yields a great revenue of
pleasure and satisfaction to the inhabitants; it not
only benefits every individual of them every hour,
but it invites residents from abroad; it is a standing invitation to persons of taste and good sense.
The wisest thing the city of New York ever did,
next to the introduction of the Croton water, was
the creation of the Central Park; the one feature which redeems the city from the disgrace of

its dirty streets and its agonizing tenement region.

This John Bromfield, merchant, was just such a thoughtful and benevolent man as we should naturally expect to find him from his bequest. He belonged to a class of merchants which is rapidly becoming extinct. The cable telegraph and the steam freight ship are superseding the merchants of moderate capital, and are concentrating the great business of interchanging commodities in the hands of a few houses who reckon their capital by millions. Born at Newburyport, in 1779, he was brought up by excellent parents near Boston, who practiced the old-fashioned system of making him hardy and self-helpful. His mother used to say that when he was old enough to wear leather shoes she bored holes in the soles in order to accustom him to wet feet, so that he might be made less liable to catch cold from that cause. This appears to have been a custom of that generation, for it is recorded of the mother of Josiah Quincy that she would never let him take off his wet shoes, regarding it as an effeminate practice.

On approaching the time of entering college his father met with misfortunes and could not bear the expense. Two aunts of his, who could well afford it, offered to pay his expenses in college. He firmly declined the offer. The foundation of his character and career was a love of independence. He asked to be apprenticed, as the custom then was, to a mercantile house, and remained in it as long as it held together. After its failure he tried for months to obtain a clerkship, but, not succeeding, he arranged with a carpenter to learn his trade. Just before putting on the carpenter's apron an opening occurred in his own business, and he became a merchant. About the year 1801 he went out to China as supercargo, and continued to visit that part of the world in similar capacities for many years, occasionally making small ventures of his own, and slowly accumulating a little capital. He had a series of the most discouraging misfortunes. In the year 1813 he wrote to his sister from Cadiz : —

"It is a melancholy truth that in the whole course of my life I never arrived at a good market."

On that occasion everything promised well. He had a ship full of valuable goods, and the market to which he was carrying them was in an excellent condition for his purpose, but within twenty-four hours of his port he was captured, and detained ten weeks a prisoner. After the peace of 1815, merchants could send their ships across the ocean without fear of their being taken by English or French cruisers. From that time he had better luck, and gradually gained a moderate fortune, upon which he retired. He never kept a store, or had any sort of warehouse, but made his fortune by sending or taking merchandise from a port which had too much of it to one that was in want of it.

On one of his winter passages to Europe he found the sailors suffering extremely from handling frozen ropes, as they were not provided with mittens. Being a Yankee, and having been brought up to *do* things as well as read about them, he took one of his thick overcoats and made with his own hands a pair of mittens for every sailor.

On another occasion, in the ship Atahualpa, in 1809, bound to China, the vessel was attacked off Macao by pirates, in twenty-two junks, some of them being twice the tonnage of the vessel. Captain Sturgis, who commanded the vessel, defended her with signal ability and courage, and kept the pirates off for forty minutes, until the vessel gained the protection of the fort. John Bromfield, a passenger on board, took command of a gun, and seconded the endeavors of the captain with such coolness and promptitude as to contribute essentially to the protection of the vessel.

In retirement he lived a quiet life in Boston, unmarried, fond of books, and practicing unusual frugality for a person in liberal circumstances. He had a singular abhorrence of luxury, waste, and ostentation. He often said that the cause of more than half the bankruptcies was spending too much money. Nothing could induce him to accept personal service. He was one of those men who wait upon themselves, light their own fire, reduce their wants to the necessaries of civilized life, and all with a view to a more perfect independence. He would take trouble to oblige others, but could not bear to put any one else to trouble. This love of independence was carried to excess by him, and was a cause of sorrow to his relations and friends.

He was a man of maxims, and one of them was : —

> "The good must merit God's peculiar care,
> And none but God can tell us who they are."

Another of his favorite couplets was Pope's : —

> "Reason's whole pleasure, all the joys of sense,
> Lie in three words : health, peace, and competence."

He used to quote Burns's stanza about the desirableness of wealth : —

> "Not to hide it in a hedge,
> Nor for a train attendant ;
> But for the glorious privilege
> Of being independent."

He was utterly opposed to the way in which business was then conducted — hazardous enterprises undertaken upon borrowed capital. The excessive credit formerly given was the frequent theme of his reprobation.

How changed the country, even in the short space of sixty years! In 1825 he made a journey from Boston to New Orleans, and his letters show curious glimpses of life and travel as they then were. Leaving Boston at four o'clock on a Friday morning, he reached New York at ten o'clock on Saturday morning, and he speaks of this performance with astonishment. Boston to New York in thirty hours! He was in New York November 4, 1825, when the opening of the Erie Canal was celebrated. He did not care much for the procession.

"There was, however," he adds, "an interesting exhibition of steamboats, probably greater than could be found at any other place in the world; say, *from twenty-five to thirty*, and most of them of a large class."

He was in the valley of the Ohio that year, and he spoke of it "as the land of cheapness:" flour, two dollars and a quarter a barrel; oats, twelve and a half cents a bushel; corn and rye, twenty cents; coal, three cents. He found all the region from Louisville to Louisiana "one vast wilderness," with scarcely any settlements, and now and then a log hut on the banks, occupied by the people who cut wood for the steamboats. On the prairies of Missouri he rode miles and miles without seeing a house. Indiana was an almost unbroken wilderness: corn ten cents a bushel, a wild turkey twelve and half cents, and other things in proportion.

Nevertheless, travelers at that day had some pleasures which could be advantageously compared with the ease and comfort of the Pullman car. The Alleghanies were then crossed by open wagons drawn by splendid Pennsylvania horses, six in a team, gayly decorated with ribbons, bells, and trappings. He used to repeat, in a peculiarly buoyant and delightful manner, a popular song of the day, called "The Wagoner," suggested by the apparently happy lot of the boys who rode and drove these horses. Some readers may remember the old song, beginning: —

> "I 've often thought if I were asked
> 	Whose lot I envied most,
> What one I thought most lightly tasked
> 	Of man's unnumbered host,
> I 'd say I 'd be a mountain boy
> And drive a noble team — wo hoy !
> 		Wo hoy ! I 'd cry,
> 		And lightly fly
> 			Into my saddle seat ;
> 		My rein I 'd slack,
> 		My whip I 'd crack —
> 			What music is so sweet ?
> Six blacks I 'd drive, of ample chest,
> 	All carrying high their head.
> All harnessed tight, and gaily dressed
> 	In winkers tipped with red.
> Oh, yes ! I 'd be a mountain boy,
> And such a team I 'd drive — wo hoy !
> 		Wo hoy ! I 'd cry ;
> 		The lint should fly.
> 		Wo hoy ! Dobbin, Ball.
> 		Their feet should ring,
> 		And I would sing,
> 			I 'd sing my fal-de-roll."

We have almost forgotten that such a gay mode of crossing the Alleghanies was ever practiced ; and yet a person need not be very old to have enjoyed the experience. I myself, for example, can just remember riding from Buffalo to New York by a line of stages that came round by the Alleghany Mountains, and crossed the State of New Jersey, passing through Morristown. We were just six days in performing the journey.

This excellent man, after a tranquil and happy life, died in 1849, aged seventy, and left considerable sums to benevolent societies. His estate proved to be of about two hundred thousand dollars value, which was then considered very large, and he bestowed something more than half of it upon institutions for mitigating human woe. Ten thousand of it he gave for the promotion of pleasure, and the evidences of his forethought and benevolence are waving and rustling above my head as these lines are written. His memory is green in Newburyport. All the birds and all the lovers, all who walk and all who ride, the gay equestrian and the dusty wayfarer, the old and the invalid who can only look out of the window, all owe his name a blessing.

FREDERICK TUDOR,

ICE EXPORTER.

EDWARD EVERETT used to relate a curious anecdote of the time when he was the American minister
at London. He was introduced one day to an
Eastern prince, who greeted him with a degree of
enthusiasm that was altogether unusual and unexpected. The prince launched into eulogium of the
United States, and expressed a particular gratitude
for the great benefit conferred upon the East Indies by Mr. Everett's native Massachusetts. The
American minister, who was a good deal puzzled by
this effusion, ventured at length to ask the prince
what special benefit Massachusetts had conferred
upon the East Indies, wondering whether it was
the missionaries, or the common school system, or
Daniel Webster's Bunker Hill oration.

"I refer," said the prince, "to the great quantity of excellent ice which comes to us from Boston."

Mr. Everett bowed with his usual politeness, but
was much amused at the excessive gratitude of the
prince for the service named.

The founder of this foreign ice business, which has now attained such large proportions, was a Boston merchant named Frederick Tudor, son of that Colonel William Tudor who studied law under John Adams, and who served his country on the staff of General Washington, and afterwards became a judge. Frederick Tudor, who was born in 1783, the year of the peace between England and the United States, entered early into business, being at twenty-two already owner of a vessel trading with the West Indies.

It was in 1805 that the idea of exporting ice first occurred to him — an idea which, as he was accustomed to relate in his old age, was received with derision by the whole town as a "mad project." He had made his calculations too carefully, however, to be disturbed by a little ridicule; and that same year he sent out his first cargo of a hundred and thirty tons, to the Island of Martinique.

The result justified his confidence. The ice arrived in perfect condition, and he was encouraged to follow up his single cargo with many others larger and more profitable. During the war of 1812 business was somewhat interrupted by the English cruisers, which were ever on the alert for prizes in the West Indian waters, but, after peace was declared, his trade increased rapidly. He supplied ice to Charleston and New Orleans also, those cities at first requiring but a ship-load each per annum, although the demand increased so rapidly that a few years later New Orleans alone consumed thirty cargoes.

Almost from the first, Mr. Tudor had believed that ice could be transported as safely and profitably to Calcutta as to Havana; but he could not bring others to share this opinion — at least, not to the point of risking money upon it. It was not, therefore, until 1834, twenty-nine years later than his Martinique experiment, that he sent his first cargo of one hundred and eighty tons of ice to India. Notwithstanding a waste of one third of the whole cargo during the voyage, he was able to sell this Massachusetts ice at one half the price charged for the artificially frozen ice formerly used in Calcutta by the few families who could afford such a luxury.

The cold commodity which he provided met, therefore, with a warm welcome from the English inhabitants. They recognized the boon afforded them, and expressed their gratitude by raising a subscription and presenting to the enterprising Yankee merchant a fire-proof building in which to store his ice. He met them in the same spirit of wise liberality, and sold the article at no more than a reasonable profit — about three cents a pound — which enabled the great body of English residents to use the ice habitually. Mr. Tudor used to boast that in Jamaica he sold the best Wenham ice at half the price which an inferior article brought in London; and even at Calcutta he made ice cheaper

than it was in London or Paris. On the passage
to the East Indies, ice is four or five months at sea,
traverses sixteen thousand miles of salt water, and
crosses the equator twice; and on its arrival it is
stored in massive double-walled houses, which are
covered by four or five separate roofs. It has also
to be unloaded in a temperature of ninety to one
hundred degrees. Notwithstanding all this, the inhabitants of the most distant tropical seaports are
supplied with ice every day of the year at the moderate price mentioned above.

It was Frederick Tudor also who originated and
developed the best methods of cutting, packing,
storing, and discharging ice, so as to reduce the
waste to the minimum. I am assured by a gentleman engaged in the business that the blocks of ice
now reach Calcutta, after the long voyage from Boston, with a waste scarcely noticeable. The vessels
are loaded during the cold snaps of January, when
water will freeze in the hold of a vessel, and when
the entire ship is penetrated with the intensest cold.
The glittering blocks of ice, two feet thick, at a
temperature below zero, are brought in by railroad
from the lakes, and are placed on board the ships
with a rapidity which must be seen to be appreciated. The blocks are packed in sawdust, which
is used very much as mortar is used in a stone wall.
Between the topmost layer of ice and the deck there
is sometimes a layer of closely packed hay, and
sometimes one of barrels of apples. It has occa-

sionally happened that the profit upon the apples
has paid the freight upon the ice, which usually
amounts to about ten thousand dollars, or five dollars a ton.

The arrival of an ice ship at Calcutta is an ex-
hilarating scene.   Clouds of dusky natives come on
board to buy the apples, which are in great request,
and bring from ten to thirty cents each, according
to the supply.   Happy is the native who has capital enough to buy a whole barrel of the fruit.   Off
he trudges with it on his back to the place of sale,
or else puts it on a little cart and peddles the apples
about the streets.   In a day or two that portion of
the cargo has disappeared, and then the ice is to be
unloaded.   It was long before a native could be induced to handle the crystal blocks.   Tradition reports that they ran away affrighted, thinking the
ice was something bewitched and fraught with danger.   But now they come on board in a long line,
and each of them takes a huge block of ice upon
his head and conveys it to the adjacent ice-house,
moving with such rapidity that the blocks are exposed to the air only a few seconds.   Once deposited there, the waste almost ceases again, and the
ice which cost in Boston four dollars a ton is worth
fifty dollars.

When Frederick Tudor had been employed
twenty-five years in this trade, finding it inconvenient to be separated from the great body of merchants, he embarked again in general mercantile

business, by way of re-uniting himself to his former associates. The experiment resulted in ruinous losses. In less than three years he was a bankrupt, and owed his creditors two hundred and ten thousand dollars more than he could pay. The ice business being still profitable and growing, it was proposed to him that he should conduct it as the agent of his creditors, retaining a specified sum per annum for his personal expenses. To this he objected, and said to them : —

" Allow me to proceed, and I will work for you better than I can under any restriction. Give me the largest liberty, and I will pay the whole in time with interest."

He was then fifty-two years of age, and he had undertaken to pay an indebtedness, the mere interest of which was about ten thousand dollars a year. By the time he had got fairly at work the treachery of an agent whom he had raised from poverty to wealth lost him his Havana monopoly, his principal source of profit. Then it became necessary to buy land bordering the lakes from which he gathered ice, and to erect in Calcutta, New Orleans, and elsewhere expensive and peculiarly constructed buildings for storage. Occasionally, too, he experienced the losses and adverse incidents from which no business is exempt. Nevertheless, in fourteen years from the date of his bankruptcy he had paid his debts, principal and interest, amounting to two hundred and eighty thousand dollars, besides having

11

acquired a large quantity of real estate, some of which had increased in value tenfold. Thus, while paying his debts, and in the very process of paying, and while thinking only of his creditors' interest, he had gained for himself a very large fortune. He continued an ice merchant for more than fifty years; or, as he said himself: —

"I began this trade in the youthful hopes attendant on the age of twenty-two. I have followed it until I have a head with scarcely a hair that is not white."

It was this enterprising merchant who may be said to have created the beautiful seaside retreat near Boston called Nahant, where he invented many ingenious expedients for protecting trees and shrubs from the east winds which lacerate that rock-bound coast. His gardens and plantations in Nahant were famous many years before his death. He died in 1864, aged eighty-one, leaving to his children and to his native State a name which was honorable when he inherited it, and the lustre of which his life increased.

yours
Myron Holley

MYRON HOLLEY,

MARKET-GARDENER.

———◆———

FIFTY years ago, this man used to sell vegetables
and fruit from door to door in the streets of Rochester, N. Y. He had a small farm a few miles out of
town, upon which he raised the produce which he
thus disposed of. An anecdote is related of a fine
lady who had recently come to Rochester as the
wife of one of its most distinguished clergymen.
She ran up into her husband's study one morning,
and said to him : —

"Why, Doctor, I've just seen the only gentleman I have yet met with in Rochester, and he was
at our basement door selling vegetables. How wonderful! Who is it? Who can it be?"

"It must be Myron Holley," said her husband.

Another of his lady customers used to say that
he sold early peas and potatoes in the morning with
as much grace as he lectured before the Lyceum in
the evening. Nor was it the ladies alone who admired him. The principal newspaper of the city,
in recording his death in 1841, spoke of him as
"an eminent citizen, an accomplished scholar, and

noble man, who carried with him to the grave the love of all who knew him."

In reflecting upon the character of this truly remarkable person, I am reminded of a Newfoundland dog that I once had the honor of knowing near the spot on the shore of Lake Ontario where Myron Holley hoed his cabbages and picked his strawberries. It was the largest and most beautiful dog I have ever seen, of a fine shade of yellow in color, and of proportions so extraordinary that few persons could pass him without stopping to admire. He had the strength and calm courage of a lion, with the playfulness of a kitten, and an intelligence that seemed sometimes quite human. One thing this dog lacked. He was so destitute of the evil spirit that he would not defend himself against the attacks of other dogs. He seemed to have forgotten how to bite. He has been known to let a smaller dog draw blood from him without making the least attempt to use his own teeth in retaliation. He appeared to have lost the instinct of self-assertion, and walked abroad protected solely, but sufficiently, by his vast size and imposing appearance.

Myron Holley, I say, reminds me of this superb and noble creature. He was a man of the finest proportions both of body and of mind, beautiful in face, majestic in stature, fearless, gifted with various talents, an orator, a natural leader of men. With all this, he was destitute of the personal ambition which lifts the strong man into publicity, and gives him commonplace success. If he had been only half as good as he was, he might have been ten times as famous.

He was born at Salisbury, Conn., in 1779, the son of a farmer who had several sons that became notable men. The father, too, illustrated some of the best traits of human nature, being one of the men who make the strength of a country without asking much from the country in return. He used to say to his sons that the height of human felicity was "to be able to converse with the wise, to instruct the ignorant, to pity and despise the intriguing villain, and to assist the unfortunate." His son Myron enjoyed this felicity all the days of his life.

After graduating at Williams, and studying law at New Haven, he set his face toward western New York, then more remote from New England than Oregon now is. He made an exquisite choice of a place of residence, the village of Canandaigua, then only a hamlet of log huts along the border of one of the lakes for which that part of the State is famous. The first step taken by the young lawyer after his arrival fixed his destiny. He was assigned by the court to defend a man charged with murder — a capital chance for winning distinction in a frontier town. Myron Holley, however, instead of confining himself to his brief and his precedents, began by visiting the jail and interviewing the prisoner. He became satisfied of his guilt. The next morning he came into court, resigned the case, and never after made any attempt to practice his profession.

He was, in fact, constitutionally disqualified for the practice of such a calling. Having a little property, he bought out a bookseller of the village, laid out a garden, married, was soon elected county clerk, and spent the rest of his life in doing the kind of public service which yields the maximum of good to the country with the minimum of gain to the individual doing it.

The war of 1812 filled all that region with distress and want. It was he who took the lead in organizing relief, and appealed to the city of New York for aid with great success. As soon as the war was over, the old scheme of connecting Lake Erie with the Hudson by a canal was revived. It was an immense undertaking for that day, and a great majority of the prudent farmers of the State opposed the enterprise as something beyond their strength. It was Myron Holley who went to the legislature year after year, and argued it through. His winning demeanor, his persuasive eloquence, his intimate knowledge of the facts involved, his entire conviction of the wisdom of the scheme, his tact, good temper, and, above all, his untiring persistence, prevailed at length, and the canal was begun.

He was appointed one of the commissioners to superintend the construction of the canal at a sal-

ary of twenty-five hundred dollars a year. The
commissioners appointed him their treasurer, which
threw upon him for eight years an inconceivable
amount of labor, much of which had to be done in
situations which were extremely unhealthy. At one
time, in 1820, he had a thousand laborers on his
hands sick with malaria. He was a ministering
angel to them, friend, physician, and sometimes
nurse. He was obliged on several occasions to
raise money for the State on his personal credit,
and frequently he had to expend money in circumstances which made it impossible for him to secure the legal evidence of his having done so.

In 1825 the work was done. A procession of
boats floated from Lake Erie to New York Harbor,
where they were received by a vast fleet of steamboats and other vessels, all dressed with flags and
crowded with people. In the midst of this triumph,
Myron Holley, who had managed the expenditures
with the most scrupulous economy, was unable to
furnish the requisite vouchers for a small part of
the money which had passed through his hands.
He at once gave up his small estate, and appealed
to the legislature for relief. He was completely
vindicated; his estate was restored to him; but he
received no compensation either for his services or
his losses.

He returned to his garden, however, a happy
man, and during the greater part of the rest of his
life he earned a modest subsistence by the beauti-

ful industry which has since given celebrity and wealth to all that fertile region. He remained, however, to the end of his days, one of those brave and unselfish public servants who take the laboring oar in reforms which are very difficult or very odious. After the abduction of Morgan, he devoted some years to anti-masonry, and he founded what was called the Liberty Party, which supported Mr. Birney, of Kentucky, for the presidency.

One of his fellow-workers, the Hon. Elizur Wright, of Boston, has recently published an interesting memoir of him, which reveals to us a cast of character beautiful and rare in men; a character in which the moral qualities ruled with an easy and absolute sway, and from which the baser traits appeared to be eliminated. He was like that great, splendid, yellow king of dogs which escaped perfection by not having just a spice of evil in his composition.

Let me add, however, that he was as far as possible from being a "spoony." Mr. Wright says:—

"He had the strength of a giant, and did not abstain from using it in a combative sense on a fit occasion. When his eldest daughter was living in a house not far from his own, with her first child in her arms, he became aware that she was in danger from a stout, unprincipled tramp who had called on her as a beggar and found her alone. Hastening to the house, without saying a word he grasped the fellow around body and both arms, and

carried him, bellowing for mercy, through the yard
and into the middle of the street, where he set him
down. Greatly relieved, the miserable wretch ran
as if he had escaped from a lion."

Mr. Wright adds another trait: "Once in Lyons (N. Y.) when there was great excitement about
the 'sin of dancing,' the ministers all preaching
and praying against it, Myron Holley quietly said:
'It is as natural for young people to like to dance
as for the apple trees to blossom in the spring.'"

THE FOUNDERS OF LOWELL.

WE do not often hear of strikes at Lowell. Some men tell us it is because there are not as many foreigners there as at certain manufacturing centres where strikes are frequent. This cannot be the explanation; for out of a population of seventy-one thousand, there are more than twenty thousand foreign-born inhabitants of Lowell, of whom more than ten thousand are natives of Ireland. To answer the question correctly, we must perhaps go back to the founding of the town in 1821, when there were not more than a dozen houses on the site.

At that time the great water-power of the Merrimac River was scarcely used, and there was not one cotton manufactory upon its banks. At an earlier day this river and its tributaries swarmed with beaver and other fur-yielding creatures, which furnished a considerable part of the first capital of the Pilgrim Fathers. The Indians trapped the beaver, and carried the skins to Plymouth and Boston; and this is perhaps the reason why the Merrimac and most of its branches retain their Indian names.

Merrimac itself is an Indian word meaning sturgeon, and of its ten tributaries all but two appear to have Indian names: Contoocook, Soucook, Suncook, Piscatagoug, Souhegan, Nashua, Concord, Spiggot, Shawshine, and Powow.

Besides these there are the two rivers which unite to form it, the names of which are still more peculiar: Pemigewassett and Winnepiseogee. The most remarkable thing with regard to these names is, that the people who live near see nothing remarkable in them, and pronounce them as naturally as New Yorkers do Bronx and Croton. It is difficult for us to imagine a lover singing, or saying, "Meet me by the Pemigewasset, love," or asking her to take a row with him on the lovely Winnepiseogee. But lovers do such things up there; and beautiful rivers they are, flowing between mountains, and breaking occasionally into falls and rapids. The Merrimac, also, loses its serenity every few miles, and changes from a tranquil river into a — water-power.

In November, 1821, a light snow already covering the ground, six strangers stood on the banks of the Merrimac upon the site of the present city of Lowell. A canal had been dug around the falls for purposes of navigation, and these gentlemen were there with a view to the purchase of the dam and canal, and erecting upon the site a cotton mill. Their names were Patrick T. Jackson, Kirk Boott, Warren Dutton, Paul Moody, John W. Boott, and

Nathan Appleton; all men of capital or skill, and since well known as the founders of a great national industry. They walked about the country, observed the capabilities of the river, and made up their minds that that was the place for their new enterprise.

"Some of us," said one of the projectors, "may live to see this place contain twenty thousand inhabitants."

The enterprise was soon begun. In 1826 the town was incorporated and named. It is always difficult to name a new place or a new baby. Mr. Nathan Appleton met one of the other proprietors, who told him that the legislature was ready to incorporate the town, and it only remained for them to fill the blank left in the act for the name.

"The question," said he, "is narrowed down to two, Lowell or Derby."

"Then," said Mr. Appleton, "Lowell, by all means."

It was so named from Mr. Francis C. Lowell, who originated the idea. He had visited England and Scotland in 1811, and while there had observed and studied the manufacture of cotton fabrics, which in a few years had come to be one of the most important industries of the British Empire. The war of 1812 intervened; but before the return of peace Mr. Lowell took measures for starting the business in New England. A company was formed with a capital of four hundred thousand dollars, and Mr.

Lowell himself undertook the construction of the power loom, which was still guarded in Europe as a precious secret. After having obtained all possible information about it, he shut himself up in a Boston store with a man to turn his crank, and experimented for months till he had conquered the difficulties. In the fall of 1814 the machine was ready for inspection.

"I well recollect," says Mr. Appleton, "the state of admiration and satisfaction with which we sat by the hour watching the beautiful movement of this new and wonderful machine, destined as it evidently was to change the character of all textile industry."

In a few months the first manufactory was established in Waltham, with the most wonderful success. Henry Clay visited it, and gave a glowing account of it in one of his speeches, using its success as an argument against free trade. It is difficult to see what protection the now manufacture required. The company sold its cotton cloth at thirty cents a yard, and they afterwards found that they could sell it without loss at less than seven cents. The success of the Waltham establishment led to the founding of Lowell, Lawrence, Nashua, and Manchester. There are now at Lowell eighty mills and factories, in which are employed sixteen thousand men and women, who produce more than three million yards of fabric every week. The city has a solid inviting appearance, and there

are in the outskirts many beautiful and commanding sites for residences, which are occupied by men
of wealth.

But now as to the question above proposed.
Why are the operatives at Lowell less discontented
than elsewhere?   It is in part because the able
men who founded the place bestowed some thought
upon the welfare of the human beings whom they
were about to summon to the spot. They did not,
it is true, bestow thought enough; but they *thought*
of it, and they made some provision for proper and
pleasant life in their proposed town. Mr. Appleton, who many years ago took the trouble to record
these circumstances, mentions that the probable
effect of this new kind of industry upon the character of the people was most attentively considered
by the founders. In Europe, as most of them
had personally seen, the operatives were unintel-
ligent and immoral, made so by fifteen or sixteen
hours' labor a day, and a beer-shop on every corner. They caused suitable boarding-houses to be
built, which were placed under the charge of women known to be competent and respectable. Land
was assigned and money subscribed for schools,
for churches, for a hospital. Systematic care was
taken to keep away immoral persons, and rules
were established, some of which carried the super-
vision of morals and manners perhaps too far.
The consequence was that the daughters of farmers, young women well educated and well-bred,

came from all quarters, and found the factory life something more than endurable.

But for one thing they would have found it salutary and agreeable. The plague of factory life is the extreme monotony of the employment, and this is aggravated in some mills by high temperature and imperfect ventilation. At that time the laws of health were so little understood that few persons saw any hardship in young girls standing on their feet thirteen, fourteen, fifteen, and even sixteen hours a day! It was considered a triumph when the working-day was reduced to thirteen hours. Thirty years ago, after prodigious agitation, the day was fixed at eleven hours. That was too much. It has now been reduced to ten hours; but it is yet to be shown that a woman of average strength and stamina can work in a cotton mill ten hours a day for years at a stretch, without deteriorating in body, in mind, or in character.

During the first years the girls would come from the country, work in the mill a few months, or two or three years, and then return to their country homes. Thus the injury was less ruinous than it might have been. The high character of the Lowell operatives was much spoken of in the early day. Some of the boarding-houses contained pianos upon which the boarders played in the evening, and there was a magazine called the " Lowell Offering," to which they contributed all the articles. These things seemed so astonishing that Charles Dickens, when he was first in the United States, in 1842, visited Lowell to behold the marvels for himself. How changed the world in forty years! Few persons now living can remember even the cars of forty years ago, when there were but a few hundred miles of railroad in the United States.

The train which conveyed the great novelist from Boston to Lowell consisted of three cars, a gentlemen's car in which smoking was allowed, a ladies' car in which no one smoked, and "a negro car," which the author describes as a "great, blundering, clumsy chest, such as Gulliver put to sea in from the kingdom of Brobdingnag." Where is now the negro car? It is gone to rejoin its elder brother, the negro pew. The white people's cars he describes as "large, shabby omnibuses," with a red-hot stove in the middle, and the air insufferably close.

He happened to arrive at his first factory in Lowell just as the dinner hour was over, and the girls were trooping up the stairs as he himself ascended. How strange his comments now appear to us! If we read them by the light of to-day, we find them patronizing and snobbish; but at that day they were far in advance of the feelings and opinions of the comfortable class. He observed that the girls were all well-dressed, extremely clean, with serviceable bonnets, good warm cloaks and shawls, and their feet well protected both against wet and cold. He felt it necessary, as he was writing for English readers, to *apologize* for their pleasant appearance.

" To my thinking," he remarks, " they were not dressed above their condition ; for I like to see the humbler classes of society careful of their dress and appearance, and even, if they please, decorated with such little trinkets as come within the compass of their means."

He alluded to the " Lowell Offering," a monthly magazine, " written, edited, and published," as its cover informed the public, " by female operatives employed in the mills." Mr. Dickens praised this magazine in an extremely ingenious manner. He could not claim that the literature of the work was of a very high order, because that would not have been true. He said : —

" Its merits will compare advantageously with a great many English Annuals."

That is really an exquisite touch of satire. He went on to say : —

" Many of its tales inculcate habits of self-denial and contentment, and teach good doctrines of enlarged benevolence. A strong feeling for the beauties of nature, as displayed in the solitudes the writers have left at home, breathes through its pages like wholesome village air. . . . It has very scant allusion to fine clothes, fine marriages, fine houses, or fine life."

I am so happy as to possess a number of the " Lowell Offering," for August, 1844. It begins with a pretty little story called "A Flower Dream," which confirms Mr. Dickens's remarks. There are two or three amiable pieces of poetry, a very moral article upon "Napoleon at St. Helena," one upon the tyranny of fashion, in which young ladies are advised to "lay aside all glittering ornaments, all expensive trappings," and to present instead the charms of a cultivated mind and good disposition. There is one article in the number which Mr. Dickens would have enjoyed for its own sake. It is "A Letter from Susan;" Susan being a "mill girl," as she honestly calls herself. She describes the life of the girls in the mill and in the boarding-house. She gives an excellent character both to her companions and to the overseers, one of whom had lately given her a bouquet from his own garden; and the mills themselves, she remarks, were surrounded with green lawns kept fresh all the summer by irrigation, with beds of flowers to relieve their monotony.

According to Susan, the mills themselves were pleasant places, the rooms being "high, very light, kept nicely whitewashed, and extremely neat, with many plants in the window-seats, and white cotton curtains to the windows."

"Then," says Susan, "the girls dress so neatly, and are so pretty. The mill girls are the prettiest in the city. You wonder how they can keep so neat. Why not? There are no restrictions as to the number of pieces to be washed in the boarding-houses. You say you do not see how we can have so many conveniences and comforts at the price we pay for board. You must remember that the boarding-houses belong to the company, and are let to the tenants far below the usual city rents."

Much has changed in Lowell since that day, and it is probable that few mill girls would now describe their life as favorably as Susan did in 1844. Nevertheless, the present generation of operatives derive much good from the thoughtful and patriotic care of the founders. More requires to be done. A large public park should be laid out in each of those great centres of industry. The abodes of the operatives in many instances are greatly in need of improvement. There is need of half-day schools for children who are obliged to assist their parents. Wherever it is possible, there should be attached to every house a piece of ground for a garden. The saying of the old philosopher is as true now as it was in the simple old times when it was uttered: "The way to have good servants is to be a good master."

ROBERT OWEN,
COTTON-MANUFACTURER.

———◆———

THE agitation of labor questions recalls attention to Robert Owen, who spent a great fortune and a long life in endeavoring to show workingmen how to improve their condition by coöperation. A more benevolent spirit never animated a human form than his; his very failures were more creditable than some of the successes which history vaunts.

At the age of ten years, Robert Owen, the son of a Welsh saddler, arrived in London, consigned to the care of an elder brother, to push his fortune. His school-days were over, and there was nothing for him but hard work in some lowly occupation. At the end of six weeks he found a situation as shop-boy in a dry-goods store at Stamford, in the east of England; wages, for the first year, his board and lodging; for the second year, eight pounds in addition; and a gradual increase thereafter. In this employment he remained four years, and then, although very happily situated, he made up his mind to return to London to push his fortune more rapidly.

Being large and forward for his age, a handsome, prompt, active, engaging youth, he soon obtained a situation in a dry-goods store on old London Bridge, at a salary of twenty-five pounds a year and his board. But he had to work unreasonably hard, often being obliged to sit up half the night putting away the goods, and sometimes going to bed so tired that he could hardly crawl up stairs. All the clerks had to be in the store ready for business at eight in the morning. This was about the year 1786, when men were accustomed to have their hair elaborately arranged.

" Boy as I was," he once wrote, " I had to wait my turn for the hair-dresser to powder and pomatum and curl my hair — two large curls on each side and a stiff pigtail. And until this was all nicely done no one thought of presenting himself behind the counter."

The lad endured this painful servitude for six months, at the end of which he found a better situation in Manchester, the seat of the rising cotton trade, and there he remained until he was nearly nineteen. He appeared to have had no " wild oats " to sow, being at all times highly valued by his employers, and acquiring in their service habits of careful industry, punctuality, and orderliness. He must have been a young man both of extraordinary virtues and more extraordinary abilities ; for when he was but nineteen, one of his masters offered to take him as an equal partner, to furnish all the capital, and leave him the whole business in a few years. There was also an agreeable niece in the family, whose affections he had gained without knowing it.

"If I had accepted," he says, "I should most likely have married the niece, and lived and died a rich Stamford linen-draper."

I doubt it. I do not believe that the best shop in Christendom could have held him long. When he declined this offer he was already in business for himself manufacturing cotton machinery. This business was a failure, his partner proving incompetent; and he abandoned the enterprise in a few months, taking, as his share of the stock, three cotton-spinning machines. With these he began business for himself as a cotton spinner, hiring three men to work his machines, while he superintended the establishment. He made about thirty dollars a week profit, and was going along at this rate, not ill satisfied with his lot, when he read one morning in the paper an advertisement for a factory manager. He applied for the place in person.

"You are too young," said the advertiser.

"They used to object to me on that score four or five years ago," was his reply, "but I did not expect to have it brought up now."

"Why, what age are you?"

"I shall be twenty in May next."

"How often do you get drunk in the week?"

" I never," said Owen, blushing, " was drunk in my life."

" What salary do you ask ? "

" Three hundred (pounds) a year."

" Three hundred a year! Why, I have had I don't know how many after the place here this morning, and all their askings together would not come up to what you want."

" Whatever others may ask, I cannot take less. I am making three hundred a year by my own business."

He got the place. A few days after, this lad of twenty, who had never so much as entered a large factory in his life, was installed manager of an establishment which employed five hundred people. He conducted himself with consummate prudence and skill. For the first six weeks he went about the building grave, silent, and watchful, using his eyes much and his tongue little, answering questions very briefly, and giving no positive directions. When evening came, and the hands were dismissed, he studied the machinery, the product, and all the secrets of the business. In six weeks he was a competent master, and every one felt that he was a competent master. Of large frame, noble countenance, and sympathizing disposition, he won affection, as well as confidence and respect. In six months there was not a better - managed mill in Manchester.

Now began his connection with America, a coun-

try to which, by and by, he was to give three valuable sons. While managing this mill he bought the
first two bales of American Sea Island cotton ever
imported into England, and he advanced one hundred and seventy pounds to Robert Fulton, his
fellow-boarder, to help him with his inventions. I
cannot relate all the steps by which he made his
way, while still a very young man, to the ownership
of a village of cotton mills in Scotland, and to a
union with the daughter of David Dale, a famous
Scotch manufacturer and philanthropist of that
day. He was but twenty-nine years of age when
he found himself at the head of a great community
of cotton spinners at New Lanark in Scotland.

Here he set on foot the most liberal and far-reaching plans for the benefit of the working people and
their children. He built commodious and beautiful
school-rooms, in which the children were taught
better, in some respects, than the sons of the nobility were taught at Eton or Harrow. Besides the
usual branches, he had the little sons and daughters
of the people drilled regularly in singing, dancing,
military exercises, and polite demeanor. He made
one great mistake, due rather to the ignorance of
the age than his own: he over-taught the children
— the commonest and fatalest of errors to new-born
zeal. But his efforts generally for the improvement
of the people were wonderfully successful.

"For twenty-nine years," as he once wrote to
Lord Brougham, "we did without the necessity for

magistrates or lawyers; without a single legal punishment; without any known poors' rates; without intemperance or religious animosities. We reduced the hours of labor, well educated all the children from infancy, greatly improved the condition of the adults, and cleared upward of three hundred thousand pounds profit."

Having won this great success, he fell into an error to which strong, self-educated men are peculiarly liable, — *he judged other people by himself*. He thought that men in general, if they would only try, could do as well for themselves and others as he had. He thought there could be a New Lanark without a Robert Owen. Accustomed all his life to easy success, he was not aware how exceptional a person he was, and he did not perceive that the happiness of the people who worked for him was due as much to his authority as a master as to his benevolence as a man. The consequence was that he devoted the rest of his life to going about the world telling people how much better they would be off if they would stop competing with one another, and act together for their common good. Why have one hundred kitchens, one hundred ovens, and one hundred cooks, when the work done in them could be better done in one kitchen, with one oven, by five cooks? This was one question that he asked.

Here is the steam engine, he would say, doing as much work in Great Britain as the labor power of two worlds as populous as ours could do without it.

Yet the mass of the people find life more difficult than it was centuries ago. How is this? Such questions Robert Owen pondered day and night, and the results he reached were three in number: —

1. The steam engine necessitates radical changes in the structure of society.

2. Cooperation should take the place of competition.

3. Civilized people should no longer live in cities and separate homes, but in communities of fifteen hundred or two thousand persons each, who should own houses and lands in common, and labor for the benefit of the whole.

In spreading abroad these opinions he spent forty of the best years of his life, and the greater part of a princely income. At first, and for a considerable time, such was the magnetism of his presence, and the contagion of his zeal, that his efforts commanded the sympathy, and even the approval, of the ruling classes of England, — the nobility and clergy. But in the full tide of his career as a reformer he deliberately placed himself in opposition to religion. At a public meeting in London he declared in his bland, impressive way, without the least heat or ill-nature, that all the religions of the world, whether ancient or modern, Christian or pagan, were erroneous and hurtful.

Need I say that from that moment the influential classes, almost to a man, dropped him? One of the few who did not was the Duke of Kent, the

father of Queen Victoria. He remained a steadfast friend to Owen as long as he lived. Mr. Owen
founded a community on his own system. Its failure was speedy and complete, as all experiments
must be which are undertaken ages too soon. He
came to America and repeated the experiment. That
also failed in a remarkably short period. Associated with him in this undertaking was his son,
Robert Dale Owen, who has since spent a long and
honorable life among us.

Returning to England, Mr. Owen continued to
labor in the dissemination of his ideas until the
year 1858, when he died at the age of eighty-seven.

Mr. Holyoake, author of "The History of Cooperation in England," attributes to the teaching
of Robert Owen the general establishment in Great
Britain of cooperative stores, which have been successful. As time goes on it is probable that other
parts of his system may become available ; and,
perhaps, in the course of time, it may become possible for men to live an associated life in communities such as he suggested. But they will never do
it until they can get Robert Owens at their head,
and learn to submit loyally and proudly to the just
discipline essential to success where a large number
of persons work together.

JOHN SMEDLEY,

STOCKING-MANUFACTURER.

I wonder men in a factory town should ever
have the courage to strike; it brings such woe and
desolation upon them all. The first few days, the
cessation from labor may be a relief and a pleasure
to a large number — a holiday, although a dull and
tedious holiday, like a Sunday without any of the
alleviations of Sunday — Sunday without Sunday
clothes, Sunday bells, Sunday church, Sunday walks
and visits. A painful silence reigns in the town.
People discover that the factory bell calling them
to work, though often unwelcome, was not a hundredth part as disagreeable as the silence that now
prevails. The huge mills stand gaunt and dead;
there is no noise of machinery, no puff of steam, no
faces at the windows.

By the end of the first week the novelty has
passed, and the money of some of the improvident
families is running low. All are upon short allow·
ance, the problem being to prolong life at the minimum of expense. The man goes without his meat,
the mother without her tea the children without

the trifling, inexpensive luxuries with which parental fondness usually treated them. Before the end of the second week a good many are hungry, and the workers begin to pine for employment. Their muscles are as hungry for exercise as their stomachs are for food. The provision dealers are more and more cautious about giving credit. The bank accounts, representing months or years of self-denying economy, begin to lessen rapidly, and careful fathers see that the bulwarks which they have painfully thrown up to defend their children against the wolf are crumbling away a hundred times faster than they were constructed. If the strike lasts a month, one half the population suffers every hour, and suffers more in mind than in body. Anxiety gnaws the soul. Men go about pale, gloomy, and despairing; women sit at home suffering even more acutely; until at last the situation becomes absolutely intolerable; and the strikers are fortunate indeed if they secure a small portion of the advance which they claimed.

Terrible as all this is, I am afraid we must admit that to just such miseries, sometimes rashly encountered, often heroically endured, the workingman owes a great part of the improvement in his condition which has taken place during the last seventy-five years. A strike is like war. It should be the last resort. It should never be undertaken except after long deliberation, and when every possible effort has been made to secure justice by other means.

In many instances it is better to submit to a certain degree of injustice than resort to a means of redress which brings most suffering upon the least guilty.

Does the reader know how the industrial classes were treated in former times? Mr. George Adcroft, president of an important coöperative organization in England, began life as a coal miner. He has recently given to Mr. Holyoake, author of the " History of Coöperation," some information about the habits and treatment of English miners only forty years ago : —

" They worked absolutely naked, and their daughters worked by their side. He and others were commonly compelled to work sixteen hours a day; and, from week's end to week's end, they never washed either hands or face. One Saturday night (he was then a lad of fifteen) he and others had worked till midnight, when there were still wagons at the pit's mouth. They had at last refused to work any later. The foreman told the employer, who waited till they were drawn up to the mouth, and beat them with a stout whip as they came to the surface."

So reports Mr. Holyoake, who could produce, if necessary, from the records of parliamentary investigations, many a ream of similar testimony. In truth, workingmen were scarcely regarded — nay, they were *not* regarded — as members of the human family. We find proof of this in the ancient laws of every country in Europe. In the reign of Edward VI. there was a law against idle workmen which shows how they were regarded. Any laboring man or servant loitering or living idly for the space of three days could be branded on the breast with the latter V (vagabond) and sentenced to be the slave of the person who arrested him for two years; and that person could "give him bread, water, or small drink, and refuse him meat, and cause him to work by beating, chaining, or otherwise." If he should run away from this treatment, he could be branded on the face with a hot iron with the letter S, and was to be the slave of his master for life.

Nor does there appear to have been any radical improvement in the condition of the workingman until within the memory of men now alive. When Robert Owen made his celebrated journey in 1815 among the factory towns of Great Britain, for the purpose of collecting evidence about the employment of children in factories, he gathered facts which his son, who traveled with him, speaks of as being too terrible for belief.

"As a rule," says that son (Robert Dale Owen), "we found children of ten years old worked regularly fourteen hours a day, with but half an hour's interval for dinner, which was eaten in the factory. . . . Some mills were run fifteen, and in exceptional cases sixteen hours a day, with a single set of hands; and they did not scruple to employ children of both sexes from the age of eight. . . . Most

of the overseers carried stout leather thongs, and
we frequently saw even the youngest children severely beaten."

This as recently as 1815! Mr. Holyoake himself remarks that, in his youth, he never heard one
word which indicated a kindly or respectful feeling
between employers and employed; and he speaks
of the workshops and factories of those days as
"charnel-houses of industry." If there has been
great improvement, it is due to these causes: The
resistance of the operative class; their growth in
self-respect, intelligence, and sobriety; and the humanity and wisdom of some employers of labor.

The reader has perhaps seen an article lately
printed in several newspapers entitled: "Strikes
and How to Prevent Them," by John Smedley, a
stocking manufacturer of Manchester, who employs
about eleven hundred persons. He is at the head
of an establishment founded about the time of the
American Revolution by his grandfather; and during all this long period there has never been any
strike, nor even any disagreement between the proprietors and the work-people.

"My ancestors' idea was," says Mr. Smedley,
"that those who ride inside the coach should make
those as comfortable as possible who are compelled,
from the mere accident of birth, to ride outside."

That is the secret of it. Mr. Smedley mentions
some of their modes of proceeding, one of which is
so excellent that I feel confident it will one day be

generally adopted in large factories. A cotton or
woolen mill usually begins work in this country at
half-past six, and frequently the operatives live
half an hour's walk or ride from it. This obliges
many of the operatives, especially family men and
women, to be up soon after four in the morning, in
order to get breakfast, and be at the mill in time.
It is the breakfast which makes the difficulty here.
The meal will usually be prepared in haste and
eaten in haste; late risers will devour it with one
eye on the clock; and of course it cannot be the
happy, pleasant thing a breakfast ought to be. But
in Mr. Smedley's mill the people go to work at six
without having had their breakfast. At eight the
machinery stops, and all hands, after washing in a
comfortable wash-room, assemble in what they call
the dinner-house, built, furnished, and run by the
proprietors. Here they find good coffee and tea
for sale at two cents a pint, oatmeal porridge with
syrup or milk at about ten cents a week; good
bread and butter at cost.

In addition to these articles, the people bring
whatever food they wish from home. The meal is
enjoyed at clean, well-ordered tables. The employers keep in their service a male cook and
female assistants, who will cook anything the people choose to bring. After breakfast, for fifteen
minutes, the people knit, sew, converse, stroll out
of doors, or amuse themselves in any way they
choose. At half-past eight, the manager takes his

13

stand at a desk in the great dinner-room, gives out a hymn, which the factory choir sings. Then he reads a passage from a suitable book, — sometimes from the Bible, sometimes from some other book. Then there is another hymn by the choir; after which all hands go to work, the machinery starting up again at nine.

There is similar accommodation for dinner, and at six work is over for the day. On Saturdays the mill is closed at half-past twelve, and the people have the whole afternoon for recreation. All the other rules and arrangements are in harmony with this exquisite breakfast scheme.

"We pay full wages," adds Mr. Smedley, "the hands are smart and effective. No man ever loses a day from drunkenness, and rarely can a hand be tempted to leave us. We keep a supply of dry stockings for those women to put on who come from a distance and get their feet wet; and every overlooker has a stock of waterproof petticoats to lend the women going a distance on a wet night."

I would like to cross the sea once more for the purpose of seeing John Smedley, and placing wreaths upon the tombs of his grandfather and father. He need not have told us that whenever he goes through the shops all the people recognize him, and that it is a pleasure to him to be so recognized.

"I wish," he says, "I could make their lot easier, for, with all we can do, factory life is a hard one."

RICHARD COBDEN,

CALICO PRINTER.

An American citizen presented to the English town of Bradford a marble statue of Richard Cobden. It was formally uncovered by Mr. John Bright, in the presence of the mayor and town council, and a large assembly of spectators. The figure is seven feet in height, and it rests upon a pedestal of Scotch granite polished, which bears the name of COBDEN encircled by an inscription, which summarizes the aims of his public life : —

" FREE TRADE, PEACE, AND GOOD WILL AMONG NATIONS."

The giver of this costly and beautiful work was Mr. G. H. Booth, an American partner in a noted Bradford firm. Unhappily Mr. Booth did not live to behold his own gift and share in the happiness of this interesting occasion.

We ought not to be surprised that an American should have paid this homage to the memory of an English statesman. There are plenty of good Americans in this world who were not born in America, and Richard Cobden was one of them.

Wherever there is a human being who can intelligently adopt, not as a holiday sentiment merely, but as a sacred principle to be striven for, the inscription borne upon the Cobden statue: "Free trade, peace, and good will among nations," *there* is an American. And this I say although we have not yet adopted, as we shall soon adopt, the principle of Free Trade.

Cobden was one of the best exemplifications which our times afford of that high quality of a free citizen which we name public spirit. The force of this motive drew him away from a business which yielded a profit of a hundred thousand dollars a year, to spend time, talent, fortune, and life itself, for the promotion of measures which he deemed essential to the welfare of his countrymen.

He did this because he could not help doing it. It was his nature so to do. Circumstances made him a calico printer, but by the constitution of his mind he was a servant of the State.

His father was an English yeoman; that is, a farmer who owned the farm he tilled. During the last century such farmers have become in England fewer and fewer, until now there are scarcely any left; for there is such a keen ambition among rich people in England to own land that a small proprietor cannot hold out against them. A nobleman has been known to give four or five times its value for a farm bordering upon his estate, because in an old country nothing gives a man so much social importance as the ownership of the soil. Cobden's father, it appears, lost his property, and died leaving nine children with scarcely any provision for their maintenance; so that Richard's first employment was to watch the sheep for a neighboring farmer, and this humble employment he followed on the land and near the residence of the Duke of Richmond, one of the chiefs of that protectionist party which Cobden destroyed. With regard to his education, he was almost entirely self-taught, or, as Mr. Bright observed, in his most cautious manner : —

"He had no opportunity of attending ancient universities, and availing himself of the advantages, and, I am afraid I must say, in some degree, of suffering from some of the disadvantages, from which some of those universities are not free."

This sly satire of the eloquent Quaker was received by the men of Bradford with cheers; and, indeed, it is true that college education sometimes weakens more than it refines, and many of the masters of our generation have been so lucky as to escape the debilitating process.

From tending sheep on his father's farm, he was sent away at ten years of age to a cheap Yorkshire boarding-school, similar in character to the Dotheboys Hall described by Dickens many years after in "Nicholas Nickleby." Five miserable years he spent at that school, ill-fed, harshly treated, badly taught, without once going home, and permitted to write to his parents only once in three months. In after life he could not bear to speak of his life at school; nor was he ever quite the genial and happy man he might have been if those five years had been spent otherwise.

But here again we see that hardship does not so radically injure a child as unwise indulgence. At fifteen he entered as a clerk into the warehouse of an uncle in London, an uncomfortable place, from which, however, he derived substantial advantages. The great city itself was half an education to him. He learned French in the morning before going to business. He bought cheap and good little books which are thrust upon the sight of every passer-by in cities, and, particularly, he obtained a clear insight into the business of his uncle, who was a wholesale dealer in muslins and calicoes.

From clerk he was advanced to the post of commercial traveler, an employment which most keenly gratified his desire to see the world. This was in 1826, before the days of the railroad, when commercial travelers usually drove their own gigs. The ardent Cobden accomplished his average of forty miles a day, which was then considered very rapid work. He traversed many parts of Great Britain, and not only increased his knowledge of the business, but found time to observe the natural beauties of his country, and to inspect its ancient monuments. He spent two or three years in this mode of life, being already the chief support of his numerous and unusually helpless family.

At the early age of twenty-four he thought the time had come for him to sell his calicoes and muslins on his own account. Two friends in the same business and himself put together their small capitals, amounting to five hundred pounds, borrowed another five hundred, rode to Manchester on the top of the coach named the Peveril of the Peak, boldly asked credit from a wealthy firm of calico manufacturers, obtained it, and launched into business. It proved to be a good thing for them all. In two years the young men were selling fifty or sixty thousand pounds' worth of the old men's calicoes every six months. In after years Cobden often asked them how they could have the courage to trust to such an extent three young fellows not worth two hundred pounds apiece. Their answer was : —

"We always prefer to trust young men with connections and with a knowledge of their trade, if we know them to possess character and ability, to those who start with capital without these advantages, and we have acted on this principle successfully in all parts of the world."

The young firm gained money with astonishing rapidity, one presiding over the warehouse in London, one remaining in Manchester, and the other free to go wherever the interests of the firm required. Cobden visited France and the United

States. He was here in 1835, when he thought the American people were the vainest in the world of their country. He said it was almost impossible to praise America enough to satisfy the people. He evidently did not think much of us then. American men, he thought, were a most degenerate race. And as for the women : —

"My eyes," said he, "have not found one resting place that deserves to be called a wholesome, blooming, pretty woman, since I have been here. One fourth part of the women look as if they had just recovered from a fit of the jaundice, another quarter would in England be termed in a stage of decided consumption, and the remainder are fitly likened to our fashionable women when haggard and jaded with the dissipation of a London season."

This was forty-nine years ago. Let us hope that we have improved since then. I think I could now find some American ladies to whom no part of this description would apply.

After a prosperous business career of a few years he left its details more and more to his partners, and devoted himself to public affairs.

Richard Cobden, I repeat, was a public man by nature. He belonged to what I call the natural nobility of a country ; by which I mean the individuals, whether poor or rich, high or low, learned or unlearned, who have a true public spirit, and take care of the public weal. As soon as he was free from the trammels of poverty he fell into the habit of taking extensive journeys into foreign countries, a thing most instructive and enlarging to a genuine nobleman. His first public act was the publication of a pamphlet called, " England, Ireland and America," in which he maintained that American institutions and the general policy of the American government were sound, and could safely be followed ; particularly in two respects, in maintaining only a very small army and navy, and having no entangling alliances with other countries.

" Civilization," said the young pamphleteer, " is *peace ;* war is barbarism. If the great states should devote to the development of business and the amelioration of the common lot only a small part of the treasure expended upon armaments, humanity would not have long to wait for glorious results."

He combated with great force the ancient notion that England must interfere in the politics of the continent ; and if England was not embroiled in the horrible war between Russia and Turkey, she owes it in part to Richard Cobden. He wrote also a pamphlet containing the results of his observations upon Russia, in which he denied that Russia was as rich as was generally supposed. He was the first to discover what all the world now knows, that Russia is a vast but poor country, not to be feared by neighboring nations, powerful to defend herself, but weak to attack. In a word, he adopted a line of argument with regard to Russia very similar to that recently upheld by Mr. Gladstone.

Like a true American, he was a devoted friend to universal education, and it was in connection with this subject that he first appeared as a public speaker. Mr. Bright said in his oration:—

"The first time I became acquainted with Mr. Cobden was in connection with the great question of education. I went over to Manchester to call upon him and invite him to Rochdale to speak at a meeting about to be held in the school-room of the Baptist chapel in West Street. I found him in his counting-house. I told him what I wanted. His countenance lighted up with pleasure to find that others were working in the same cause. He without hesitation agreed to come. He came and he spoke."

Persons who heard him in those days say that his speaking then was very much what it was afterward in Parliament — a kind of conversational eloquence, simple, clear, and strong, without rhetorical flights, but strangely persuasive. One gentleman who was in Parliament with him mentioned that he disliked to see him get up to speak, because he was sure that Cobden would convince him that his own opinion was erroneous; "and," said he, "a man does not like that to be done."

Soon after coming upon the stage of active life, he had arrived at the conclusion that the public policy of his country was fatally erroneous in two particulars, namely, the protective system of duties, and the habit of interfering in the affairs of other nations. At that time even the food of the people, their very bread and meat, was stopped at the custom houses until a high duty was paid upon them, for the "protection" of the farmers and landlords. In other words, the whole population of Great Britain was taxed at every meal, for the supposed benefit of two classes, those who owned and those who tilled the soil.

Richard Cobden believed that the policy of protection was not beneficial even to the protected classes, while it was most cruel to people whose wages were barely sufficient to keep them alive. For several years, aided by Mr. Bright and many other enlightened men, he labored by tongue and pen, with amazing tact, vigor, persistence, and good temper, to convince his countrymen of this.

The great achievement of his life, as all the world knows, was the repeal of those oppressive Corn Laws by which the duty on grain rose as the price declined, so that the poor man's loaf was kept dear, however abundant and cheap wheat might be in Europe and America. It was in a time of deep depression of trade that he began the agitation. He called upon Mr. Bright to enlist his coöperation, and he found him overwhelmed with grief at the loss of his wife, lying dead in the house at the time. Mr. Cobden consoled his friend as best he could; and yet even at such a time he could not forget his mission. He said to Mr. Bright: —

" There are thousands and thousands of homes

in England at this moment, where wives, mothers, and children are dying of hunger! Now when the first paroxysm of your grief is past, I would advise you to come with me, and we will never rest until the Corn Laws are repealed."

Mr. Bright joined him. The Anti-Corn-Law-League was formed; such an agitation was made as has seldom been paralleled; but, so difficult is it to effect a change of this kind against *interested* votes, that, after all, the Irish famine was necessary to effect the repeal. As a writer remarks: —

" It was hunger that at last ate through those stone walls of protection!"

Sir Robert Peel, the prime minister, a protectionist, as we may say, from his birth, yielded to circumstances as much as to argument, and accomplished the repeal in 1846. When the great work was done, and done, too, with benefit to every class, he publicly assigned the credit of the measure to the persuasive eloquence and the indomitable resolution of Richard Cobden.

Mr. Cobden's public labors withdrew his attention from his private business, and he became embarrassed. His friends made a purse for him of eighty thousand pounds sterling, with which to set him up as a public man. He accepted the gift, bought back the farm upon which he was born, and devoted himself without reserve to the public service. During our war he was the friend and champion of the United States, and he owed his premature death to his zeal and friendly regard for this country. There was a ridiculous scheme coming up in Parliament for a line of fortresses to defend Canada against the United States. On one of the coldest days of March he went to London for the sole purpose of speaking against this project. He took a violent cold, under which he sank. He died on that Sunday, the second of April, 1865, when Abraham Lincoln, with a portion of General Grant's army, entered the city of Richmond. It was a strange coincidence. Through four years he had steadily foretold such an ending to the struggle; but though he lived to see the great day he breathed his last a few hours before the news reached the British shore.

There is not in Great Britain, as Mr. Bright observed, a poor man's home that has not in it a bigger and a better loaf through Richard Cobden's labors. His great measure relieved the poor, and relieved the rich. It was a good without alloy, as free trade will, doubtless, be to all nations when their irrepressible Cobdens and their hungry workmen force them to adopt it.

The time is not distant when we, too, shall be obliged, as a people, to meet this question of Free Trade and Protection. In view of that inevitable discussion I advise young voters to study Cobden and Bright, as well as men of the opposite school, and make up their minds on the great question of the future.

HENRY BESSEMER.

NERVOUS persons who ride in sleeping-cars are much indebted to Henry Bessemer, to whose invent-ive genius they owe the beautiful steel rails over which the cars glide so steadily. It was he who so simplified and cheapened the process of making steel that it can be used for rails.

Nine people in ten, I suppose, do not know the chemical difference between iron and steel. Iron is iron ; but steel is iron mixed with carbon. But, then, what is carbon ? There is no substance in nature of which you can pick up a piece and say, This is carbon. And hence it is difficult to explain its nature and properties. Carbon is the principal ingredient in coal, charcoal, and diamond. Carbon is not diamond, but a diamond is carbon crystal-lized. Carbon is not charcoal, but in some kinds of charcoal it is almost the whole mass. As crys-tallized carbon or diamond is the hardest of all known substances, so also the blending of carbon with iron hardens it into steel.

The old way of converting iron into steel was slow, laborious, and expensive. In India for ages the process has been as follows : pieces of forged iron are put into a crucible along with a certain quantity of wood. A fire being lighted underneath, three or four men are incessantly employed in blowing it with bellows. Through the action of the heat the wood becomes charcoal, the iron is melted and absorbs carbon from the charcoal. In this way small pieces of steel were made, but made at a cost which confined the use of the article to small objects, such as watch-springs and cutlery. The plan pursued in Europe and America, until about twenty-five years ago, was similar to this in principle. Our machinery was better, and pure charcoal was placed in the crucible instead of wood ; but the process was long and costly, and only small pieces of steel were produced at a time.

Henry Bessemer enters upon the scene. In 1831, being then eighteen years of age, he came up to London from a country village in Hertfordshire to seek his fortune, not knowing one person in the metropolis. He was, as he has since said, " a mere cipher in that vast sea of human enterprise." He was a natural inventor, of studious and observant habits. As soon as he had obtained a footing in London he began to invent. He first devised a process for copying bas-reliefs on cardboard, by which he could produce embossed copies of such works in thousands at a small expense. The process was so simple that in ten minutes a person without skill could produce a die from an embossed stamp at a cost of one penny.

When his invention was complete he thought with dismay and alarm that, as almost all the expensive stamps affixed to documents in England are raised from the paper, any of them could be forged by an office-boy of average intelligence. The English government has long obtained an important part of its revenue by the sale of these stamps, many of which are high priced, costing as much as twenty-five dollars. If the stamp on a will, a deed, or other document is not genuine, the document has no validity. As soon as he found what mischief had been done, he set to work to devise a remedy. After several months' experiment and reflection he invented a stamp which could neither be forged nor removed from the document and used a second time. A large business, it seems, had been done in removing stamps from old parchments of no further use, and selling them to be used again.

The inventor called at the stamp office and had an interview with the chief, who frankly owned that the government was losing half a million dollars a year by the use of old stamps; and he was then considering methods of avoiding the loss. Bessemer exhibited his invention, the chief feature of which was the perforation of the stamp in such a way that forgery and removal were equally impossible. The commissioner finally agreed to adopt it. The next question was as to the compensation of the young inventor, and he was given his choice either to accept a sum of money or an office for life in the stamp office of four thousand dollars a year. As he was engaged to be married, he chose the office, and went home rejoicing, feeling that he was a made man. Nor did he long delay to communicate the joyful news to the young lady. To her also he explained his invention, dwelling upon the fact that a five-pound stamp a hundred years old could be taken off a document and used a second time.

"Yes," said she, "I understand that; but, surely, if all stamps had a DATE put upon them they could not at a future time be used again without detection."

The inventor was startled. He had never thought of an expedient so simple and so obvious. A lover could not but be pleased at such ingenuity in his affianced bride; but it spoiled his invention! His perforated stamp did not allow of the insertion of more than one date. He succeeded in obviating this difficulty, but deemed it only fair to communicate the new idea to the chief of the stamp office. The result was that the government simply adopted the plan of putting a date upon all the stamps afterwards issued, and discarded Bessemer's fine scheme of perforation, which would have involved an expensive and troublesome change of machinery and methods. But the worst of it was that the inventor lost his office, since his services were not needed. Nor did he ever receive compensation for the service rendered.

14

Thus it was that a young lady changed the stamp system of her country, and ruined her lover's chances of getting a good office. She rendered him, however, and rendered the world, a much greater service in throwing him upon his own resources. They were married soon after, and Mrs. Bessemer is still living to tell how she married and made her husband's fortune.

Twenty years passed, with the varied fortune which young men of energy and talent often experience in this troublesome world. We find him then experimenting in the conversion of iron into steel. The experiments were laborious as well as costly, since his idea was to convert at one operation many tons' weight of iron into steel, and in a few minutes. As iron ore contains carbon, he conceived the possibility of making that carbon unite with the iron during the very process of smelting. For nearly two years he was building furnaces and pulling them down again, spending money and toil with just enough success to lure him on to spend more money and toil; experimenting sometimes with ten pounds of iron ore, and sometimes with several hundredweight. His efforts were at length crowned with such success that he was able to make five tons of steel at a blast, in about thirty-five minutes, with comparatively simple machinery, and with a very moderate expenditure of fuel.

This time he took the precaution to patent his process, and offered rights to all the world at a royalty of a shilling per hundredweight. His numerous failures, however, had discouraged the iron men, and no one would embark capital in the new process. He therefore began himself the manufacture of steel on a small scale, and with such large profit, that the process was rapidly introduced into all the iron-making countries, and gave Mrs. Bessemer ample consolation for her early misfortune of being too wise. Money and gold medals have rained in upon them. At the French Exhibition of 1868 Mr. Bessemer was awarded a gold medal weighing twelve ounces. His process has been improved upon both by himself and others, and has conferred upon all civilized countries numerous and solid benefits. We may say of him that he has added to the resources of many trades a new material.

The latest device of Henry Bessemer, if it had succeeded, would have been a great comfort to the Marquis of Lorne and other persons of weak digestion who cross the ocean. It was a scheme for suspending the cabin of a ship so that it should swing free and remain stationary, no matter how violent the ship's motion. The idea seems promising, but we have not yet heard of the establishment of a line of steamers constructed on the Bessemer principle. We may yet have the pleasure of swinging from New York to Liverpool.

JOHN BRIGHT.

MANUFACTURER.

FORTY-FIVE years ago, when John Bright was first elected to the British Parliament, he spoke thus to his constituents : —

" I am a working man as much as you. My father was as poor as any man in this crowd. He was of your own body entirely. He boasts not, nor do I, of birth, nor of great family distinctions. What he has made, he has made by his own industry and successful commerce. What I have comes from him and from my own exertions. I come before you as the friend of my own class and order, as one of the people."

When these words were spoken, his father, Jacob Bright, a Quaker, and the son of a Quaker, was still alive, a thriving cotton manufacturer of Rochdale, ten miles from Manchester. Jacob Bright had been a "Good Apprentice," who married one of the daughters of his master, and had been admitted as a partner in his business. He was a man of much force and ability, who became in a few years the practical head of the concern,

John Bright.
August 10. 1883

finally its sole proprietor, and left it to his sons, who have carried it on with success for about half a century longer.

Four years ago, on the celebration of John Bright's seventieth birthday, he stood face to face with fifteen hundred persons in the employment of his firm, and repeated in substance what he had said once before, that, during the seventy-three years of the firm's existence, there had been, with one brief exception, uninterrupted harmony and confidence between his family and those who had worked for them.

He made another remark on that birthday which explains a great deal in his career. It was of particular interest to me, because I have long been convinced that no man can give himself up to the service of the public, with advantage to the public, and safety to himself, unless he is practically free from the burdens and trammels of private business.

"I have been greatly fortunate," said Mr. Bright, "in one respect — that, although connected with a large and increasing and somewhat intricate business, yet I have been permitted to be free from the employments and engagements and occupations of business by the constant and undeviating generosity and kindness of my brother, Thomas Bright."

The tribute was well deserved. Certainly, no individual can successfully direct the industry of fifteen hundred persons, and spend six months of the year in London, working night and day as a member of Parliament. Richard Cobden tried it, and brought a flourishing business to ruin by the attempt, and probably shortened his own life. Even with the aid rendered him by his brother, Mr. Bright was obliged to withdraw from public life for three years in order to restore an exhausted brain.

John Bright enjoyed just the kind of education in his youth which experience has shown to be the best for the development of a leader of men. At fifteen, after attending pretty good Quaker schools in the country, where, besides spelling and arithmetic, he learned how to swim, to fish, and to love nature, he came home, went into his father's factory, and became a man of business. He had acquired at school love of literature, particularly of poetry, which he continued to indulge during his leisure hours. You will seldom hear Mr. Bright speak twenty minutes without hearing him make an apt and most telling quotation from one of the poets. He possesses in an eminent degree the talent of quotation, which is one of the happiest gifts of the popular orator. It is worthy of note that this manufacturer, this man of the people, this Manchester man, shows a familiarity with the more dainty, outlying, recondite literature of the world than is shown by any other member of a house composed chiefly of college-bred men.

In his early days he belonged to a debating society, spoke at temperance meetings, was an ardent

politician, and, in short, had about the sort of training which an American young man of similar cast
of mind would have enjoyed. John Bright, in fact,
is one of that numerous class of Americans whom
the accident of birth and the circumstances of their
lot have prevented from treading the soil of America. In his debating society he had good practice
in public speaking, and on all questions took what
we may justly call *the Quaker side, i. e.*, the side
which he thought had most in it of humanity and
benevolence. He sided against capital punishment, against the established church, and defended
the principle of equal toleration of all religions.

Next to Mr. Gladstone, the most admired
speaker in Great Britain is John Bright, and there
are those who even place him first among the living orators of his country. His published speeches
reveal to us only part of the secret of his power,
for an essential part of the equipment of an orator
is his bodily attributes, his voice, depth of chest,
eye, demeanor, presence.

The youngest portrait of him which has been
published represents him as he was at the age of
thirty-one. If an inch or two could have been added to his stature he would have been as perfect a
piece of flesh and blood as can ordinarily be found.
His face was strikingly handsome, and bore the
impress both of power and of serenity. It was a well-
balanced face ; there being a full development of
the lower portion without any bull-dog excess.

His voice was sonorous and commanding ; his manner tranquil and dignified. As he was never a student at either university, he did not acquire the Cambridge nor the Oxford sing - song, but has always spoken the English language as distinctly and naturally as though he were a native American citizen.

Although of Quaker family, and himself a member of the Society of Friends, he has never used the Quaker *thee* and *thou*, nor persisted in wearing his hat where other men take off theirs. In the House of Commons he conforms to the usages of the place, and speaks of " the noble lord opposite," and " my right honorable friend near me," just as though the Quakers never had borne their testimony against such vanity. In his dress, too, there is only the faintest intimation of the Quaker cut. He is a Quaker in his abhorrence of war and in his feeling of the substantial equality of men. He is a Quaker in those few sublime principles in which the Quakers, two centuries ago, were three centuries in advance of the time.

For the benefit of young orators, I will mention also that he has taken excellent care of his bodily powers. As a young man he was a noted cricketer and an enthusiastic angler. At all periods of his life he has played a capital game at billiards. Angling, however, has been his favorite recreation, and he has fished in almost all the good streams of the northern part of his native island.

Nor does he find it necessary to carry a brandy flask with him on his fishing excursions. He mentioned some time ago, at a public meeting, that he had been a tee-totaler from the time when he set up housekeeping thirty-four years before. He said he had in his house no decanters, and, so far as he knew, no wineglasses.

Edward Everett used to say that a speaker's success before an audience depended chiefly upon the thoroughness of his previous preparation. Mr. Bright has often spoken extempore with great effect, when circumstances demanded it. But his custom is to prepare carefully, and in his earlier days he used frequently to write his speech and learn it by heart. He received his first lesson in oratory from a Baptist clergyman of great note, whom he accompanied to a meeting of the Bible Society, and who afterwards gave an account of their conversation. John Bright was then twenty-one years of age.

"Soon a slender, modest young gentleman came, who surprised me by his intelligence and thoughtfulness. I took his arm on the way to the meeting, and I thought he seemed nervous. I think it was his first public speech. It was very eloquent and powerful, and carried away the meeting, but it was elaborate, and had been committed to memory. On our way back, as I congratulated him, he said that such efforts cost him too dear, and asked me how I spoke so easily. I said that in his case, as in most, I thought it would be best not to burden the memory too much, but, having carefully prepared and committed any portion when special effect was desired, merely to put down other things in the desired order, leaving the wording of them to the moment."

The young man remembered this lesson, and acted upon it. He no longer finds it best to learn any portions of his speeches by heart, but his addresses show a remarkable thoroughness of preparation, else they could not be so thickly sown as they are with pregnant facts, telling figures, and apt illustrations. His pudding is too full of plums to be the work of the moment. Such aptness of quotation as he displays is sometimes a little too happy to be spontaneous; as when, in alluding to the difference between men's professions out of office and their measures in office, he quoted Thomas Moore: —

> "As bees on flowers alighting cease to hum,
> So, settling upon places, Whigs grow dumb."

So also, in referring to the aristocratic composition of the English government, he quoted Mr. Lowell's "Biglow Papers": —

> "It is something like fulfilling the prophecies
> When the first families have all the best offices."

Again, when lamenting the obstacles put in the way of universal education by the rivalries of sect, he produced a great effect in the House of Commons by saying: —

" We are, after all, of one religion."

And then he quoted in illustration an impressive sentence from William Penn, to the effect that just and good souls were everywhere of one faith, and "when death has taken off the mask, they will know one another, though the diverse liveries they wear here make them strangers."

No man has less need to quote the brilliant utterances of others than John Bright ; for he possesses himself the power to speak in epigrams, and to make sentences which remain long in the memory. Once in his life he found himself in opposition to the workingmen of his district, and during the excitement of an election he was greeted with hoots and hisses. He made a remark on the platform which all public men making head against opposition would do well to remember : —

" Although there are here many of the operative classes who consider me to be their enemy, I would rather have their ill-will now, while defending their interests, than have their ill-will hereafter because I have betrayed them."

One of his homely similes uttered thirty years ago, to show the waste and folly of the Crimean War, has become a familiar saying in Great Britain.

"Some men," said he, " because they have got government contracts, fancy that trade is good, and that war is good for trade. Why, it is but endeavoring to keep a dog alive by feeding him with his own tail."

This homeliness of speech, when there is strong conviction and massive sense behind it, has a prodigious effect upon a large meeting. Once, during his warfare upon the Corn Laws, he exclaimed : —

" This is not a party question, for men of all parties are united upon it. It is a pantry question — a knife-and-fork question — a question between the working millions and the aristocracy."

So in addressing the work-people of his native town, who were on a strike for higher wages at a time when it was impossible for the employers to accede to their demands without ruin, he expressed an obvious truth very happily in saying : —

" Neither act of parliament nor act of a multitude can keep up wages."

I need scarcely say that no combination of physical and intellectual powers can make a truly great orator. Moral qualities are indispensable. There must be courage, sincerity, patriotism, humanity, faith in the future of our race.

His Quaker training was evidently the most influential fact of his whole existence, for it gave him the key to the moral and political problems of his day. It made him, as it were, the natural enemy of privilege and monopoly in all their countless forms. It suffused his whole being with the sentiment of human equality, and showed him that no class can be degraded without lowering all other classes. He seems from the first to have known that human brotherhood is not a mere sentiment not a conviction of the mind, but a fact of nature, from which there is no escape; so that no individual can be harmed without harm being done to the whole. When he was a young man he summed up all this class of truths in a sentence : —

"The interests of all classes are so intimately blended that none can suffer without injury being inflicted upon the rest, and the true interest of each will be found to be advanced by those measures which conduce to the prosperity of the whole."

Feeling thus, he was one of the first to join the movement for Free Trade. When he came upon the public stage the Corn Laws, as they were called, which sought to protect the interests of farmers and landlords by putting high duties upon imported food, had consigned to the poor-houses of Great Britain and Ireland more than two millions of paupers, and reduced two millions more to the verge of despair. John Bright was the great orator of the movement for the repeal of those laws. After six years of the best sustained agitation ever witnessed in a free country, the farmers and land-owners were not yet convinced. In 1846, however, an event occurred which gave the reasoning of Cobden and the eloquence of Bright their due effect upon the minds of the ruling class. This event was the Irish famine of 1846, which lessened the population of Ireland by two millions in one year. This awful event prevailed, though it would not have prevailed unless the exertions of Cobden and

Bright had familiarized the minds of men with the true remedy, — which was the free admission of those commodities for the want of which people were dying.

On his seventieth birthday Mr. Bright justified what he called the policy of 1846. He said to his townsmen :—

"I was looking the other day at one of our wages books of 1840 and 1841. I find that the throttle-piecers were then receiving eight shillings a week, and they were working twelve hours a day. I find that now the same class of hands are receiving thirteen shillings a week at ten hours a day — exactly double. At that time we had a blacksmith, whom I used to like to see strike the sparks out. His wages were twenty-two shillings a week. Our blacksmiths now have wages of thirty-four shillings, and they only work ten hours."

Poor men alone know what these figures mean. They know what an amount of improvement in the lot of the industrial class is due to the shortened day, the cheaper loaf, the added shillings.

In a word, the effort of John Bright's life has been to apply Quaker principles to the government of his country. He has called upon ministers to cease meddling with the affairs of people on the other side of the globe, to let Turkey alone, to stop building insensate ironclads, and to devote their main strength to the improvement and elevation of their own people. He says to them in substance :

You may have an historical monarchy and a splendid throne ; you may have an ancient nobility, living in spacious mansions on vast estates ; you may have a church hiding with its pomp and magnificence a religion of humility ; and yet, with all this, if the mass of the people are ignorant and degraded, the whole fabric is rotten, and is doomed at last to sink into ruin.

THOMAS EDWARD,
COBBLER AND NATURALIST.

THE strangest story told for a long time is that of Thomas Edward, shoemaker and naturalist, to whom the Queen of England recently gave a pension of fifty pounds a year. He was not a shoemaker who kept a shop and gave out work to others, but actually worked at the bench from childhood to old age, supporting a very large family on the eight or nine or ten shillings a week that he earned. And yet we find him a member of several societies of naturalists, the Linnæan Society among others, and an honored pensioner of the Queen.

His father was a Scottish linen weaver, and for some time a private soldier in a militia regiment which was called into active service during the wars with Napoleon; and it was while the regiment was stationed at an English sea-port that this remarkable child was born. A few months after, when the Waterloo victory had given peace to Europe, the regiment was ordered home and disbanded, and this family settled at Aberdeen, where the father resumed his former occupation. Now the peculiar character of Thomas Edward began to exhibit itself. He showed an extraordinary fondness for animals, to the sore distress and torment of his parents and their neighbors.

It was a taste purely natural, for not only was it not encouraged, it was strongly discouraged by every one who could be supposed to have influence over the boy. He disappeared one day when he was scarcely able to walk, and when he had been gone for some hours he was found in a pig-sty fast asleep, near a particularly savage sow and her pigs. As soon as he could walk well enough his delight was to ramble along the shore and into the country, gathering tadpoles, beetles, frogs, crabs, mice, rats, and spiders, to the horror of his mother, to say nothing of the neighbors, for these awful creatures escaped into houses near by and appeared to the inmates at the most unexpected moments.

His parents scolded and whipped him, but his love of animal life was unconquerable, and the only effect of opposing it was to make him more cunning in its gratification. They tied the little fellow by his leg to a table, but he drew the table up near the fire, burnt the rope in halves, and was off for the fields. They hid his coat, but he took his elder brother's coat and ran. Then they hid all his clothes, but he slipped on an old petticoat and had another glorious day out of doors, returning with a fever in his veins which brought him to death's door.

All these things, and many others like them, happened when he was still a boy under five years of age. Recovering from his fever he resumed his old tricks, and brought home one day, wrapped in his shirt, a wasp's nest, which his father took from him and plunged into hot water. Between four and five he was sent to school, his parents thinking to keep him out of mischief of this kind. But he had not the least interest in school knowledge, and constantly played truant; and when he did come to school he brought with him all kinds of horrid insects, reptiles, and birds. One morning during prayers a jackdaw began to caw, and as the bird was traced to the ownership of Thomas Edward, he was dismissed from the school in great disgrace. His perplexed parents sent him to another school, the teacher of which used more vigorous measures to cure him of his propensity, applying to his back an instrument of torture called " the taws." It was in vain. From this second school he was expelled, because some horse-leeches, which he had brought to school in a bottle, escaped, crept up the legs of the other boys, and drew blood from them.

" I would not take him back for twenty pounds ! " said the schoolmaster in horror.

A third time his father put him at school ; and now he experienced the ill consequences of having a bad name. A centipede was found upon another boy's desk, and he was of course suspected of having brought it into the schoolroom. But it so happened that on this one occasion he was innocent; it was another boy's centipede; and Thomas denied the charge. The schoolmaster whipped him severely for the supposed falsehood, and sent him away saying: —

"Go home, and tell your father to get you on board a man-of-war, as that is the best school for irreclaimables such as you."

He went home and declared he would go to no more schools, but would rather work. He had now reached the mature age of six years, and had been turned out of school three times, without having learned to write his own name. Soon after, he went to work in a tobacco factory on the river Don, a short distance out of Aberdeen, and there for two happy years he was free to employ all his leisure time in investigating animated nature around him. His love of natural history grew with his growth and strengthened with his strength, so that by the time he had completed his eighth year he was familiarly acquainted with the animals of that region, and had the most lively admiration for the more interesting specimens. He watched with delight the kingfisher, and loved to distinguish the voices of the different birds.

But his parents objecting to the tobacconist's trade, he was apprenticed about his ninth year to a shoemaker, — a violent, disreputable character, who made ruthless war upon the lad's birds and reptiles, searching his pockets for them, and killing them whenever found. The lad bore this misery for three years, and then his patience being exhausted, and having in his pocket the sum of seven pence, he ran away and walked a hundred miles into the country to the house of one of his uncles. His uncle received him kindly, entertained him a day or two, and gave him eighteen pence, upon which the boy returned home, and made a bargain with his master by which he received small wages and had complete control of his leisure time. At eighteen we may regard him as fairly launched upon life, a journeyman shoemaker, able to earn in good times nine shillings a week by laboring from six in the morning till nine at night. At that time all mechanics worked more hours than they do at present, and particularly shoemakers, whose sedentary occupation does not expend vitality so rapidly as out-of-door trades. And what made his case the more difficult was, he was a thorough-going Scotchman, and consequently a strict observer of Sunday. Confined though he was to his work fifteen hours a day, he abstained on principle from pursuing his natural studies on the only day he could call his own.

He was a night-bird, this Thomas Edward; and as in Scotland the twilight lasts till ten in the evening and the day dawns at three in the morning, there were some hours out of the twenty-four which he could employ, and did employ, in his rambles. At twenty-three he fell in love with a pretty girl, and married her, his income being still but nine and sixpence a week. His married life was a happy one, for his wife had the good sense to make no opposition to his darling pursuits, and let him fill their cottage and garden with as many creatures as he chose, not even scolding him for his very frequent absences during the night. Some one asked her recently about this, and her reply was:—

" Weel, he took such an interest in beasts that I didna compleen. Shoemakers were then a very drucken set, but his beasts keepit him frae them. My mon 's been a sober mon all his life, and he never negleckit his wark. Sae I let him be." —

Children were born to them, eleven in all, and yet he found time to learn to write, to read some books, and to increase constantly his knowledge of nature. In order to procure specimens for his collection, he bought an old shot-gun for a sum equal to about a dollar, — such a battered old piece that he had to tie the barrel to the stock with a piece of string. A cow's horn served for his powder; he measured his charge with a tobacco pipe, and carried his shot in a paper-bag. About nine in the evening, carrying his supper with him, he would start out and search the country round for animals and rare plants as long as he could see; then eat his supper and lie down and sleep till the light returned, when he would continue his hunting till it was time for work. Many a fight he had in the darkness with badgers and pole-cats.

When he had thus been employed eight or nine

years, his collection contained two thousand specimens of animals and two thousand plants, all nicely arranged in three hundred cases made with his own hands. Upon this collection he had founded hopes of getting money upon which to pursue his studies more extensively. So he took it to Aberdeen, six cart loads in all, accompanied by the whole family, — wife and five children. It needs scarcely to be said that his collection did not succeed, and he was obliged to sell the fruit of nine years' labor for twenty pounds. Nothing daunted, he returned to his cobbler's stall, and began again to collect, occasionally encouraged by a neighboring naturalist, and sometimes getting a little money for a rare specimen. Often he tried to procure employment as a naturalist, but unsuccessfully, and as late as 1875 we find him writing thus : —

" As a last and only remaining resource, I betook myself to my old and time-honored friend, a friend of fifty years' standing, who has never yet forsaken me nor refused help to my body when weary, nor rest to my limbs when tired — my well-worn cobbler's stool. And although I am now like a beast tethered to his pasture, with a portion of my faculties somewhat impaired, I can still appreciate and admire as much as ever the beauties and wonders of nature as exhibited in the incomparable works of our adorable Creator."

These are cheerful words to come from an old man who has enriched the science of his country by additions to its sources of knowledge. In another letter, written a year or two since, he says : —

" Had the object of my life been money instead of nature, I have no hesitation in saying that by this time I would have been a rich man. But it is not the things I have done that vex me so much as the things I have not done. I feel that I could have accomplished so much more. I had the will, but I wanted the means."

It is in this way that such men feel toward the close of their lives. Thomas Edward still lives, in his sixty-seventh year, at Banff, in Scotland, rich in his pension of fifty pounds a year, which is more than twice as much as the income he had when he supported by his labor a wife and eleven children. Even his specimens now command a price, and he is every way a prosperous gentleman. It seems a pity that such men cannot have their precious little fifty pounds to begin with, instead of to end with. But who could pick them out ? What mortal eye can discern in a man the *genuine* celestial fire before he has proved its existence by the devotion of a lifetime to his object ? And even if it could be discerned in a young man, the fifty pounds a year might quench it.

ROBERT DICK,

BAKER AND NATURALIST.

———◆———

THE most northern county of Scotland is Caithness, a wild region of mountain, marsh, and rock-
ribbed headlands, in which the storms of the Atlantic have worn every variety of fantastic indentation.
Much of the land has been reclaimed in modern
days by rich proprietors. There are manufactures
of linen, wool, rope, and straw, besides important
fisheries; so that forty thousand people now find
habitation and subsistence in the county. There
are castles, too, ancient and modern, — some in
ruins, some of yesterday, — the summer home of
wealthy people from the south.

The coast is among the most picturesque in the
world, bearing a strong resemblance to the coast of
Maine. The reader, perhaps, has never seen the
coast of Maine. Then let him do so speedily, and
he will know, as he sails along its bold headlands,
and its seamed walls of rock rising here and there
into mountains, how the coast of Caithness looked
to one of the noblest men that ever lived in it,
Robert Dick, baker of Thurso. Thurso is the

most northern town of this most northern county. It is situated on Thurso Bay, which affords a good harbor, and it has thus grown to be a place of three or four thousand inhabitants. From this town the Orkney Islands can be seen, and a good walker can reach in a day's tramp Dunnet Head, the lofty promontory which ends the Island.

Here lived, labored, studied, and died, Robert Dick, a man whose name should never be pronounced by intelligent men but with respect.

He did not look like a hero. When the boys of the town saw him coming out of his baker's shop, in a tall stove-pipe hat, an old-fashioned dress coat and jean trousers, they used to follow him to the shore, and watch him as he walked along it with his eyes fixed upon the ground. Suddenly he would stop, fall upon his hands and knees, crawl slowly onward, and then with one hand catch something on the sand; an insect, perhaps. He would stick it upon a pin, put it in his hat, and go on his way; and the boys would whisper to one another that there was a mad baker in Thurso. Once he picked up a nut upon the beach, and said to his companion : —

" That has been brought by the ocean current and the prevailing winds all the way from one of the West India Islands."

He made the most astonishing journeys about that fag end of the universe in the pursuit of knowledge. We read of his walking thirty-two miles in a soaking rain to the top of a mountain, and bringing home only a plant of white heather. On another day he walked thirty-six miles to find a peculiar kind of fern. Again he walked for twenty-four hours in hail, rain, and wind, reaching home at three o'clock in the morning. But at seven he was up and ready for work as usual. He carried heavy loads, too, when he went searching for minerals and fossils. In one of his letters we read : —

"Shouldering an old poker, a four-pound hammer, and with two chisels in my pocket, I set out. . . . What hammering! what sweating! Coat off; got my hands cut to bleeding."

In another letter he speaks of having "three pounds of iron chisels in his trousers pocket, a four-pound hammer in one hand and a fourteen-pound sledge-hammer in the other, and his old beaver hat filled with paper and twine."

But who and what was this man, and why was he performing these laborious journeys? Robert Dick, born in 1811, was the son of an excise officer, who gave his children a hard stepmother when Robert was ten years old. The boy's own mother, all tenderness and affection, had spoiled him for such a life as he now had to lead under a woman who loved him not, and did not understand his unusual cast of character, his love of nature, his wanderings by the sea, his coming home with his pockets full of wet shells and his trousers damaged by the mire. She snubbed him; she whipped him. He

bore her ill treatment with wonderful patience;
but it impaired the social side of him forever.
Nearly fifty years after he said to one of his few
friends : —

"All my naturally buoyant, youthful spirits were
broken. To this day I feel the effects. I cannot
shake them off. It is this that still makes me
shrink from the world."

At thirteen he escaped from a home blighted by
this woman, and went apprentice to a baker; and
when he was out of his time served as a journeyman for three years; then set up a small business
for himself in Thurso. It was a very small business indeed; for at that day bread was a luxury
which many people of Caithness only allowed themselves on Sundays: their usual fare being oatmeal.
He was a baker all the days of his life, and his
business never increased so as to oblige him to
employ even a baker's boy. He made his bread,
his biscuit, and his gingerbread without any assistance, and when it was done, it was sold in his little
shop by an old housekeeper, who lived with him
till he died.

The usual course of his day was this: He was
up in the morning very early, at any time from
three to six, according to his plans for the after
part of the day. He kneaded his bread, worked
the dough into loaves, put the whole into the oven,
waited till it was baked, and drew it out. His
work was then usually done for the day. The old

housekeeper sold it as it was called for, and, in case
her master did not get home in time, she could set
the sponge in the evening. Usually, he could get
away from the bake-shop soon after the middle of
the day, and he had then all the afternoon, the evening, and the night for studying nature in Caithness. His profits were small, but his wants were
few, and during the greater part of his life he was
able to spare a small sum per annum for the purchase of books.

If this man had enjoyed the opportunities he
would have had but for his mother's death, he
might have been one of the greatest naturalists
that ever lived. Nature had given him every requisite: a frame of iron, Scotch endurance, a poet's
enthusiasm, the instinct of not believing anything
in science till he was *sure* of it, till he had put it
to the test of repeated observation and experiment.
Although a great reader, he derived most of his
knowledge directly from nature's self. He began
by merely picking up shells, as a child picks them
up, because they were pretty; until, while still a
lad, he had a very complete collection all nicely
arranged in a cabinet and labeled. Youth being
past, the shy and lonely young man began to study
botany, which he pursued until he had seen and
felt everything that grew in Caithness. Next he
studied insects, and studied with such zeal that in
nine months he had collected, of beetles alone, two
hundred and fifty-six specimens. There are still

in the Thurso museum two hundred and twenty varieties of bees, and two hundred and forty kinds of butterflies, collected by him.

Early in life he was powerfully attracted to astronomy, and read everything he could find upon the subject. But he was one of those students whom books alone can never satisfy; and as a telescope was very far beyond his means he was obliged to devote himself to subjects more within his own reach. He contrived out of his small savings to buy a good microscope, and found it indispensable. Geology was the subject which occupied him longest and absorbed him most. He pursued it with untiring and intelligent devotion for thirty years. He found the books full of mistakes, because, as he said, so many geologists study nature from a gig and are afraid to get a little mud on their trousers.

"When," said he, " I want to know what a rock is, I go to it; I hammer it; I dissect it. I then know what it really is. . . . The science of geology! No, no; we must just work patiently on, *collect facts*, and in course of time geology may develop into a science."

I suppose there never was a man whose love of knowledge was more disinterested. He used to send curious specimens to Hugh Miller, editor of "The Witness" as well as a geologist, and Mr. Miller would acknowledge the gifts in his paper; but Robert Dick entreated him not to do so.

"I am a quiet creature," he wrote, "and do not

like to see myself in print at all. So leave it to be understood who found the old bones, and let them guess who can."

As long as he was in unimpaired health he continued this way of life cheerfully enough, refusing all offers of assistance. His brother-in-law once proposed to send him a present of whiskey.

" No," said he in reply, " spirits never enter this house save when I cannot help it."

His brother-in-law next offered to send him some money. He answered : —

" God grant you more sense ! I want no sovereigns. It 's of no use sending anything down here. Nothing is wanted. Delicacies would only injure health. *Hardy* is the word with working people. Pampering does no good, but much evil."

And yet the latter days of this great-souled man were a woeful tragedy. He was the best baker in the place, gave full weight, paid for his flour on the day, and was in all respects a model of fair dealing. But his trade declined. Competition reduced his profits and limited his sales. When the great split occurred in Scotland between the old and the free church, he stuck to the old, merely saying that the church of his forefathers was good enough for him. But his neighbors and customers were zealous for the free church ; and one day, when the preacher aimed a sermon at him for taking his walks on Sunday, he was offended, and rarely went again. And so, for various reasons, his business declined; some losses befell him; and he injured his constitution by exposure and exhausting labors in the study of geology.

There were rich and powerful families near by who knew his worth, or would have known it if they had themselves been worthy. They looked on and saw the noblest heart in Scotland break in this unequal strife. They should have set him free from his bake-shop as soon as he had given proof of the stuff he was made of. He was poet, artist, philosopher, hero, and they let him die in his bake-house in misery. After his death they performed over his body the shameful mockery of a pompous funeral, and erected in his memory a paltry monument, which will commemorate their shame as long as it lasts. His name has been rescued from oblivion by the industry and tact of Samuel Smiles, who, in writing his life, has revealed to us a rarer and higher kind of man than Robert Burns.

JOHN DUNCAN,

WEAVER AND BOTANIST.

MANY young men ask nowadays what is the secret of "success." It were better to inquire also how to do without success, since that is the destiny of most of us, even in the most prosperous communities.

Could there be imagined a more complete "failure" than this John Duncan, a Scottish weaver, always very poor, at last a pauper, short-sighted, bent, shy, unlettered, illegitimate, dishonored in his home, not unfrequently stoned by the boys of the roadside, and in every particular, according to the outward view, a wretched fag-end of human nature !

Yet, redeemed and dignified by the love of knowledge, he passed, upon the whole, a joyous and even a triumphant life. He had a pursuit which absorbed his nobler faculties, and lifted him far above the mishaps and inconveniences of his lowly lot. The queen of his country took an interest in his pursuits, and contributed to the ease of his old age. Learned societies honored him,

John Duncan

and the illustrious Charles Darwin called him " my fellow botanist."

The mother of John Duncan, a " strong, pretty woman," as he called her, lived in a poor tenement at Stonehaven, on the Scottish coast, and supported herself by weaving stockings at her own home, and in the summer went into the harvest field. He always held his mother in honor and tenderness, as indeed he ought, for she stood faithfully by the children she ought not to have borne.

As a boy the future botanist developed an astonishing faculty of climbing. There was a famous old castle upon the pinnacle of a cliff, inaccessible except to cats and boys. He was the first to gain access to the ancient ruin, and after him the whole band of boys explored the castle, from the deep dungeons to the topmost turret.

His first employment led him directly to what became a favorite pursuit of his lifetime. By way of adding to the slender gains of his mother, he extracted the white pith from certain rushes of the region, which made very good lamp-wicks for the kind of lamps then in use in Scotland. These wicks of pith he sold about the town in small penny bundles. In order to get his supply of rushes he was obliged to roam the country far and wide, and along the banks of streams. When he had gathered as many as he could carry he would bring them home to be stripped. To the end of his days, when he knew familiarly every plant that

16

grew in his native land, he had a particular fondness for all the varieties of rush, and above all for the kind that gave him his first knowledge.

Then he went to a farmer's to tend cattle, and in this employment he experienced the hard and savage treatment to which hired boys were so frequently subjected at that day. Drenched with rain after tending his herd all day, the brutal farmer would not permit him to go near the fire to dry his clothes. He had to go to his miserable bed in an out-house, where he poured the water from his shoes, and wrung out his wet clothes as dry as he could. In that foggy climate his garments were often as wet in the morning as he left them in the evening, and so days would pass without his having a dry thread upon him.

But it did not rain always. Frequently his herd was pastured near the old castle, which, during the long summer days, he studied more intelligently, and in time learned all about its history and construction. And still he observed the flowers and plants that grew about his feet. It seemed natural to him to observe them closely and to learn their names and uses.

In due time he was apprenticed to a weaver. This was before the age of the noisy, steaming factory. Each weaver then worked at home, at his own loom, and could rent, if he chose, a garden and a field, and keep a cow, and live a man's life upon his native soil. Again our poor, shy apprentice had one of the hardest of masters. The boy was soon able to do the work of a man, and the master exacted it from him. On Saturdays the loom was usually kept going till midnight, when it stopped at the first sound of the clock, for this man, who had less feeling for a friendless boy than for a dog or a horse, was a strict Sabbatarian. In the depth of the Scotch winter he would keep the lad at the river-side, washing and wringing out the yarn, a process that required the arms to be bare and the hands to be constantly wet. His hands would be all chilblains and frost-bitten.

But again we may say it was not always winter. In the most dismal lot there are gleams of sunshine. The neighbors pitied and comforted him. His tyrant's wife was good to him as far as she dared. It was she, indeed, who inspired him with the determination to learn to read, and another friendly woman gave him regular instruction. He was sixteen years old when he learned his alphabet. A school-girl, the daughter of another weaver, would come into his shop to hear him read his lesson, and tell him how to pronounce the hard words. This bright, pretty girl of twelve would take her seat on the loom beside the bashful, lanky boy, who, with the book close to his eyes and his finger on the page, would grope his way through the paragraph.

Other children helped him, and he was soon able to get the meanings from the few books at his command. His solitary walks were still cheered by his observation of nature, although as yet he did not know there was such a thing as a science of botany. He could give no account of the interest he took in plants, except that he " loved the pretty little things," and liked to know their names, and to classify in his rude way those that were alike.

The exactions of his despot wore out at length even his astonishing patience. He ran away at twenty, and entered upon the life which he lived all the rest of his days, that of a weaver, wandering about Scotland according to his need of work. At this period he was not the possessor of a single book relating to his favorite pursuit, and he had never seen but one, an old-fashioned work of botany and astrology, of nature and superstition, by the once famous Culpepper. It required extra work for months, at the low wages of a hand-loom weaver, to get the money required for the purchase of this book, about five dollars. The work misled him in many ways, but it contained the names and properties of many of his favorite herbs. Better books corrected these errors by and by, and he gradually gathered a considerable library, each volume won by pinching economy and hard labor.

The sorrow of his life was his most woeful, disastrous marriage. His wife proved false to him, abandoned his home and their two daughters, and became a drunken tramp. Every now and then she returned to him, appealing to his compassion for assistance. I think Charles Dickens must have had John Duncan's case in his mind when he wrote those powerful scenes of the poor man cursed with a drunken wife in " Hard Times."

But the more miserable his outward life, the more diligently he resorted for comfort to his darling plants. For many years he groped in the dark; but at length he was put upon the right path by one of those accomplished gardeners so common in Scotland, where the art of gardening is carried to high perfection. He always sought the friendship of gardeners wherever he went. Nevertheless he was forty years old before he became a scientific botanist.

During the rest of his life of forty-four years, besides pursuing his favorite branch, he obtained a very considerable knowledge of the kindred sciences and of astronomy. Being obliged to sell his watch in a time of scarcity, he made for himself a pocket sun-dial, by which he could tell the time to within seven or eight minutes.

During this period steam was gaining every year upon hand power; his wages grew less and less; and, as his whole heart was in science, he had no energy left for seeking more lucrative employment. When he was past eighty-three he would walk twelve miles or more to get a new specimen, and hold on his way, though drenched with a sudden storm.

At length, old age and lack of work reduced him to actual suffering for the necessaries of life. Mr. William Jolly, a contributor to periodicals, heard his story, sought him out, and found him so poor as to be obliged to accept out-door relief, of which the old man was painfully ashamed. He published a brief history of the man and of his doings in the newspapers.

"The British people," says Voltaire, "may be very stupid, but they know how to give."

Money rained down upon the old philosopher, until a sum equal to about sixteen hundred dollars had reached him, which abundantly sufficed for his maintenance during the short residue of his life. For the first time in fifty years he had a new and warm suit of clothes, and he again sat down by his own cheerful fire, an independent man, as he had been all his life until he could no longer exercise his trade.

He died soon after, bequeathing the money he had received for the foundation of scholarships and prizes for the encouragement of the study of natural science among the boys and girls of his country. His valuable library, also, he bequeathed for the same object.

JAMES LACKINGTON,

SECOND-HAND BOOKSELLER.

———◆———

It would seem not to be so very difficult a matter to buy an article for fifty cents and sell it for seventy-five. Business men know, however, that to live and thrive by buying and selling requires a special gift, which is about as rare as other special gifts by which men conquer the world. In some instances, it is easier to make a thing than to sell it, and it is not often that a man who excels in the making succeeds equally well in the selling. General George P. Morris used to say: —

"I know a dozen men in New York who could make a good paper, but among them all I do not know one who could sell it."

The late Governor Morgan of New York had this talent in a singular degree even as a boy. His uncle sent him to New York, to buy, among other things, two or three hundred bushels of corn. He bought two cargoes, and sold them to advantage in Hartford on his way from the stage office to his uncle's store, and he kept on doing similar things all his life. He knew by a sort of intuition when it was safe to buy twenty thousand bags of coffee, or all the coffee there was for sale in New York, and he was very rarely mistaken; he had a genius for buying and selling.

I have seen car-boys and news-boys who had this gift.   There are boys who will go through a train and hardly ever fail to sell a book or two.   They improve every chance.   If there is a passenger who wants a book, or can be made to think he wants one, the boy will find him out.

Now James Lackington was a boy of that kind. In the preface to the Memoirs which he wrote of his career he described himself as a person " who, a few years since, began business with five pounds, and now sells one hundred thousand volumes annually."   But in fact he did not begin business with five pounds, but with nothing at all.

He was the son of a drunken shoemaker who lived in an English country town, and he had no schooling except a few weeks at a dame's school, at twopence a week.   He had scarcely learned his letters at that school when his mother was obliged to take him away to help her in tending his little brothers and sisters.   He spent most of his childhood in doing that, and, as he remarks, " in running about the streets getting into mischief."   When he was ten years old he felt the stirring of an inborn genius for successful traffic.

He noticed, and no doubt with the hungry eyes of a growing boy, an old pie-man, who sold his pies about the streets in a careless, inefficient way, and the thought occurred to him that, if he had pies to sell, he could sell more of them than the ancient pie-man. He went to a baker and acquainted him with his thoughts on pie-selling, and the baker soon sent him out with a tray full of pies. He showed his genius at once. The spirited way in which he cried his pies, and his activity in going about with them, made him a favorite with the pie-buyers of the town ; so that the old pie-man in a few weeks lost all his business, and shut up his shop. The boy served his baker more than a year, and sold so many pies and cakes for him as to save him from impending bankruptcy. In the winter time he sold almanacs with such success that the other dealers threatened to do him bodily mischief.

But this kind of business would not do to depend on for a lifetime, and therefore he was bound apprentice to a shoemaker at the age of fourteen years, during which a desire for more knowledge arose within him. He learned to read and write, but was still so ashamed of his ignorance that he did not dare to go into a bookstore because he did not know the name of a single book to ask for. One of his friends bought for him a little volume containing a translation from the Greek philosopher Epictetus, a work full of wise maxims about life and duty. Then he bought other ancient authors, Plato, Plutarch, Epicurus, and others. He became a sort of Methodist philosopher, for he heard the Methodist preachers diligently on Sundays, and read his Greek philosophy in the evenings. He tells us that the account of Epicurus living in his garden upon a halfpenny a day, and considering a little cheese on his bread as a great treat, filled him with admiration, and he began forthwith to live on bread and tea alone, in order to get money for his books. After ending his apprenticeship and working for a short time as a journeyman, he married a buxom dairymaid, with whom he had been in love for seven years. It was a bold enterprise, for when they went to their lodgings after the wedding they searched their pockets carefully to discover the state of their finances, and found that they had one halfpenny to begin the world with. They had laid in provisions for a day or two, and they had work by which to procure more, so they began their married life by sitting down to work at shoemaking and singing together the following stanza :

> "Our portion is not large indeed,
> But then how little do we need !
> For nature's wants are few.
> In this the art of living lies,
> To want no more than may suffice,
> And make that little do."

They were as happy as the day was long. Twenty times, reports this jolly shoemaker, he and his wife sang an ode by Samuel Wesley, beginning : —

> "No glory I covet, no riches I want,
> Ambition is nothing to me ;

The one thing I beg of kind Heaven to grant
Is a mind independent and free. ''

They needed their cheerful philosophy, for all
they had to spend on food and drink for a week
was a sum about equal to one of our dollars. Even
this small revenue grew smaller, owing to the hard
times, and poor James Lackington saw his young
wife pining away under insufficient food and sedentary employment. His courage again saved him.
After enduring extreme poverty for three years,
he got together all the money he could raise, gave
most of it to his wife, and set out for London,
where he arrived in August, 1774, with two and
sixpence in his pocket.

It was a fortunate move for our brave shoemaker.
He obtained work and good wages at once, soon
sent for his wife, and their united earnings more
than supplied their wants. A timely legacy of ten
pounds from his grandfather gave them a little
furniture, and he became again a frequenter of
second-hand bookstores. He could scarcely resist
the temptation of a book that he wanted. One
Christmas Eve he went out with money to buy
their Christmas dinner, but spent the whole sum
for a copy of Young's "Night Thoughts." His
wife did not relish this style of Christmas repast.

"I think," said he to his disappointed spouse,
" that I have acted wisely ; for had I bought a dinner we should have eaten it to-morrow, and the
pleasure would have been soon over ; but should we

live fifty years longer we shall have the ' Night Thoughts ' to feast upon."

It was his love of books that gave him abundant Christmas dinners for the rest of his life. Having hired a little shop in which to sell the shoes made by himself and his wife, it occurred to him that he could employ the spare room in selling old books, his chief motive being to have a chance to read the books before he sold them. Beginning with a stock of half a hundred volumes, chiefly of divinity, he invested all his earnings in this new branch, and in six months he found his stock of books had increased fivefold. He abandoned his shoemaking, moved into larger premises, and was soon a thriving bookseller. He was scrupulous not to sell any book which he thought calculated to injure its readers, although about this time he found the Methodist Society somewhat too strict for him. He makes a curious remark on this subject : —

" I well remember," he says, " that some years before, Mr. Wesley told his society at Bristol, in my hearing, that he could never keep a bookseller six months in his flock."

His trade increased with astonishing rapidity, and the reason was that he knew how to buy and sell. He abandoned many of the old usages and traditions of the book trade. He gave no credit, which was itself a startling innovation ; but his master-stroke was selling every book at the lowest price he could afford, thus giving his customers a fair portion of the benefit of his knowledge and activity. He appears to have begun the system by which books have now become a part of the furniture of every house. He bought with extraordinary boldness, spending sometimes as much as sixty thousand dollars in an afternoon's sale.

As soon as he began to live with some liberality kind friends foretold his speedy ruin. Or, as he says: —

" When by the advice of that eminent physician, Dr. Lettsom, I purchased a horse, and saved my life by the exercise it afforded me, the old adage, ' Set a beggar on horseback and he 'll ride to the devil,' was deemed fully verified."

But his one horse became two horses, and his chaise a chariot with liveried servants, in which vehicle, one summer, he made the round of the places in which he had lived as a shoemaker, called upon his old employers, and distributed liberal sums of money among his poor relations. So far from being ashamed of his business, he caused to be engraved on all his carriage doors the motto which he considered the secret of his success : —

SMALL PROFITS DO GREAT THINGS.

In his old age he rejoined his old friends the Methodists, and he declares in his last edition that, if he had never heard the Methodists preach, in all probability he should have remained through life " a poor, ragged, dirty cobbler."

HORACE GREELEY'S START.

I HAVE seldom been more interested than in hearing Horace Greeley tell the story of his coming to New York in 1831, and gradually working his way into business there.

He was living at the age of twenty years with his parents in a small log-cabin in a new clearing of Western Pennsylvania, about twenty miles from Erie. His father, a Yankee by birth, had recently moved to that region and was trying to raise sheep there, as he had been accustomed to do in Vermont. The wolves were too numerous there.

It was part of the business of Horace and his brother to watch the flock of sheep, and sometimes they camped out all night, sleeping with their feet to the fire, Indian fashion. He told me that occasionally a pack of wolves would come so near that he could see their eyeballs glare in the darkness and hear them pant. Even as he lay in the loft of his father's cabin he could hear them howling in the fields. In spite of all their care, the wolves killed in one season a hundred of his father's sheep, and then he gave up the attempt.

The family were so poor that it was a matter of doubt sometimes whether they could get food enough to live through the long winter; and so Horace, who had learned the printer's trade in Vermont, started out on foot in search of work in a village printing-office. He walked from village to village, and from town to town, until at last he went to Erie, the largest place in the vicinity.

There he was taken for a runaway apprentice, and certainly his appearance justified suspicion. Tall and gawky as he was in person, with tow-colored hair, and a scanty suit of shabbiest homespun, his appearance excited astonishment or ridicule wherever he went. He had never worn a good suit of clothes in his life. He had a singularly fair, white complexion, a piping, whining voice, and these peculiarities gave the effect of his being wanting in intellect. It was not until people conversed with him that they discovered his worth and intelligence. He had been an ardent reader from his childhood up, and had taken of late years the most intense interest in politics and held very positive opinions, which he defended in conversation with great earnestness and ability.

A second application at Erie procured him employment for a few months in the office of the Erie "Gazette," and he won his way, not only to the respect, but to the affection, of his companions and his employer. That employer was Judge J. M. Sterrett, and from him I heard many curious particulars of Horace Greeley's residence in Erie. As he was only working in the office as a substitute, the return of the absentee deprived him of his place, and he was obliged to seek work elsewhere. His employer said to him one day : —

"Now, Horace, you have a good deal of money coming to you ; don't go about the town any longer in that outlandish rig. Let me give you an order on the store. Dress up a little, Horace."

The young man looked down at his clothes as though he had never seen them before, and then said, by way of apology : —

"You see, Mr. Sterrett, my father is on a new place, and I want to help him all I can."

In fact, upon the settlement of his account at the end of his seven months' labor, he had drawn for his personal expenses six dollars only. Of the rest of his wages he retained fifteen dollars for himself, and gave all the rest, amounting to about a hundred and twenty dollars, to his father, who, I am afraid, did not make the very best use of all of it.

With the great sum of fifteen dollars in his pocket, Horace now resolved upon a bold movement. After spending a few days at home, he tied up his spare clothes in a bundle, not very large, and took the shortest road through the woods that led to the Erie Canal. He was going to New York, and he was going cheap !

A walk of sixty miles or so, much of it through the primeval forest, brought him to Buffalo, where he took passage on the Erie Canal, and after various detentions, he reached Albany on a Thursday morning just in time to see the regular steamboat of the day move out into the stream. At ten o'clock on the same morning he embarked on board of a tow-boat, which required nearly twenty-four hours to descend the river, and thus afforded him ample time to enjoy the beauty of its shores.

On the 18th of August, 1831, about sunrise, he set foot in the city of New York, then containing about two hundred thousand inhabitants, one sixth of its present population. He had managed his affairs with such strict economy that his journey of six hundred miles had cost him little more than five dollars, and he had ten left with which to begin life in the metropolis. This sum of money and the knowledge of the printer's trade made up his capital. There was not a person in all New York, so far as he knew, who had ever seen him before.

His appearance, too, was much against him, for although he had a really fine face, a noble forehead, and the most benign expression I ever saw upon a human countenance, yet his clothes and bearing quite spoiled him. His round jacket made him look like a tall boy who had grown too fast for his strength; he stooped a little and walked in a loose-jointed manner. He was very bashful, and totally destitute of the power of pushing his way, or arguing with a man who said "No" to him. He had brought no letters of recommendation, and had

17

no kind of evidence to show that he had even learned his trade.

The first business was, of course, to find an extremely cheap boarding-house, as he had made up his mind only to try New York as an experiment, and, if he did not succeed in finding work, to start homeward while he still had a portion of his money. After walking awhile he went into what looked to him like a low-priced tavern, at the corner of Wall and Broad Streets.

"How much do you charge for board?" he asked the bar-keeper, who was wiping his decanters and putting his bar in trim for the business of the day.

The bar-keeper gave the stranger a look-over and said to him : —

"I guess we 're too high for you."

"Well how much do you charge?"

"Six dollars."

"Yes, that 's more than I can afford."

He walked on until he descried on the North River, near Washington Market, a boarding-house so very mean and squalid that he was tempted to go in and inquire the price of board there. The price was two dollars and a half a week.

"Ah!" said Horace, "that sounds more like it."

In ten minutes more he was taking his breakfast at the landlord's table. Mr. Greeley gratefully remembered this landlord, who was a friendly Irish man by the name of McGorlick. Breakfast done, the new-comer sallied forth in quest of work, and began by expending nearly half of his capital in improving his wardrobe. It was a wise action. He that goes courting should dress in his best, particularly if he courts so capricious a jade as Fortune.

Then he began the weary round of the printing-offices, seeking for work and finding none, all day long. He would enter an office and ask in his whining note : —

" Do you want a hand ? "

" No," was the invariable reply ; upon receiving which he left without a word. Mr. Greeley chuckled as he told the reception given him at the office of the " Journal of Commerce," a newspaper he was destined to contend with for many a year in the columns of the " Tribune."

" Do you want a hand ? " he said to David Hale, one of the owners of the paper.

Mr. Hale looked at him from head to foot, and then said : —

" My opinion is, young man, that you 're a runaway apprentice, and you 'd better go home to your master."

The applicant tried to explain, but the busy proprietor merely replied : —

" Be off about your business, and don't bother us."

The young man laughed good-humoredly and resumed his walk. He went to bed Saturday night thoroughly tired and a little discouraged. On Sunday he walked three miles to attend a church, and remembered to the end of his days the delight he had, for the first time in his life, in hearing a sermon that he entirely agreed with. In the mean time he had gained the good will of his landlord and the boarders, and to that circumstance he owed his first chance in the city. His landlord mentioned his fruitless search for work to an acquaintance who happened to call that Sunday afternoon. That acquaintance, who was a shoemaker, had accidentally heard that printers were wanted at No. 85 Chatham Street.

At half-past five on Monday morning Horace Greeley stood before the designated house, and discovered the sign, " West's Printing-Office," over the second story ; the ground floor being occupied as a bookstore. Not a soul was stirring up stairs or down. The doors were locked, and Horace sat down on the steps to wait. Thousands of workmen passed by ; but it was nearly seven before the first of Mr. West's printers arrived, and he, too, finding the door locked, sat down by the side of the stranger, and entered into conversation with him.

" I saw." said this printer to me many years after, " that he was an honest, good young man, and, being a Vermonter myself, I determined to help him if I could."

Thus, a second time in New York already, *the native quality of the man* gained him, at the critical moment the advantage that decided his destiny. His new friend did help him, and it was very much through his urgent recommendation that the foreman of the printing-office gave him a chance. The foreman did not in the least believe that the green-looking young fellow before him could set in type one page of the polyglot Testament for which help was needed.

" Fix up a case for him," said he, " and we'll see if he *can* do anything."

Horace worked all day with silent intensity, and when he showed to the foreman at night a printer's proof of his day's work, it was found to be the best day's work that had yet been done on that most difficult job. It was greater in quantity and much more correct. The battle was won. He worked on the Testament for several months, making long hours and earning only moderate wages, saving all his surplus money, and sending the greater part of it to his father, who was still in debt for his farm and not sure of being able to keep it.

Ten years passed. Horace Greeley from journeyman printer made his way slowly to partnership in a small printing-office. He founded the " New Yorker," a weekly paper, the best periodical of its class in the United States. It brought him great credit and no profit.

In 1840, when General Harrison was nominated for the presidency against Martin Van Buren, his feelings as a politician were deeply stirred, and he started a little campaign paper called " The Log-Cabin," which was incomparably the most spirited thing of the kind ever published in the United States. It had a circulation of unprecedented extent, beginning with forty-eight thousand, and rising week after week until it reached ninety thousand. The price, however, was so low that its great sale proved rather an embarrassment than a benefit to the proprietors, and when the campaign ended, the firm of Horace Greeley & Co. was rather more in debt than it was when the first number of " The Log-Cabin " was published.

The little paper had given the editor two things which go far towards making a success in business, — great reputation and some confidence in himself. The first penny paper had been started. The New York " Herald " was making a great stir. The " Sun " was already a profitable sheet. And now the idea occurred to Horace Greeley to start a daily paper which should have the merits of cheapness and abundant news, without some of the qualities possessed by the others. He wished to found a cheap daily paper that should be good and salutary, as well as interesting. The last number of " The Log-Cabin " announced the forthcoming " Tribune," price one cent.

The editor was probably not solvent when he conceived the scheme, and he borrowed a thousand dollars of his old friend, James Coggeshall, with which to buy the indispensable material. He began with six hundred subscribers, printed five thousand of the first number, and found it difficult to give them all away. The "Tribune" appeared on the day set apart in New York for the funeral procession in commemoration of President Harrison, who died a month after his inauguration.

It was a chilly, dismal day in April, and all the town was absorbed in the imposing pageant. The receipts during the first week were ninety-two dollars; the expenses five hundred and twenty-five. But the little paper soon caught public attention, and the circulation increased for three weeks at the rate of about three hundred a day. It began its fourth week with six thousand; its seventh week, with eleven thousand. The first number contained four columns of advertisements; the twelfth, nine columns; the hundredth, thirteen columns.

In a word, the success of the paper was immediate and very great. It grew a little faster than the machinery for producing it could be provided. Its success was due chiefly to the fact that the original idea of the editor was actually carried out. He aimed to produce a paper which should morally benefit the public. It was not always right, but it always meant to be.

JAMES GORDON BENNETT,

AND HOW HE FOUNDED HIS HERALD.

———

A CELLAR in Nassau Street was the first office of the "Herald." It was a real cellar, not a basement, lighted only from the street, and consequently very dark except near its stone steps. The first furniture of this office, — as I was told by the late Mr. Gowans, who kept a bookstore near by, — consisted of the following articles : —

Item, one wooden chair. Item, two empty flour barrels with a wide, dirty pine board laid upon them, to serve as desk and table. End of the inventory.

The two barrels stood about four feet apart, and one end of the board was pretty close to the steps, so that passers-by could see the pile of "Heralds" which were placed upon it every morning for sale. Scissors, pens, inkstand, and pencil were at the other end, leaving space in the middle for an editorial desk.

This was in the summer of 1835, when General Jackson was President of the United States, and Martin Van Buren the favorite candidate for the succession. If the reader had been in New York then, and had wished to buy a copy of the saucy little paper, which every morning amused and offended the decorous people of that day, he would have gone down into this underground office, and there he would have found its single chair occupied by a tall and vigorous-looking man about forty years of age, with a slight defect in one of his eyes, dressed in a clean, but inexpensive suit of summer clothes.

This was James Gordon Bennett, proprietor, editor, reporter, book-keeper, clerk, office-boy, and everything else there was appertaining to the control and management of the New York " Herald," price one cent. The reader would perhaps have said to him, " I want to-day's ' Herald.' " Bennett would have looked up from his writing, and pointed, without speaking, to the pile of papers at the end of the board. The visitor would have taken one and added a cent to the pile of copper coin adjacent. If he had lingered a few minutes, the busy writer would not have regarded him, and he could have watched the subsequent proceedings without disturbing him. In a few moments a woman might have come down the steps into the subterranean office, who answered the editor's inquiring look by telling him that she wanted a place as cook, and wished him to write an advertisement for her. This would have been entirely a matter of course, for in the prospectus of the paper it was expressly stated that persons could have their advertisements written for them at the office.

The editor himself would have written the advertisement for her with the velocity of a practiced hand, then read it over to her, taking particular pains to get the name spelled right, and the address correctly stated.

" How much is it, sir? "

"Twenty-five cents."

The money paid, the editor would instantly have resumed his writing. Such visitors, however, were not numerous, for the early numbers of the paper show very few advertisements, and the paper itself was little larger than a sheet of foolscap. Small as it was, it was with difficulty kept alive from week to week, and it was never too certain as the week drew to a close whether the proprietor would be able to pay the printer's bill on Saturday night, and thus secure its reappearance on Monday morning.

There were times when, after paying all the unpostponable claims, he had twenty-five cents left, or less, as the net result of his week's toil. He worked sixteen, seventeen, eighteen hours a day, struggling unaided to force his little paper upon an indifferent if not a hostile public.

James Gordon Bennett, you will observe, was forty years old at this stage of his career. Generally a man who is going to found anything extraordinary has laid a deep foundation, and got his structure a good way above ground before he is forty years of age. But there was he, past forty, and still wrestling with fate, happy if he could get three dollars a week over for his board. Yet he was a strong man, gifted with a keen intelligence, strictly temperate in his habits, and honest in his dealings. The only point against him was, that he had no power and apparently no desire to make personal friends. He was one of those who cannot easily ally themselves with other men, but must fight their fight alone, victors or vanquished.

A native of Scotland, he was born a Roman Catholic, and was partly educated for the priesthood in a Catholic seminary there; but he was diverted from the priestly office, as it appears, by reading Byron, Scott, and other literature of the day. At twenty he was a romantic, impulsive, and innocent young man, devouring the Waverley novels, and in his vacations visiting with rapture the scenes described in them. The book, however, which decided the destiny of this student was of a very different description, being no other than the "Autobiography of Benjamin Franklin," a book which was then read by almost every boy who read at all. One day, at Aberdeen, a young acquaintance met him in the street, and said to him : —

" I am going to America, Bennett."

" To America! When ? Where?"

" I am going to Halifax on the 6th of April."

"My dear fellow," said Bennett, " I 'll go with

you. I want to see the place where Franklin was born."

Three months after he stepped ashore at the beautiful town of Halifax in Nova Scotia, with only money enough in his pocket to pay his board for about two weeks. Gaunt poverty was upon him soon, and he was glad to earn a meagre subsistence for a few weeks, by teaching. He used to speak of his short residence in Halifax as a time of severe privation and anxiety, for it was a place then of no great wealth, and had little to offer to a penniless adventurer, such as he was.

He made his way to Portland, in Maine, before the first winter set in, and thence found passage in a schooner bound to Boston. In one of the early numbers of his paper he described his arrival at that far-famed harbor, and his emotions on catching his first view of the city. The paragraph is not one which we should expect from the editor of the " Herald," but I have no doubt it expressed his real feelings in 1819.

" I was alone, young, enthusiastic, uninitiated. In my more youthful days I had devoured the enchanting life of Benjamin Franklin written by himself, and Boston appeared to me as the residence of a friend, an associate, an acquaintance. I had also drunk in the history of the holy struggle for independence, first made on Bunker Hill. Dorchester Heights were to my youthful imagination almost as holy ground as Arthur's Seat or Salis-

bury Craigs. Beyond was Boston, her glittering
spires rising into the blue vault of heaven like bea-
cons to light a world to liberty."

In the glow of his first enthusiasm, and having
nothing else to do, he spent several days in visiting
the scenes of historic events with which his reading had made him familiar. But his slender purse
grew daily more attenuated, and he soon found
himself in a truly desperate situation, a friendless,
unprepossessing young man, knowing no trade or
profession, and without an acquaintance in the city.
His last penny was spent. A whole day passed
without his tasting food. A second day went by,
and still he fasted. He could find no employment,
and was too proud to beg. In this terrible strait
he was walking upon Boston Common, wondering
how it could be that he, so willing to work, and
with such a capacity for work, should be obliged
to pace the streets of a wealthy city, idle and starv-
ing!

"How shall I get something to eat?" he said to
himself.

At that moment he saw something glittering
upon the ground before him, which proved to be a
silver coin of the value of twelve and a half cents.
Cheered by this strange coincidence, and refreshed
by food, he went with renewed spirit in search of
work. He found it almost immediately. A coun-
tryman of his own, of the firm of Wells & Lilly,
publishers and booksellers, gave him a situation as

clerk and proof-reader, and thus put him upon the track which led him to his future success.

This firm lasted only long enough to give him the means of getting to New York, where he arrived in 1822, almost as poor as when he left Scotland. He tried many occupations, — a school, lectures upon political economy, instruction in the Spanish language; but drifted at length into the daily press as drudge-of-all-work, at wages varying from five to eight dollars a week, with occasional chances to increase his revenue a little by the odd jobbery of literature.

Journalism was then an unknown art in the United States, and no newspaper had anything at all resembling an editorial corps. The most important daily newspapers of New York were carried on by the editor, aided by one or two ill-paid assistants, with a possible correspondent in Washington during the session of Congress. And that proved to be James Gordon Bennett's opportunity of getting his head a little above water. He filled the place one winter of Washington corespondent to the New York "Enquirer;" and while doing so he fell in by chance in the Congressional library with a volume of Horace Walpole's gossiping society letters. He was greatly taken with them, and he said to himself: "Why not try a few letters on a similar plan from Washington, to be published in New York?"

He tried the experiment. The letters, which

were full of personal anecdotes, and gave descriptions of noted individuals, proved very attractive, and gave him a most valuable hint as to what readers take an interest in. The letters being anonymous, he remained poor and unknown. He made several attempts to get into business for himself. He courted and served the politicians. He conducted party newspapers for them, without political convictions of his own. But when he had done the work of carrying elections and creating popularity, he did not find the idols he had set up at all disposed to reward the obscure scribe to whom they owed their elevation.

But all this while he was learning his trade, and though he lived under demoralizing influences, he never lapsed into bad habits. What he said of himself one day was strictly true, and it was one of the most material causes of his final victory: —

"Social glasses of wine are my aversion; public dinners are my abomination; all species of gormandizing, my utter scorn and contempt. When I am hungry, I eat; when thirsty, drink. Wine and viands, taken for society, or to stimulate conversation, tend only to dissipation, indolence, poverty, contempt, and death."

At length, early in 1835, having accumulated two or three hundred dollars, he conceived the notion of starting a penny paper. First he looked about for a partner. He proposed the scheme to a struggling, ambitious young printer and journalist, beginning to be known in Nassau Street, named Horace Greeley. I have heard Mr. Greeley relate the interview.

"Bennett came to me," he said, "as I was standing at the case setting type, and putting his hand in his pocket pulled out a handful of money. There was some gold among it, more silver, and I think one fifty-dollar bill. He said he had between two and three hundred dollars, and wanted me to go in with him and set up a daily paper, the printing to be done in our office, and he to be the editor.

"I told him he had n't money enough. He went away, and soon after got other printers to do the work and the 'Herald' appeared."

This was about six years before the "Tribune" was started. Mr. Greeley was right in saying that his future rival in journalism had not money enough. The little "Herald" was lively, smart, audacious, and funny; it pleased a great many people and made a considerable stir; but the price was too low, and the range of journalism then was very narrow. It is highly probable that the editor would have been baffled after all, but for one of those lucky accidents which sometimes happen to men who are bound to succeed.

There was a young man then in the city named Brandreth, who had brought a pill over with him from England, and was looking about in New York for some cheap, effective way of advertising his pill. He visited Bennett in his cellar and made an

arrangement to pay him a certain sum every week
for a certain space in the columns of the " Herald."
It was the very thing he wanted, a little *certainty*
to help him over that awful day of judgment which
comes every week to struggling enterprises, — Saturday night !

Still, the true cause of the final success of the
paper was the indomitable character of its founder,
his audacity, his persistence, his power of continuous labor, and the inexhaustible vivacity of his
mind. After a year of vicissitude and doubt, he
doubled the price of his paper, and from that time
his prosperity was uninterrupted. He turned everything to account. Six times he was assaulted
by persons whom he had satirized in his newspaper,
and every time he made it tell upon his circulation.
On one occasion, for example, after relating how
his head had been cut open by one of his former
employers, he added : —

" The fellow no doubt wanted to let out the never
failing supply of good-humor and wit which has
created such a reputation for the ' Herald.' . . .
He has not injured the skull. My ideas in a few
days will flow as freshly as ever, and he will find
it so to his cost."

In this humble, audacious manner was founded
the newspaper which, in the course of forty-eight
years, has grown to be one of national and international importance. Its founder died in 1872, aged
seventy-seven years, in the enjoyment of the largest

revenue which had ever resulted from journalism in the United States, and leaving to his only son the most valuable newspaper property, perhaps, in the world.

That son, the present proprietor, has greatly improved the " Herald." He possesses his father's remarkable journalistic tact, with less objectionable views of the relation of the daily paper to the public. His great enterprises have been bold, far-reaching, almost national in their character. Mr. Frederick Hudson, who was for many years the managing editor of the paper, has the following interesting paragraph concerning father and son: —

" Somewhere about the year 1866, James Gordon Bennett, Sr., inducted James Gordon Bennett, Jr., into the mysteries of journalism. One of his first *coups* was the Prusso-Austrian war. The cable transmitted the whole of the King of Prussia's important speech after the battle of Sadowa and peace with Austria, costing in tolls seven thousand dollars in gold."

He has followed this bold *coup* with many similar ones, and not a few that surpassed it. Seven thousand dollars seems a good deal of money to pay for a single feature of one number of a daily paper. It was not so much for a paper, single issues of which have yielded half as much as that in clear profit. And the paper was born in a cellar !

THREE JOHN WALTERS,

AND THEIR NEWSPAPER.

THE reader, perhaps, does not know why the London " Times " is the first journal of Europe. I will tell him.

The starting of this great newspaper ninety-nine years ago was a mere incident in the development of another business. Almost every one who has stood in a printing-office watching compositors set type must have sometimes asked himself, why not have whole words cast together, instead of obliging the printer to pick up each letter separately? Such words as *and*, *the*, *but*, *if*, *is*, and even larger words, like *although* and *notwithstanding*, occur very often in all compositions. How easy it would be, inexperienced persons think, to take up a long word, such as *extraordinary*, and place it in position at one stroke. I confess that I had this idea myself, long before I knew that any one else had ever had it.

In the year 1785 there was a printer in London named John Walter, well-established in business, who was fully resolved on giving this system a trial.

At great expense and trouble he had all the commonest words and phrases cast together. He would give his type-founder an order like this: —

Send me a hundredweight, made up in separate pounds, of *heat, cold, wet, dry, murder, fire, dreadful robbery, atrocious outrage, fearful calamity,* and *alarming explosion.*

This system he called logographic printing, — logographic being a combination of two Greek words signifying word-writing. In order to give publicity to the new system, on which he held a patent, as well as to afford it a fuller trial, he started a newspaper, which he called the "Daily Universal Register." The newspaper had some little success from the beginning; but the logographic printing system would not work. Not only did the compositors place obstacles in the way, but the system itself presented difficulties which neither John Walter nor any subsequent experimenter has been able to surmount.

"The whole English language," said Walter, in one of his numerous addresses to the public, "lay before me in a confused arrangement. It consisted of about ninety thousand words. This multitudinous mass I reduced to about five thousand, by separating the parcels, and removing the obsolete words, technical terms, and common terminations."

After years of labor this most resolute and tenacious of men was obliged to give it up. It was too expensive, too cumbersome, too difficult; it required a vast amount of space; and, in short, it was a system which could not, and cannot, be worked to profit. But though the logographic printing was a failure, the "Daily Universal Register" proved more and more successful. It was a dingy little sheet, about twice as large as a sheet of foolscap, without a word of editorial, and containing a small number of well-selected paragraphs of news. It had also occasionally a short notice of the plays of the night before, and a few items of what we now call society gossip. The advertisements, after the paper had been in existence three years, averaged about fifty a day, most of them very short. Its price was threepence, English, equal to about twelve cents of our present currency. The paper upon which it was printed was coarse and cheap. In the third year of its existence, on the first of January, 1788, the name was changed to "The Times." The editor humorously explained the reasons for changing the name: —

" ' Boy, bring me the "Register." ' The waiter answers, 'Sir, we have no library, but you may see it in the New Exchange Coffee House.' 'Then I will see it there,' answers the disappointed politician, and he goes to the New Exchange Coffee House, and calls for the 'Register'; upon which the waiter tells him he cannot have it, as he is not a subscriber; or presents him with the 'Court and City Register,' the 'Old Annual Register,' or the 'New Annual Register.' "

John Walter was not what is commonly called an educated man. He was a brave and honest Englishman, instinctively opposed to jobbery, and to all the other modes by which a corrupt government plunders a laborious people. The consequence was that during the first years of his editorial life he was frequently in very hot water. When "The Times" had been in existence little more than a year, he took the liberty of making a remark upon the Duke of York, one of the king's dissolute sons, saying that the conduct of his Royal Highness had been such as to incur His Majesty's just disapprobation.

For this offense he was arrested and put on trial for libel. Being convicted, he was sentenced to pay a fine of fifty pounds, to undergo a year's imprisonment in Newgate, to stand in the pillory for one hour, and give bonds for his good behavior for the next seven years. While he was still in prison, he was convicted of two libels: first for saying that both the Prince of Wales and the Duke of York had incurred the just disapprobation of the king; and secondly, for saying that the Duke of Clarence, another son of George III., an officer in the navy, had left his station without the permission of his commanding officer. For these offenses he was condemned to pay fines amounting to two hundred pounds, and to suffer a second year's imprisonment. His first year he served out fully, and four months of the second, when by the intercession of the Prince of Wales he was released.

From this period the newspaper appears to have gone forward, without any interruption, to the present day. In due time John Walter withdrew from the management, and gave it up to his eldest son, John Walter the second, who seems to have possessed his father's resolution and energy, with more knowledge of the world and a better education. It was he who took the first decisive step toward placing "The Times" at the head of journalism. For many years the Walters had been printers to the custom house, a post of considerable profit. In 1810 the newspaper discovered and exposed corrupt practices in the Navy Department, — practices which were subsequently condemned by an investigatmg commission. The administration deprived the fearless editor of the custom house business. As this was not in accordance with the usages of English politics, it made a great outcry, and the editor was given to understand that, if ho would wink at similar abuses in future, the public printing should be restored to him. This offer he declined, saying that he would enter into no engagements and accept no favors which would diminish, in any degree whatever, the independence of the paper.

This was an immense point gained. It was, as I have said, the first step toward greatness. Nor do I believe that any newspaper has ever attained a genuine and permanent standing in a community until it has first conquered a substantial independence. The administration then tried to accomplish its purpose in another way. During the gigantic wars of Napoleon Bonaparte, extending over most of the first fifteen years of the present century, "The Times" surpassed all newspapers in procuring early intelligence from the seat of war. The government stooped to the pettiness of stopping at the outposts all packages addressed to "The Times," while allowing dispatches for the ministerial journals to pass. Foreign ships bound to London were boarded at Gravesend, and papers addressed to "The Times" were taken from the captain. The editor remonstrated to the Home Secretary. He was informed that he might receive his foreign papers *as a favor* from government. Knowing that this would be granted in the expectation of its modifying the spirit and tone of the newspaper, he declined to accept as a favor that which he claimed as a right. The consequence was that the paper suffered much inconvenience from the loss or delay of imported packages. But this inconvenience was of small account compared with the prestige which such complimentary persecution conferred.

Another remarkable feature of the system upon which "The Times" has been conducted is the liberality with which it has compensated those who served it. Writing is a peculiar kind of industry, and demands so strenuous and intense an exertion of the vital forces, that no one will ever get good writing done who compensates it on ordinary commercial principles. The rule of supply and demand can never apply to this case. There are two things which the purchaser of literary labor can do towards getting a high quality of writing. One is, to give the writer the amplest motive to do his best; and the other is, to prevent his writing too much. Both these things the conductors of "The Times" have systematically done. It is their rule to pay more for literary labor than any one else pays for the same labor, more than the writer himself would think of demanding, and also to afford intervals of repose after periods of severe exertion.

Until the year 1814, all the printing in the world was done by hand, and "The Times" could only be struck off at the rate of four hundred and fifty copies an hour. Hence the circulation of the paper, when it had reached three or four thousand copies a day, had attained the utmost development then supposed to be possible; and when such news came as that of the battle of Austerlitz, Trafalgar, or Waterloo, the edition was exhausted long before the demand was supplied. There was a compositor in the office of "The Times," named Thomas Martyn, who, as early as 1804, conceived the idea of applying Watt's improved steam-engine to a printing press. He showed his model to John Walter, who furnished him with money and room in which to continue his experiments, and perfect his machine. But the pressmen pursued the inventor with such blind, infuriate hate, that the man was in terror of his life from day to day, and the scheme was given up.

Ten years later another ingenious inventor, named König, procured a patent for a steam-press, and Mr. Walter determined to give his invention a trial at all hazards. The press was secretly set up in another building, and a few men, pledged to secrecy, were hired and put in training to work it. On the night of the trial the pressmen in "The Times" building were told that the paper would not go to press until very late, as important news was expected from the Continent. At six in the morning John Walter went into the press-room, and announced to the men that the whole edition of "The Times" had been printed by steam during the night, and that thenceforward the steam-press would be regularly used. He told the men that if they attempted violence there was a force at hand to suppress it, but if they behaved well no man should be a loser by the invention. They should either remain in their situations, or receive full wages until they could procure others. This conduct in a rich and powerful man was no more than decent. The men accepted his terms with alacrity.

A great secret of "The Times'" popularity has been its occasional advocacy of the public interest to its own temporary loss. Early in its history it ridiculed the advertisers of quack medicines, and has never hesitated to expose unsound projects though ever so profusely advertised. During the railroad mania of 1845, when the railroad advertisements in "The Times" averaged sixty thousand dollars a week, it earnestly, eloquently, and every day, week after week, exposed the empty and ruinous nature of the railway schemes. It continued this course until the mighty collapse came which fulfilled its own prophecies, and paralyzed for a time the business of the country.

Was this pure philanthropy? It was something much rarer than that — it was good sense. It was sound judgment. It was *not* killing the goose that laid the golden egg.

Old readers of the London "Times" were a little surprised, perhaps, to see the honors paid by that journal to its late editor-in-chief. An obituary notice of several columns was surrounded by black lines; a mark of respect which the paper would pay only to members of the royal family, or to some public man of universal renown. Never before, I believe, did this newspaper avow to the world that its editor had a name; and the editor himself usually affected to conceal his professional character. Former editors, in fact, would flatly deny their connection with the paper, and made a great secret of a fact which was no secret at all.

Mr. Carlyle, in his "Life of Sterling," gives a curious illustration of this. Sir Robert Peel, in 1835, upon resigning his ministry, wrote a letter to the editor of "The Times," thanking him for the powerful support which his administration had received from that journal. Sir Robert Peel did not presume to address this letter to any individual by name, and he declared in this letter that the editor was unknown to him even by sight. Edward Sterling replied in a lofty tone, very much as one king might reply to another, and signed the letter simply "The Editor of 'The Times.'"

But all this is changed. The affectation of secrecy, long felt to be ridiculous, has been abandoned, and the editor now circulates freely among his countrymen in his true character, as the conductor of the first journal in Europe. At his death he receives the honors due to the office he holds and the power he exerts, and his funeral is publicly attended by his associates. This is as it should be. Journalism has now taken its place as one of the most important of the liberal professions. Next to statesmanship, next to the actual conduct of public affairs, the editor of a leading newspaper fills, perhaps, the most important place in the practical daily life of the community in which he lives; and the influence of the office is likely to increase, rather than diminish.

Mr. Delane was probably the first individual who was ever educated with a distinct view to his becoming an editor. While he was still a boy, his father, a solicitor by profession, received an appointment in the office of "The Times," which led to young

Delane's acquaintance with the proprietors of the
journal. It seems they took a fancy to the lad.
They perceived that he had the editorial cast of
character, since, in addition to uncommon industry
and intelligence, he had a certain eagerness for information, an aptitude for acquiring it, and a dis-
crimination in weighing it, which marks the journalistic mind. The proprietors, noting these traits,
encouraged, and, I believe, assisted him to a university education, in the expectation that he would
fit himself for the life editorial.

Having begun this course of preparation early,
he entered the office of "The Times" as editorial
assistant soon after he came of age, and acquitted
himself so well that, in 1841, when he was not yet
twenty-five, he became editor-in-chief. He was
probably the youngest man who ever filled such a
post in a daily paper of anything like equal importance. This rapid promotion will be thought the
more remarkable when it is mentioned that he
never wrote an editorial in his life. "The Times"
itself says of him : —

"He never was a writer. He never even attempted to write anything, except reports and letters. These he had to do, and he did them well.
He had a large staff of writers, and it was not
necessary he should write, except to communicate
with them."

His not being a writer was one of his strongest
points. Writing is a career by itself. The com-

position of one editorial of the first class is a very hard day's work, and one that leaves to the writer but a small residue of vital force. Writing for the public is the most arduous and exhausting of all industries, and cannot properly be combined with any other. Nor can a man average more than two or three editorial articles a week such as "The Times" prints every day. It was an immense advantage to the paper to have an editor who was never tempted to waste any of his strength upon the toil of composition. "The Times" prints daily three editorial articles, which cost the paper on an average fifty dollars each. Mr. Delane himself mentioned this during his visit to this country.

There was one quality of his editorship which we ought not to overlook. It was totally free from personalities. I have been in the habit for a long time of reading "The Times" — not regularly but very frequently, and sometimes every day for a considerable period; but I have never seen an individual disrespectfully mentioned in the paper. An opinion may be denounced; but the individual holding that opinion is invariably spoken of with decency. "The Times" has frequently objected to the course pursued by Mr. Gladstone; but the man himself is treated with precisely the same respect as he would be if he were an invited guest at the editor's table.

"The Times," being a human institution, has plenty of faults, and has made its ample share of

mistakes; but it owes its eminent position chiefly to
its good qualities, its business ability, its patriotism, its liberal enterprise, and wise treatment of
those who serve it. The paper is still chiefly
owned and conducted by John Walter, the grandson of the founder.

GEORGE HOPE.

———•———

THE story of this stalwart and skillful Scotch farmer, George Hope, enables us to understand what agitators mean by the term "landlordism." It is a very striking case, as the reader will admit.

George Hope, born in 1811, was the son of a tenant farmer of the county of East Lothian, now represented in Parliament by Mr. Gladstone. The farm on which he was born, on which his ancestors had lived, and upon which he spent the greater part of his own life, was called Fenton Barns. With other lands adjacent, it made a farm of about eight hundred acres. Two thirds of it were of a stiff, retentive clay, extremely hard to work, and the rest was little better than sand, of a yellow color and incapable of producing grain.

Two or three generations of Hopes had spent life and toil unspeakable upon this unproductive tract, without making the least profit by it; being just able to pay their rent, and keep their heads above water. They subsisted, reared families, and died, worn out with hard work, leaving to their sons, besides an honest name, only the same inheritance of struggle and despair. George Hope's mother tried for years to squeeze out of her butter and eggs the price of a table large enough for all her family to sit round at once, but died without obtaining it.

At the age of eighteen years, George Hope took hold of this unpromising farm; his parents being in declining health, nearly exhausted by their long struggle with it. He brought to his task an intelligent and cultivated mind. He had been for four years in a lawyer's office. He had read with great admiration the writings of the American Channing; and he now used his intelligence in putting new life into this old land.

The first thing was to acquire more capital; and the only way of accomplishing this was to do much of the work himself. Mere manual labor, however, would not have sufficed; for he found himself baffled by the soil. Part of the land being wet, cold clay, and part yellow sand, he improved both by mixing them together. He spread sand upon his clay, and clay upon his sand, as well as abundant manure, and he established a kiln for converting some of the clay into tiles, with which he drained his own farm, besides selling large quantities of tiles to the neighboring farmers. For a time, he was in the habit of burning a kiln of eleven thousand tiles every week, and he was thus enabled to expend in draining his own farms about thirteen thousand dollars, without going in debt for it.

He believed in what is called " high farming,"

19

and spent enormous sums in fertilizing the soil. For a mere top-dressing of guano, bones, nitrate of soda, or sulphate of ammonia, he spent one spring eight thousand dollars. These large expenditures, directed as they were by a man who thoroughly understood his business, produced wonderful results. He gained a large fortune, and his farm became so celebrated, that travelers arrived from all parts of Europe, and even from the United States, to see it. An American called one day to inspect the farm, when Mr. Hope began, as usual, to express his warm admiration for Dr. Channing. The visitor was a nephew of the distinguished preacher, and he was exceedingly surprised to find his uncle so keenly appreciated in that remote spot.

It is difficult to say which of his two kinds of land improved the most under his vigorous treatment. His sandy soil, the crop of which in former years was sometimes blown out of the ground, was so strengthened by its dressing of clay as to produce excellent crops of wheat; and his clay fields were made among the most productive in Scotland by his system of combined sanding, draining and fertilizing.

One of his secrets was that he treated his laborers with justice and consideration. His harvest-homes were famous in their day. When he found that certain old-fashioned games caused some of his weak teetotalers to fall from grace, he changed them for others; and, instead of beer and toddy, provided abundance of tea, coffee, strawberries, and other dainties. When the time came for dancing, he took the lead, and could sometimes boast that he had not missed one dance the whole evening. In addressing a public meeting of farmers and landlords in 1861, he spoke on the subject of improving the cottages of farm laborers. These were some of the sentences which fell from his lips : —

"Treat your laborers with respect, as men ; encourage their self-respect. Never enter a poor man's house any more than a rich man's unless invited, and then go not to find fault, but as a friend. If you can render him or his family a service, by advice or otherwise, let it be more delicately done than to your most intimate associate. Remember how hard it is for a poor man to respect himself. He hears the wealthy styled the respectable, and the poor, the lower classes ; but never call a man low. His being a *man* dwarfs, and renders as nothing, all the distinctions of an earthly estate."

The reader sees what kind of person this George Hope was. He was as nearly a perfect character as our very imperfect race can ordinarily exhibit. He was a great farmer, a true captain of industry, an honest, intelligent, just, and benevolent man. He was, moreover, a good citizen, and this led him to take an interest in public matters, and to do his utmost in aid of several reasonable reforms. He was what is called a Liberal in politics. He did what he could to promote the reform bill of Lord

John Russell, and he was a conspicuous ally of Cobden and Bright in their efforts to break down the old corn laws. He remembered that there were about five thousand convictions in Great Britain every year under the game laws, and he strove in all moderate and proper ways to have those laws repealed.

And now we come to the point. A certain person named R. A. Dundas Christopher Nisbet Hamilton married the heiress of the estate to which the farm of George Hope belonged. He thus acquired the power, when a tenant's lease expired, to refuse a renewal. This person was a Tory, who delighted in the slaughter of birds and beasts, and who thought it highly impertinent in the tenant of a farm to express political opinions contrary to those of his landlord. George Hope, toward the end of his long lease, offered to take the farm again, at a higher rent than he had ever before paid, though it was himself who had made the farm more valuable. His offer was coldly declined, and he was obliged, after expending the labor and skill of fifty-three years upon that land, to leave it, and find another home for his old age.

He had fortunately made money enough to buy a very good farm for himself, and he had often said that he would rather farm fifty acres of his own than to be the tenant of the best farm in Europe. This "eviction," as it was called, of a farmer so celebrated attracted universal comment, and excited general indignation. He left his farm like a conqueror. Public dinners and services of plate were presented to him, and his landlord of many names acquired a notoriety throughout Europe which no doubt he enjoyed. He certainly did a very bold action, and one which casts a perfect glare of light upon the nature of landlordism.

George Hope died in 1876, universally honored in Scotland. He lies buried in the parish of his old farm, not far from the home of his fathers. On his tombstone is inscribed : —

"To the memory of George Hope, for many years tenant of Fenton Barns. He was the devoted supporter of every movement which tended to the advancement of civil and religious liberty, and to the moral and social elevation of mankind."

SIR HENRY COLE.

HE was an "Old Public Functionary" in the service of the British people.

When President Buchanan spoke of himself as an Old Public Functionary he was a good deal laughed at by some of the newspapers, and the phrase has since been frequently used in an opprobrious or satirical sense. This is to be regretted, for there is no character more respectable, and there are few so useful, as an intelligent and patriotic man of long standing in the public service. What *one* such man can do is shown by the example of Sir Henry Cole, who died a few months ago in London after half a century of public life.

The son of an officer in the British army, he was educated at that famous Blue-Coat School which is interesting to Americans because Lamb and Coleridge attended it. At the age of fifteen he received an appointment as clerk in the office of Public Records. In due time, having proved his capacity and peculiar fitness, be was promoted to the post of Assistant Keeper, which gave him a respectable position and some leisure.

He proved to be in an eminent sense the right man in the right place. Besides publishing, from time to time, curious and interesting documents which he discovered in his office, he called attention, by a series of vigorous pamphlets, to the chaotic condition in which the public records of Great Britain were kept. Gradually these pamphlets made an impression, and they led at length to a reform in the office. The records were rearranged, catalogued, rendered safe, and made accessible to students. This has already led to important corrections in history, and to a great increase in the sum of historical knowledge.

When the subject of cheap postage came up in 1840, the government offered four prizes of a hundred pounds each for suggestions in aid of Sir Rowland Hill's plan. One of these prizes was assigned to Henry Cole. He was one of the persons who first became converts to the idea of penny postage, and he lent the aid of his pen and influence to its adoption.

At length, about the year 1845, he entered upon the course of proceedings which rendered him one of the most influential and useful persons of his time. He had long lamented the backward condition of arts of design in England, and the consequent ugliness of the various objects in the sight and use of which human beings pass their lives. English furniture, wall - papers, carpets, curtains, cutlery, garments, upholstery, ranged from the tolerable to the hideous, and were inferior to the manufactures of France and Germany. He organized a series of exhibitions on a small scale, somewhat similar to those of the American Institute in New York, which has held a competitive exhibition of natural and manufactured objects every autumn for the last fifty years.

His exhibitions attracted attention, and they led at length to the Crystal Palace Exhibition of 1851. The merit of that scheme must be shared between Henry Cole and Prince Albert. Cole suggested that his small exhibitions should, once in five years, assume a national character, and invite contributions from all parts of the empire. Yes, said Prince Albert, and let us also invite competition from foreign countries on equal terms with native products.

The Exhibition of 1851 was admirably managed, and had every kind of success. It benefited England more than all other nations put together, because it revealed to her people their inferiority in many branches both of workmanship and design. We all know how conceited people are apt to become who have no opportunity to compare themselves with superiors. John Bull, never over-modest, surveyed the Exhibition of 1851, and discovered, to his great surprise, that he was not the unapproachable Bull of the universe which he had fondly supposed. He saw himself beaten in some things by the French, in some by the Germans, in

others by the Italians, and in a few (O wonder!)
by the Yankees.

Happily he had the candor to admit this humil-
iating fact to himself, and he put forth earnest and
steadfast exertions to bring himself up to the level
of modern times.

Henry Cole was the life and soul of the movement. It was he who called attention to the obstacles placed in the way of improvement by the
patent laws, and some of those obstacles, through
him, were speedily removed.

During this series of services to his country, he
remained in the office of Public Records. The
government now invited him to another sphere
of labor. They asked him to undertake the recon-
struction of the schools of design, and they gave
him an office which placed him practically at the
head of the various institutions designed to promote the application of art to manufacture. The
chief of these now is the Museum of South Kensington, which is to many Americans the most interesting object in London. The creation of this
wonderful museum was due more to him than to
any other individual.

It came to pass in this way: After the close of
the Crystal Palace in 1851, Parliament gave five
thousand pounds for the purchase of the objects exhibited which were thought best calculated to raise
the standard of taste in the nation. These objects,
chiefly selected by Cole, were arranged by him for

exhibition in temporary buildings of such extreme and repulsive inconvenience as to bring opprobrium and ridicule upon the undertaking. It was one of the most difficult things in the world to excite public interest in the exhibition. But by that energy which comes of strong conviction and patriotic feeling, and of the opportunity given him by his public employment, Henry Cole wrung from a reluctant Parliament the annual grants necessary to make South Kensington Museum what it now is.

Magnificent buildings, filled with a vast collection of precious and interesting objects, greet the visitor. There are collections of armor, relics, porcelain, enamel, fabrics, paintings, statues, carvings in wood and ivory, machines, models, and every conceivable object of use or beauty. Some of the most celebrated pictures in the world are there, and there is an art library of thirty thousand volumes. There are schools for instruction in every branch of art and science which can be supposed to enter into the products of industry. The prizes which are offered for excellence in design and invention have attracted, in some years, as many as two hundred thousand objects. During three days of every week admission to this superb assemblage of exhibitions is free, and on the other three days sixpence is charged.

The influence of this institution upon British manufactures has been in many branches revolutionary. As the London "Times" said some time ago : —

" There is hardly a household in the country that is not the better for the change ; there is certainly no manufacture in which design has any place which has not felt its influence."

The formation of this Museum, the chief work of Sir Henry Cole's useful life, was far from exhausting his energies. He has borne a leading part in all the industrial exhibitions held in London during the last quarter of a century, and served as English commissioner at the Paris exhibitions of 1855 and 1867.

This man was enabled to render all this service to his country, to Europe, and to us, because he was not obliged to waste any of his energies in efforts to keep his place. Administrations might change, and Parliaments might dissolve ; but he was a fixture as long as he did his duty. When his duty was fairly done, and he had completed the fortieth year of his public service, he retired on his full salary, and he was granted an honorable title ; for a title *is* honorable when it is won by good service. Henceforth he was called Sir Henry Cole, K. C. B.

To the end of his life he continued to labor in all sorts of good works — a Training School for Music, a Training School for Cookery, guilds for the promotion of health, and many others. He died in April, 1882, aged seventy-four years.

CHARLES SUMMERS.

———◆———

STRANGERS visiting Melbourne, the chief city of Australia, will not be allowed to overlook four great marble statues which adorn the public library. They are the gift of Mr. W. J. Clark, one of the distinguished public men of that growing empire. These statues represent, in a sitting posture, Queen Victoria, Prince Albert, the Prince of Wales, and the Princess of Wales. They are larger than life, and, according to the Australian press, they are admirable works in every respect.

They were executed by Charles Summers, a sculptor long resident in that colony, where he practiced his art with great success, as the public buildings and private houses of Melbourne attest. Many of his works remain in the colony, and he may be said to be the founder of his form of art in that part of the world. The history of this man's life is so remarkable that I think it will interest the reader.

Sixty years ago, Charles Summers was a little, hungry, ragged boy in English Somersetshire, who earned four cents a day by scaring the crows from the wheat fields. I have seen myself such little fellows engaged in this work, coming on duty before four in the morning, and remaining till eight in the evening, frightening away the birds by beating a tin pan with a stick, not unfrequently chasing them and throwing stones at them. He was the son of a mason, who had eight children, and squandered half his time and money in the tap-room. Hence, this boy, from the age of eight or nine years, smart, intelligent, and ambitious, was constantly at work at some such employment; and often, during his father's drunken fits, he was the chief support of the family.

Besides serving as scare-crow, he assisted his father in his mason's work, and became a hod-carrier as soon as he was able to carry a hod. Sometimes he accompanied his father to a distant place in search of employment, and he was often seen on the high-road, in charge of the drunkard, struggling to get him home before he had spent their united earnings in drink. In these deplorable circumstances, he acquired a dexterity and patience which were most extraordinary. Before he was twelve years old he began to handle the chisel and the mallet, and his work in squaring and facing a stone soon surpassed that of boys much older than himself. He was observed to have a strong propensity to do fancy stone-work. He obtained, as a boy, some local celebrity for his carved gate posts, and other ornamental objects in stone. So great was his skill and industry, that, by the time he was nineteen years of age, besides having maintained a large family for years, he had saved a sum equal to a hundred dollars.

Then a piece of good fortune happened to him. A man came from London to set up in a parish church near by a monumental figure, and looked about for a skillful mason to assist him. Charles Summers was mentioned as the best hand in the neighborhood, and upon him the choice fell. Thus he was introduced to the world of art, for this figure had been executed by Henry Weekes, a distinguished London sculptor. The hardships of his childhood had made a man of him at this early age, a thoughtful and prudent man. Taking with him ten of his twenty pounds, he went to London and applied for employment in the studio of Henry Weekes. This artist employed several men, but he had no vacant place except the humble one of stone polisher, which required little skill. He accepted the place with alacrity and delight, at a salary of five dollars a week.

He was now in his element. The lowliest employments of the studio were pleasing to him. He loved to polish the marble; the sight of the numerous models was a pleasure to him; even wetting the cloths and cleaning the model tools were pleasant tasks. His cheerfulness and industry soon made him a favorite; and when his work was done, he employed his leisure in gaining skill in carving and cutting marble. In this he had such success, that, when in after life he became himself an artist, he would sometimes execute his idea in marble without modeling it in clay.

When he had been in this studio about a year, his employer was commissioned to execute two colossal figures in bronze, and the young man was obliged to spend much of his time in erecting the foundry, and other duties which he felt to be foreign to his art. Impatient at this, he resigned his place, and visited his home, where he executed medallion portraits, first of his own relations, and afterwards of public men, such as the Mayor of Bristol, and the member of Parliament for his county. These medallions gave him some reputation, and it was a favorite branch with him as long as he lived.

Returning to London, he had no difficulty in gaining employment at good wages in a studio of a sculptor. Soon we find him competing for the prizes offered by the Royal Academy of London to young sculptors; the chief of which is a gold medal given every two years for the best group in clay of an historical character. A silver medal is also given every year for the best model from life.

At the exhibition of 1851, when he was twenty-four years of age, he was a competitor for both these prizes. For the gold medal he executed a group which he called Mercy interceding for the Vanquished. For the silver medal he offered a bust of a living person. He had the singular good fortune of winning both, and he received them in public from the hands of the President of the Academy, Sir Charles Eastlake. Cheer upon cheer greeted the modest student when he rose and went forward for the purpose. He was a young man of great self-control. Instead of joining in the usual festivities of his fellow-students after the award, he walked quietly to his lodgings, where his father and brother were anxiously waiting to hear the result of the competition. He threw himself into a chair without a word, and they began to console him for the supposed disappointment. In a few minutes they sat down to supper; whereupon, with a knowing smile, he took his medals out of his pocket, and laid one of them on each side of his plate.

From this time he had no difficulties except those inherent in the nature of his work, and in his own constitution. His early struggle with life had made him too intense. He had scarcely known what play was, and he did not know how to recreate himself. He had little taste for reading or society. He loved art alone. The consequence was that he worked with an intensity and continuity that no human constitution could long endure. Soon after winning his two medals his health was so completely prostrated that he made a voyage to Australia to visit a brother who had settled there. The voyage restored him, and he soon resumed the practice of his art at Melbourne. The people were just building their Houses of Parliament, and he was employed to execute the artistic work of the interior. He lived many years in Australia, and filled the colony with his works in marble and bronze.

In due time he made the tour of Europe, and lingered nine years in Rome, where he labored with suicidal assiduity. He did far more manual labor himself than is usual with artists of his standing, and yet, during his residence in Rome he had twenty men in his service. It was in Rome, in 1876, that he received from Melbourne the commission to execute in marble the four colossal statues mentioned above. These works he completed in something less than eighteen months, besides doing several other minor works previously ordered.

It was too much, and Nature resented the affront. After he had packed the statues, and sent them on their way to the other side of the globe, he set out for Melbourne himself, intending to take England by the way for medical advice. At Paris he visited the Exhibition, and the next day, at his hotel, he fell senseless to the floor. In three weeks he was dead, at the age of fifty-one years, in the very midst of his career.

" For him," writes one of his friends, " life consisted of but one thing — *art*. For that he lived ; and, almost in the midst of it, died. He could not have conceived existence without it. Always and under every circumstance, he was thinking of his work, and gathering from whatever sur-

20

rounded him such information as he thought would prove of service. In omnibuses, in railway carriages, and elsewhere, he found opportunities of study, and could always reproduce a likeness from memory of the individuals so observed."

I do not copy these words as commendation, but as warning. Like so many other gifted men of this age, he lived too fast and attempted too much. He died when his greatest and best life would naturally have been just beginning. He died at the beginning of the period when the capacity for high enjoyment of life is naturally the greatest. He died when he could have ceased to be a manufacturer and become an artist.

WILLIAM B. ASTOR.

HOUSE—OWNER.

In estimating the character and merits of such a
man as the late Mr. Astor, we are apt to leave out
of view the enormous harm he might have done if
he had chosen to do it.

The rich fool who tosses a dollar to a waiter for
some trifling service, debases the waiter, injures
himself, and wrongs the public. By acting in that
manner in all the transactions of life, a rich man
diffuses around him an atmosphere of corruption,
and raises the scale of expense to a point which
is oppressive to many, ruinous to some, and inconvenient to all. The late Mr. Astor, with an income
from invested property of nearly two millions a
year, could have made life more difficult than it
was to the whole body of people in New York who
are able to live in a liberal manner. He refrained
from doing so. He paid for everything which he
consumed the market price — no more, no less —
and he made his purchases with prudence and forethought. As he lived for many years next door to
the Astor Library, the frequenters of that noble

institution had an opportunity of observing that he laid in his year's supply of coal in the month of June, when coal is cheapest.

There was nothing which he so much abhorred as waste. It was both an instinct and a principle with him to avoid waste. He did not have the gas turned down low in a temporarily vacated room because he would save two cents by doing so, but because he justly regarded waste as wicked. His example in this particular, in a city so given to careless and ostentatious profusion as New York, was most useful. We needed such an example. Nor did he appear to carry this principle to an extreme. He was very far from being miserly, though keenly intent upon accumulation.

In the life of the Old World there is nothing so shocking to a republicanized mind as the awful contrast between the abodes of the poor and the establishments of the rich. A magnificent park of a thousand acres of the richest land set apart and walled in for the exclusive use of one family, while all about it are the squalid hovels of the peasants to whom the use of a single acre to a family would be ease and comfort, is the most painful and shameful spectacle upon which the sun looks down this day. Nothing can make it right. It is monstrous. It curses *equally* the few who ride in the park and the many who look over its walls; for the great lord who can submit to be the agent of such injustice is as much its victim as the degraded laborer who drowns the sense of his misery in pot-house beer. The mere fact that the lord can look upon such a scene and not stir to mend it, is proof positive of a profound vulgarity.

Nor is it lords alone who thus waste the hard earned wealth of the toiling sons of men. I read some time ago of a wedding in Paris. A thriving banker there, who is styled the Baron Alphonse de Rothschild, having a daughter of seventeen to marry, appears to have set seriously to work to find out how much money a wedding could be made to cost. In pursuing this inquiry, he caused the wedding festivals of Louis XIV's court, once so famous, to seem poverty-stricken and threadbare. He began by a burst of ostentatious charity. He subscribed money for the relief of the victims of recent inundations, and dowered a number of portionless girls; expending in these ways a quarter of a million francs. He gave his daughter a portion of five millions of francs. One of her painted fans cost five thousand francs. He provided such enormous quantities of clothing for her little body, that his house, if it had not been exceedingly large, would not have conveniently held them. For the conveyance of the wedding party from the house to the synagogue, he caused twenty-five magnificent carriages to be made, such as monarchs use when they are going to be crowned, and these vehicles were drawn by horses imported from England for the purpose. The bridal veil was composed of ineffable lace, made from an original design expressly for this bride.

And then what doings in the synagogue! A choir of one hundred and ten trained voices, led by the best conductor in Europe — the first tenor of this generation engaged, who sang the prayer from " Moses in Egypt" — a crowd of rabbis, and assistant-rabbis, with the grand rabbi of Paris at their head. To complete the histrionic performance, eight young girls, each bearing a beautiful gold-embroidered bag, and attended by a young gentleman, " took up a collection" for the poor, which yielded seven thousand francs.

Mr. Astor could, if he had chosen, have thrown his millions about in this style. He was one of a score or two of men in North America who could have maintained establishments in town and country on the dastardly scale so common among rich people in Europe. He, too, could have had his park, his half a dozen mansions, his thirty carriages, his hundred horses and his yacht as big as a man-of-war. That he was above such atrocious vulgarity as this, was much to his credit and more to our advantage. What he could have done safely, other men would have attempted to whom the attempt would have been destruction. Some discredit also would have been cast upon those who live in moderate and modest ways.

Every quarter day Mr. Astor had nearly half a million dollars to invest in the industries of the

country. To invest his surplus income in the best
and safest manner was the study of his life. His
business was to take care of and increase his estate; and that *being* his business, he was right in
giving the necessary attention to it. " William
will never make money," his father used to say;
" but he will take good care of what he has." And
so it proved. The consequence was, that all his
life he invested money in the way that was at once
best for himself and best for the country. No use-
less or premature scheme had had any encouragement from him. He invariably, and by a certainty
of judgment that resembled an instinct, "put his
money where it would do most good." Political
economists demonstrate that an investment which
is the best for the investor must of necessity be the
best for the public. Here, again, we were lucky.
When we wanted houses more than we wanted
coal, he built houses for us; and when we wanted
coal more than we wanted houses, he set his money
to digging coal; charging nothing for his trouble
but the mere cost of his subsistence.

One fault he had as a public servant — for we
may fairly regard in that light a man who wields
so large a portion of our common estate. He was
one of the most timid of men. He was even tim-
orous. His timidity was constitutional and physical. He would take a great deal of trouble to
avoid crossing a temporary bridge or scaffolding,
though assured by an engineer that it was strong

enough to bear ten elephants.   Nor can it be said
that he was morally brave.   Year after year he saw
a gang of thieves in the City Hall stealing his rev-
enues under the name of taxes and assessments, but
he never led an assault upon them nor gave the aid
he ought to those who did.   Unless he is grossly
belied, he preferred to compromise than fight, and
did not always disdain to court the ruffians who
plundered him.

This was a grave fault.   He who had the most
immediate and the most obvious interest in exposing and resisting the scoundrels, ought to have
taken the lead in putting them down.   This he
could not do.   Nature had denied him the qualities
required for such a contest.   He had his enormous
estate, and he had mind enough to take care of it
in ordinary ways ; but he had nothing more.   We
must therefore praise him less for the good he did
in his life, than for the evil which he refrained from
doing.

PETER COOPER.

PETER COOPER.

On an April morning in 1883 I was seated at breakfast in a room which commanded a view of the tall flag-staff in Gramercy Park in the city of New York. I noticed some men unfolding the flag and raising it on the mast. The flag stopped midway and dropped motionless in the still spring morning. The newspapers which were scattered about the room made no mention of the death of any person of note and yet this sign of mourning needed no explanation. For half a life-time Peter Cooper had lived in a great, square, handsome house just round the corner, and the condition of the aged philanthropist had been reported about the neighborhood from hour to hour during the previous days ; so that almost every one who saw the flag uttered words similar to those which I heard at the moment : —

"He is gone, then ! The good old man is gone. We shall never see his snowy locks again, nor his placid countenance, nor his old horse and gig jogging by. Peter Cooper is dead ! "

He had breathed his last about three o'clock that

morning, after the newspapers had gone to press; but the tidings spread with strange rapidity. When I went out of the house two hours later, the whole city seemed hung with flags at half-mast; for there is probably no city in the world which has so much patriotic bunting at command as New York. Passengers going north and west observed the same tokens of regard all along the lines of railroad. By mid-day the great State of New York, from the Narrows to the lakes, and from the lakes to the Pennsylvania line, exhibited everywhere the same mark of respect for the character of the departed. A tribute so sincere, so spontaneous and so universal, has seldom been paid to a private individual.

It was richly deserved. Peter Cooper was a man quite out of the common order even of good men. His munificent gift to the public, so strikingly and widely useful, has somewhat veiled from public view his eminent executive qualities, which were only less exceptional than his moral.

I once had the pleasure of hearing the story of his life related with some minuteness by a member of his own family, now honorably conspicuous in public life, and I will briefly repeat it here. More than ninety years ago, when John Jacob Astor kept a fur store in Water Street, and used to go round himself buying his furs of the Hudson River boatmen and the western Indians, he had a neighbor who bought beaver skins of him, and made them into hats in a little shop near by, in the

same street. This hat-maker, despite his peaceful
occupation, was called by his friends Captain
Cooper, for he had been a good soldier of the
Revolution, and had retired, after honorable service to the very end of the war, with a captain's
rank. Captain Cooper was a better soldier than
man of business. Indeed, New York was then a
town of but twenty-seven thousand inhabitants, and
the field for business was restricted. He was an
amiable, not very energetic man; but he had had
the good fortune to marry a woman who supplied
all his deficiencies. The daughter of one of the
colonial mayors of New York, she was born on the
very spot which is now the site of St. Paul's Church
at the corner of Broadway and Fulton Street, and
her memory ran back to the time when the stock-
ade was still standing which had been erected in
the early day as a defense against the Indians.

There is a vivid tradition in the surviving family of Peter Cooper of the admirable traits of his
mother. She was educated among the Moravians
in Pennsylvania, who have had particular success
in forming and developing the female character.
She was a woman in whom were blended the diverse
qualities of her eminent son, energy and tenderness, mental force and moral elevation. She was
the mother of two daughters and seven sons, her
fifth child being Peter, who was born in 1791.

To the end of his life, Peter Cooper had a clear
recollection of many interesting events which oc-

curred before the beginning of the present century.

"I remember," he used to say, "that I was
about nine years old at the time when Washington
was buried.   That is, he was buried at Mount
Vernon ; but we had a funeral service in old St
Paul's.   I stood in front of the church, and I recall
the event well, on account of his old white horse
and its trappings."

A poor hatter, with a family of nine children,
must needs turn his children to account, and the
consequence was that Peter Cooper enjoyed an
education which gave him at least great manual
dexterity.   He learned how to use both his hands
and a portion of his brain.   He learned how to do
things.   His earliest recollection was his working
for his father in pulling, picking, and cleaning the
wool used in making hat-bodies, and he was kept
at this work during his whole boyhood, except that
one year he went to school half of every day, learning a little arithmetic, as well as reading and writing.   By the time he was fifteen years old he had
learned to make a good beaver hat throughout, and
a good beaver hat of that period was an elaborate
and imposing structure.

Then his father abandoned his hat shop and removed to Peekskill on the Hudson, where he set
up a brewery, and where Peter learned the whole
art and mystery of making beer.   He was quick
to learn every kind of work, and even as a boy he

was apt to suggest improvements in tools and methods. At the age of seventeen, he was still working in the brewery, a poor man's son, and engaged in an employment which for many and good reasons he disliked. Brewing beer is a repulsive occupation.

Then, with his father's consent, he came alone to New York, intending to apprentice himself to any trade that should take his fancy. He visited shop after shop, and at last applied for employment at a carriage factory near the corner of Broadway and Chambers Street. He remembered, to his ninetieth year, the substance of the conversation which passed between him and one of the partners in this business.

" Have you room for an apprentice ? " asked Peter.

" Do you know anything about the business ? " was the rejoinder.

The lad was obliged to answer that he did not.

" Have you been brought up to work ? "

He replied by giving a brief history of his previous life.

" Is your father willing that you should learn this trade ? "

" He has given me my choice of trades."

" If I take you, will you stay with me and work out your time ? "

He gave his word that he would, and a bargain was made — twenty-five dollars a year, and his board. He kept his promise and served out his time. To use his own language : —

"In my seventeenth year I entered as apprentice to the coach-making business, in which I remained four years, till I became 'of age.' I made for my employer a machine for mortising the hubs of carriages, which proved very profitable to him, and was, perhaps, the first of its kind used in this country. When I was twenty-one years old my employer offered to build me a shop and set me up in business, but as I always had a horror of being burdened with debt, and having no capital of my own, I declined his kind offer. He himself became a bankrupt. I have made it a rule to pay everything as I go. If, in the course of business, anything is due from me to any one, and the money is not called for, I make it my business on the last Saturday before Christmas to take it to his business place."

It was during this period of his life, from seventeen to twenty-one, that he felt most painfully the defects of his education. He had acquired manual skill, but he felt acutely that this quality alone was rather that of a beaver than of a man. He had an inquisitive, energetic understanding, which could not be content without knowledge far beyond that of the most advanced beaver. Hungering for such knowledge, he bought some books : but in those days there were few books of an elementary kind adapted to the needs of a lonely, uninstructed boy.

His books puzzled more than they enlightened him; and so, when his work was done, he looked about the little bustling city to see if there was not some kind of evening school in which he could get the kind of help he needed. There was nothing of the kind, either in New York or in any city then. Nor were there free schools of any kind. He found a teacher, however, who, for a small compensation, gave him instruction in the evening in arithmetic and other branches. It was at this time that he formed the resolution which he carried out forty-five years later. He said to himself: —

"If ever I prosper in business so as to acquire more property than I need, I will try to found an institution in the city of New York, wherein apprentice boys and young mechanics shall have a chance to get knowledge in the evening."

This purpose was not the dream of a sentimental youth. It was a clear and positive intention, which he kept steadily in view through all vicissitudes until he was able to enter upon its accomplishment.

He was twenty-one years of age when the war of 1812 began, which closed for the time every carriage manufactory in the country. He was therefore fortunate in not having accepted the proposition of his employer. During the first months of the war business was dead; but as the supply of foreign merchandise gave out an impulse was given to home manufacture, especially of the fabrics used in clothing. There was a sudden demand for cloth-

making machinery of all kinds, and now Peter
Cooper put to good use his inventive faculty. He
contrived a machine for cutting away the nap on
the surface of cloth, which answered so well that he
soon had a bustling shop for making the machines,
which he sold faster than he could produce. He
found himself all at once in an excellent business,
and in December, 1813, he married Miss Sarah
Bedel of Hempstead, Long Island; he being then
twenty-two and she twenty-one.

There never was a happier marriage than this.
To old age, he never sat near her without holding
her hand in his. He never spoke to her nor of
her without some tender epithet. He attributed
the great happiness of his life and most of his success to her admirable qualities. He used to say that
she was " the day-star, the solace, and the inspira-
tion " of his life. She seconded every good impulse of his benevolence, and made the fulfillment
of his great scheme possible by her wise and resolute economy. They began their married life on a
scale of extreme frugality, both laboring together
for the common good of the family.

" In early life," he used to say, " when I was
first married, I found it necessary to rock the cradle, while my wife prepared our frugal meals. This
was not always convenient in my busy life, and I
conceived the idea of making a cradle that would
be made to rock by mechanism. I did so, and
enlarging upon my first idea, I arranged the mech-

anism for keeping off the flies, and playing a music-box for the amusement of the baby! This cradle was bought of me afterwards by a delighted peddler, who gave me his 'whole stock in trade' for the exchange and the privilege of selling the patent in the State of Connecticut."

This device in various forms and modifications is still familiar in our households. They had six children, of whom two survive, Mr. Edward Cooper, recently mayor of New York, and Sarah, wife of Hon. Abram S. Hewitt, member of Congress from the city of New York. For nearly sixty-five years this couple lived together in happy marriage.

In 1815 the peace with Great Britain, which gave such ecstasies of joy to the whole country, ruined Peter Cooper's business; as it was no longer possible to make cloth in the United States with profit. With three trades at his finger ends, he now tried a fourth, cabinet-making, in which he did not succeed. He moved out of town, and bought the stock of a grocer, whose store stood on the very site of the present Cooper Institute, at that time surrounded by fields and vacant lots. But even then he thought that, by the time he was ready to begin his evening school, that angle of land would probably be an excellent central spot on which to build it.

He did very well with his grocery store; but it never would have enabled him to endow his Insti-

21

tute. One day when he had kept his grocery about a year, and used his new cradle at intervals in the rooms above, an old friend of his accosted him, as he stood at the door of the grocery.

" I have been building," said his visitor, " a glue factory for my son ; but I don't think that either he or I can make it pay. But you are the very man to do it."

" I 'll go and see it," said Peter Cooper.

He got into his friend's wagon and they drove to the spot, which was near the corner of Madison Avenue and Twenty-ninth Street, almost on the very spot now occupied by an edifice of much note called " The Little Church Round the Corner." He liked the look of the new factory, and he saw no reason why the people of New York should send all the way to Russia for good glue. His friend asked two thousand dollars for the establishment as it stood, and Peter Cooper chanced to have that sum of money, and no more. He bought the factory on the spot, sold his grocery soon, and plunged into the manufacture of glue, of which he knew nothing except that Russian glue was very good and American very bad.

Now he studied the composition of glue, and gradually learned the secret of making the best possible article which brought the highest price in the market. He worked for twenty years without a book-keeper, clerk, salesman, or agent. He rose with the dawn. When his men came at seven o'clock to work, they found the factory fires lighted, and it was the master who had lighted them. He watched closely and always the boiling of his glue, and at midday, when the critical operation was over, he drove into the city and went the round of his customers, selling them glue and isinglass, and passed the evening in posting his books and reading to his family.

He developed the glue business until it yielded him a profit of thirty thousand dollars a year. He soon began to feel himself a capitalist, and to count the years until he would be able to begin the erection of the institution he had in his mind. But men who are known to have capital are continually solicited to embark in enterprises, and he was under a strong temptation to yield to such solicitations, for the scheme which he had projected would involve a larger expenditure than could be ordinarily made from one business in one lifetime. He used to tell the story of his getting into the business of making iron, which was finally a source of great profit to him.

" In 1828," he would say, " I bought three thousand acres of land within the city limits of Baltimore for $105,000. When I first purchased the property it was in the midst of a great excitement created by a promise of the rapid completion of the Baltimore and Ohio Railroad, which had been commenced by a subscription of five dollars per share. In the course of the first year's operations they had spent more than the five dollars per share. But the road had to make so many short turns in going around points of rocks that they found they could not complete the road without a much larger sum than they had supposed would be necessary ; while the many short turns in the road seemed to render it entirely useless for locomotive purposes. The principal stockholders had become so discouraged that they said they would not pay any more, and would lose all they had already paid in. After conversing with them, I told them that if they would hold on a little while I would put a small locomotive on the road, which I thought would demonstrate the practicability of using steam-engines on the road, even with all the short turns in it. I got up a small engine for that purpose, and put it upon the road, and invited the stockholders to witness the experiment. After a good deal of trouble and difficulty in accomplishing the work, the stockholders came, and thirty-six men were taken into a car, and, with six men on the locomotive, which carried its own fuel and water, and having to go up hill eighteen feet to a mile, and turn all the short turns around the points of rocks, we succeeded in making the thirteen miles, on the first passage out, in one hour and twelve minutes, and we returned from Ellicott's Mills to Baltimore in fifty-seven minutes. This locomotive was built to demonstrate that cars could be drawn around short curves, beyond anything believed at that time to be possible. The success of this locomotive also answered the question of the possibility of building railroads in a country scarce of capital, and with immense stretches of very rough country to pass, in order to connect commercial centres, without the deep cuts, the tunneling and leveling which short curves might avoid. My contrivance saved this road from bankruptcy."

He still had his tract of Baltimore land upon his hands, which the check to the prosperity of the city rendered for the time almost valueless; so he determined to build ironworks upon it, and a rolling-mill. In his zeal to acquire knowledge at first hand, he had a narrow escape from destruction in Baltimore.

" In my efforts to make iron," he said, " I had to begin by burning the wood growing upon the spot into charcoal, and in order to do that, I erected large kilns, twenty-five feet in diameter, twelve feet high, circular in form, hooped around with iron at the top, arched over so as to make a tight place in which to put the wood, with single bricks left out in different places in order to smother the fire out when the wood was sufficiently burned. After having burned the coal in one of these kilns perfectly, and believing the fire entirely smothered out, we attempted to take the coal out of the kiln; but when we had got it about half-way out, the coal itself took fire, and the men, after carrying water some time to extinguish it, gave up in despair.

I then went myself to the door of the kiln to see if anything more could be done, and just as I entered the door the gas itself took fire and enveloped me in a sheet of flame. I had to run some ten feet to get out, and in doing so my eyebrows and whiskers were burned, and my fur hat was scorched down to the body of the fur. How I escaped I know not. I seemed to be literally blown out by the explosion, and 1 narrowly escaped with my life."

The ironworks were finally removed to Trenton, New Jersey, where to this day, under the vigorous management of Mr. Hewitt and his partners, they are very successful.

During these active years Peter Cooper never for a moment lost sight of the great object of his life. We have a new proof of this, if proof were needed, in the Autobiography recently published of the eloquent Orville Dewey, pastor of the Unitarian Church of the Messiah, which Peter Cooper attended for many years.

"There were two men," says Dr. Dewey, "who came to our church whose coming seemed to be by chance, but was of great interest to me, for I valued them greatly. They were Peter Cooper and Joseph Curtis.[1] Neither of them then belonged to any religious society, or regularly attended any church. They happened to be walking down Broadway one Sunday evening, as the congrega-

[1] A noted philanthropist of that day, devoted to the improvement of the public schools of the city.

tion were entering Stuyvesant Hall, where we then temporarily worshiped, and they said : —

" ' Let us go in here and see what *this* is.'

" When they came out, as they both told me, they said to one another : —

" ' This is the place for *us !* '

" And they immediately connected themselves with the congregation, to be among its most valued members. Peter Cooper was even then meditating that plan of a grand educational institute which he afterwards carried out. He was engaged in a large and successful business, and his one idea — which he often discussed with me — was to obtain the means of building that institute. A man of the gentlest nature and the simplest habits; yet his religious nature was his most remarkable quality. It seemed to breathe through his life as fresh and tender as if it were in some holy retreat, instead of a life of business."

Indeed there are several aged New Yorkers who can well remember hearing Mr. Cooper speak of his project at that period.

After forty years of successful business life, he found, upon estimating his resources, that he possessed about seven hundred thousand dollars over and above the capital invested in his glue and iron works. Already he had become the owner of portions of the ground he had selected so long ago for the site of his school. The first lot he bought, as Mr. Hewitt informs me, about thirty years before he began to build, and from that time onward he continued to buy pieces of the ground as often as they were for sale, if he could spare the money; until in 1854 the whole block was his own.

At first his intention was merely to establish and endow just such an evening school as he had felt the need of when he was an apprentice boy in New York. But long before he was ready to begin, there were free evening schools as well as day schools in every ward of the city, and he therefore resolved to found something, he knew not what, which should impart to apprentices and young mechanics a knowledge of the arts and sciences underlying the ordinary trades, such as drawing, chemistry, mechanics, and various branches of natural philosophy.

While he was revolving this scheme in his mind he happened to meet in the street a highly accomplished physician who had just returned from a tour in Europe, and who began at once to describe in glowing words the Polytechnic School of Paris, wherein mechanics and engineers receive the instruction which their professions require. The doctor said that young men came from all parts of France and lived on dry bread, just to attend the Polytechnic.

He was no longer in doubt; he entered at once upon the realization of his project. Beginning to build in 1854, he erected a massive structure of brick, stone, and iron, six stories in height, and fire-proof in every part, at a cost of seven hundred thousand dollars, the savings of his lifetime up to that period. Five years after, he delivered the complete structure, with the hearty consent of his wife, his children, and his son-in-law, into the hands of trustees, thus placing it beyond his own control forever. Two thousand pupils at once applied for admission. From that day to this the Institute has continued from year to year to enlarge its scope and improve its methods. Mr. Cooper added something every year to its resources, until his entire gift to the public amounted to about two millions of dollars.

Peter Cooper lived to the great age of ninety-two. No face in New York was more familiar to the people, and surely none was so welcome to them as the benign, placid, beaming countenance of " Old Peter Cooper." The roughest cartman, the most reckless hack driver would draw up his horses and wait without a word of impatience, if it was Peter Cooper's quaint old gig that blocked the way. He was one of the most uniformly happy persons I have ever met, and he retained his cheerfulness to the very end. Being asked one day in his ninetieth year, how he had preserved so well his bodily and mental vigor, he replied : —

" I always find something to keep me busy; and to be doing something for the good of man, or to keep the wheels in motion, is the best medicine one can take. I run up and down stairs here almost as easily as I did years ago, when I never expected that my term would run into the nineties. I have occasional twinges from the nervous shock and physical injury sustained from an explosion that occurred while I was conducting some experiments with nitrogen gas years ago. In other respects my days pass as painlessly as they did when I was a boy carrying a grocer's basket about the streets. It is very curious, but somehow, though I have none of the pains and troubles that old men talk about, I have not the same luxury of life — the same relish in the mere act of living — that I had then. Age is like babyhood come back again in a certain way. Even the memories of baby-life come back — the tricks, the pranks, the boyish dreams; and things that I did not remember at forty or fifty years old I recollect vividly now. But a boy of ninety and a boy of nine are very different things, none the less. I never felt better in my life except for twinges occasioned by my nitrogen experiment. But still I hear a voice calling to me, as my mother often did, when I was a boy 'Peter, Peter, it is about bed-time,' and I have an old man's presentiment that I shall be taken soon."

He loved the Institute he had founded to the last hour of his consciousness. A few weeks before his death he said to Reverend Robert Collyer: —

"I would be glad to have four more years of life given me, for I am anxious to make some addi tional improvements in Cooper Union, and then part of my life-work would be complete. If I could only live four years longer I would die content."

Dr. Collyer adds this pleasing anecdote : —

" I remember a talk I had with him not long before his death, in which he said that a Presbyterian minister of great reputation and ability, but who has since died, had called upon him one day and among other things discussed the future life. They were old and tried friends, the minister and Mr. Cooper, and when the clergyman began to question Mr. Cooper's belief, he said : ' I sometimes think that if one has too good a time here below, there is less reason for him to go to heaven. I have had a very good time, but I know poor creatures whose lives have been spent in a constant struggle for existence. They should have some reward hereafter. They have worked here ; they should be rewarded after death. The only doubts that I have about the future are whether I have not had too good a time on earth.' "

He died in April, 1883, from a severe cold which he had not the strength to throw off. His end was as peaceful and painless as his life had been innocent and beneficial.

PARIS–DUVERNEY.

FRENCH FINANCIER.

———◆———

SOME one has remarked that the old French monarchy was a despotism tempered by epigrams. I take the liberty of adding that if the despotism of the later French kings had not been frequently tempered by something more effectual than epigrams, it would not have lasted as long as it did.

What tempered and saved it was, that, occasionally, by hook or by crook, men of sterling sense and ability rose from the ordinary walks of life to positions of influence and power, which enabled them to counteract the folly of the ruling class.

About the year 1691 there was an inn at the foot of the Alps, near the border line that divided France from Switzerland, bearing the sign, St. Francis of the Mountain. There was no village near. The inn stood alone among the mountains, being supported in part by travelers going from France to Geneva, and in part by the sale of wine to the farmers who lived in the neighborhood. The landlord, named Paris, was a man of intelligence and ability, who, besides keeping his inn, cultivated a farm; assisted in both by energetic, capable sons, of whom he had four : Antoine, aged twenty-three ; Claude, twenty-one; Joseph, seven; and Jean, an infant. It was a strong, able family, who loved and confided in one another, having no thought but to live and die near the spot upon which they were born, and in about the same sphere of life.

But such was not their destiny. An intrigue of the French ministry drew these four sons from obscurity, and led them to the high places of the world. Pontchartrain, whose name is still borne by a lake in Louisiana, was then minister of finance to Louis XIV. To facilitate the movements of the army in the war then going on between France and Savoy, he proposed to the king the formation of a company which should contract to supply the army with provisions; and, the king accepting his suggestion, the company was formed, and began operations. But the secretary of war took this movement of his colleague in high dudgeon, as the supply of the army, he thought, belonged to the war department. To frustrate and disgrace the new company of contractors, he ordered the army destined to operate in Italy to take the field on the first of May, several weeks before it was possible for the contractors by the ordinary methods to collect and move the requisite supplies. The company explained the impossibility of their feeding the army so early in the season; but the minister of war, not ill-pleased to see his rival embarrassed, held to his purpose,

and informed the contractors' agent that he must
have thirty thousand sacks of flour at a certain post
by a certain day, or his head should answer it.

The agent, alarmed, and at his wits' end, con-
sulted the innkeeper of the Alps, whom he knew to
be an energetic spirit, and perfectly well acquainted
with the men, the animals, the resources, and the
roads of the region in which he lived, and through
which the provisions would have to pass. The
elder sons of the landlord were in the field at the
time at work, and he told the agent he must
wait a few hours till he could talk the matter over
with them. At the close of the day there was a
family consultation, and the result was that they
undertook the task. Antoine, the eldest son, went
to Lyons, the nearest large city, and induced the
magistrates to lend the king the grain preserved in
the public depositories against famine, engaging to
replace it as soon as the navigation opened in the
spring. The magistrates, full of zeal for the king's
service, yielded willingly; and meanwhile, Claude,
the second of the brothers, bought a thousand
mules; and, in a very few days, in spite of the
rigor of the season, long lines of mules, each laden
with a sack of flour, were winding their way
through the defiles of the Alps, guided by peasants whom the father of these boys had selected.

This operation being insufficient, hundreds of
laborers were set to work breaking the ice in the
night, and in constructing barges, so as to be in

readiness the moment navigation was practicable.

Early in the spring two hundred barge loads were set floating down toward the seat of war; and by the time the general in command was ready to take the field, there was an abundance of tents, provisions, ammunition, and artillery within easy reach.

The innkeeper and his sons were liberally recompensed; and their talents thus being made known to the company of contractors, they were employed again a year or two after in collecting the means required in a siege, and in forwarding provisions to a province threatened with famine. These large operations gave the brothers a certain distaste for their country life, and they removed to Paris in quest of a more stirring and brilliant career than an Alpine inn with farm adjacent could afford. One of them enlisted at first in the king's guards, and the rest obtained clerkships in the office of the company of contractors. By the time they were all grown to manhood, the eldest, a man over forty, and the youngest, eighteen or twenty, they had themselves become army contractors and capitalists, noted in army circles for the tact, the fidelity, and the indomitable energy with which they carried on their business.

The reader is aware that during the last years of the reign of Louis XIV., France suffered a series of most disastrous defeats from the allied armies.

commanded by the great English general, the Duke of Marlborough. It was these four able brothers who supplied the French army with provisions during that terrible time; and I do not hesitate to say, that, on two or three critical occasions, it was their energy and intelligence that saved the independence of their country. Often the king's government could not give them a single louis-d'or in money when a famishing army was to be supplied. On several occasions they spent their whole capital in the work and risked their credit. There was one period of five months, as they used afterwards to say, when they never once went to bed *sure* of being able to feed the army the next day. During those years of trial they were sustained in a great degree by the confidence which they inspired in their honesty, as well as in their ability. The great French banker and capitalist then was Samuel Bernard. On more than one occasion Bernard saved them by lending them, on their personal security, immense sums; in one crisis as much as three million francs.

We can judge of the extent of their operations, when we learn that, during the last two years of the war, they had to supply a hundred and eighty thousand men in the field, and twenty thousand men in garrison, while receiving from the government little besides depreciated paper.

Peace came at last; and it came at a moment when the whole capital of the four brothers was in

the king's paper, and when the finances were in a
state of inconceivable confusion. The old king
died in 1715, leaving as heir to the throne a sickly
boy five years of age. The royal paper was so
much depreciated that the king's promise to pay
one hundred francs sold in the street for twenty-
five francs. Then came the Scotch inflator, John
Law, who gave France a brief delirium of paper
prosperity, ending with the most woful and wide-
spread collapse ever known. It was these four
brothers, but especially the third brother, Joseph
Paris, known in French history as Paris-Duverney,
who, by labors almost without example, restored
the finances of the country, funded the debt at a
reasonable interest, and enabled France to profit
by the twenty years of peace that lay before her.

There is nothing in the whole history of finance
more remarkable than the five years' labors of these
brothers after the Law-mania of 1710; and it is
hardly possible to overstate the value of their services at a time when the kingdom was governed by
an idle and dissolute regent, and when there was
not a nobleman about the court capable of grap-
pling with the situation. The regent died of his de-
baucheries in the midst of their work. The Duke
of Bourbon succeeded him; he was governed by
Madame de Prie; and between them they concocted
a nice scheme for getting the young king married,
who had then reached the mature age of fifteen.
The idea was to rule the king through a queen of

22

their own choosing, and who would be grateful to them for her elevation.

But it turned out quite otherwise. The king, indeed, was married, and he was very fond of his wife, and she tried to carry out the desires of those who had made her queen of France. But there was an obstacle in the way ; and that obstacle was the king's unbounded confidence in his tutor, the Abbé de Fleury, a serene and extremely agreeable old gentleman past seventy. A struggle arose between the old tutor and Madame de Prie for the possession of the young king. The tutor won the victory. The Duke of Bourbon was exiled to his country-seat, and Madame de Prie was sent packing. Paris-Duverney and his first clerk were put into the Bastille, where they were detained for two years in unusually rigorous imprisonment, and his three brothers were exiled to their native province.

Another intrigue of court set them free again, and the four brothers were once more in Paris, where they continued their career as bankers, contractors, and capitalists as long as they lived, each of them acquiring and leaving a colossal fortune, which their heirs were considerate enough to dissipate. It was Paris-Duverney who suggested and managed the great military school at Paris, which still exists. It was he also who helped make the fortunes of the most celebrated literary men of his time, Voltaire and Beaumarchais. He did this by admitting them to a share in army contracts, one of which yielded Voltaire a profit of seven hundred thousand francs, which, with good nursing, made him at last the richest literary man that ever lived.

Paris-Duverney was as good a man and patriot as a man could well be who had to work with and under such persons as Louis XV. and Madame de Pompadour. By way of showing what difficulties men had to overcome who then desired to serve their country, I will mention a single incident of his later career.

His favorite work, the École Militaire, of which he was the first superintendent, shared the unpopularity of its early patron, Madame de Pompadour, and long he strove in vain to bring it into favor. To use the narrative of M. de Loménie, the biographer of Beaumarchais : —

"He was constantly at court, laboring without cessation on behalf of the military school, and soliciting the king in vain to visit it in state, which would have given a sort of *prestige*. Coldly received by the dauphin, the queen, and the princesses, he could not, as the friend of Madame de Pompadour, obtain from the nonchalance of Louis XV. the visit which he so much desired, when the idea struck him, in his despair, of having recourse to the young harpist, who appeared to be so assiduous in his attendance on the princesses, and who directed their concert every week. Beaumarchais understood at once the advantage he might derive from rendering an important service to a clever, rich, old financier, who had still a number of affairs in hand, and who was capable of bringing him both wealth and advancement. But how could a musician without importance hope to obtain from the king what had already been refused to solicitations of much more influence than his own? Beaumarchais went to work like a man who had a genius for dramatic intrigue and a knowledge of the human heart.

" We have shown that, while he was giving his time and attention to the princesses, he never asked for anything in return. He thought that if he were fortunate enough to persuade them, in the first instance, to pay a visit to the École Militaire, the curiosity of the king perhaps would be excited by the narrative of what they had seen, and would lead him to do that which he would never have been prompted to do by justice. He accordingly represented to the princesses not only the equitable side of the question, but also the immense interest which he himself had in obtaining this favor for a man who might be of great use to him. The princesses consented to visit the École Militaire, and Beaumarchais was granted the honor of accompanying them. The director received them with great splendor ; they did not conceal from him the great interest they took in their young *protégé*, and some days afterward Louis XV., urged by his daughters, visited it himself, and thus gratified the wishes of old Duverney.

"From this moment the financier, grateful for Beaumarchais' good services, and delighted to find a person who could assist him as an intermediary in his intercourse with the court, resolved to make the young man's fortune. He began by giving him a share in one of his speculations to the amount of sixty thousand francs, on which he paid him interest at the rate of ten per cent.; after this, he gave him an interest in various other affairs. ' He initiated me,' says Beaumarchais, ' into the secrets of finance, of which, as every one knows, he was a consummate master.'"

Such was government in the good old times! I like to think of it when things go amiss in Washington or Albany. Let our rulers do as badly as they may, they cannot do worse than the rulers of the world did a century and a half ago. If any good or great thing was done in those days, it was done in spite of the government.

SIR ROWLAND HILL.

THE poet Coleridge, on one of his long walks among the English lakes, stopped at a roadside inn for dinner, and while he was there the letter-carrier came in, bringing a letter for the girl who was waiting upon him. The postage was a shilling, nearly twenty-five cents. She looked long and lovingly at the letter, holding it in her hand, and then gave it back to the man, telling him that she could not afford to pay the postage. Coleridge at once offered the shilling, which the girl after much hesitation accepted. When the carrier was gone she told him that he had thrown his shilling away, for the pretended letter was only a blank sheet of paper. On the outside there were some small marks which she had carefully noted before giving the letter back to the carrier. Those marks were the *letter*, which was from her brother, with whom she had agreed upon a short - hand system by which to communicate news without expense. "We are so poor," said she to the poet, "that we have invented this manner of corresponding and sending our letters free."

SIR ROWLAND HILL.

The shilling which the postman demanded was, in fact, about a week's wages to a girl in her condition fifty years ago. Nor was it poor girls only who then played tricks upon the post-office. Envelopes franked by honorable members of Parliament were a common article of merchandise, for it was the practice of their clerks and servants to procure and sell them. Indeed, the postal laws were so generally evaded that, in some large towns, the department was cheated of three quarters of its revenue. Who can wonder at it? It cost more then to send a letter from one end of London to the other, or from New York to Harlem, than it now does to send a letter from Egypt to San Francisco. The worst effect of dear postage was the obstacles it placed in the way of correspondence between poor families who were separated by distance. It made correspondence next to impossible between poor people in Europe and their relations in America. Think of an Irish laborer who earned sixpence a day paying *seventy-five cents* to get news from a daughter in Cincinnati! It required the savings of three or four months.

The man who changed all this, Sir Rowland Hill, died only three years ago at the age of eighty-three. I have often said that an American ought to have invented the new postal system; and Rowland Hill, though born and reared in England, and descended from a long line of English ancestors, was very much an American. He was educated on the American plan. His mind was American, and he had the American way of looking at things with a view to improving them.

His father was a Birmingham schoolmaster, a free trader, and more than half a republican. He brought up his six sons and two daughters to use their minds and their tongues. His eldest son, the recorder of Birmingham, once wrote of his father thus : —

"Perhaps the greatest obligation we owe our father is this: that, from infancy, he would reason with us, and so observe all the rules of fair play, that we put forth our little strength without fear. Arguments were taken at their just weight; the sword of authority was not thrown into the scale."

Miss Edgeworth's tales deeply impressed the boy, and he made up his mind in childhood to follow the path which she recommended, and do something which should greatly benefit mankind.

At the age of eleven he began to assist in teaching his father's pupils. At twelve he was a pupil no more, and gave himself wholly up to teaching. Long before he was of age he had taken upon himself all the mere business of the school, and managed it so well as to pay off debts which had weighed heavily upon the family ever since he was born. At the same time he invented new methods of governing the school. He was one of the first to abolish corporal punishment. He converted his school into a republic governed by a constitution and code of

laws, which filled a printed volume of more than a
hundred pages, which is still in the possession of
his family. His school, we are told, was governed
by it for many years. If a boy was accused of a
fault, he had the right of being tried by a jury of
his school-fellows. Monitors were elected by the
boys, and these monitors met to deliberate upon
school matters as a little parliament.

Upon looking back in old age upon this wonderful school, he doubted very much whether the plan
was altogether good. The democratic idea he
thought, was carried too far; it made the boys too
positive and argumentative.

"I greatly doubt," said he once, "if I should
send my own son to a school conducted on such a
complicated system."

It had, nevertheless, admirable features, which
he originated, and which are now generally adopted.
Toward middle life he became tired of this laborious business, though he had the largest private
school in that part of England. His health failed,
and he felt the need of change and rest. Having
now some leisure upon his hands he began to invent and project.

His attention was first called to the postal system merely by the high price of postage. It struck
him as absurd that it should cost thirteen pence to
convey half an ounce of paper from London to
Birmingham, while several pounds of merchandise
could be carried for sixpence. Upon studying the

subject, he found that the mere carriage of a letter between two post-offices cost scarcely anything, the chief expense being incurred at the post-offices in starting and receiving it. He found that the actual cost of conveying a letter from London to Edinburgh, four hundred and four miles, was *one eighteenth of a cent!* This fact it was which led him to the admirable idea of the uniform rate of one penny — for all distances.

At that time a letter from London to Edinburgh was charged about twenty-eight cents; but if it contained the smallest inclosure, even half a bank-note, or a strip of tissue paper, the postage was doubled. In short, the whole service was incumbered with absurdities, which no one noticed because they were old. In 1837, after an exhaustive study of the whole system, he published his pamphlet, entitled Post-Office Reforms, in which he suggested his improvements, and gave the reasons for them. The post-office department, of course, treated his suggestions with complete contempt. But the public took a different view of the matter. The press warmly advocated his reforms. The thunderer of the London " Times " favored them. Petitions poured into Parliament. Daniel O'Connell spoke in its favor.

" Consider, my lord," said he to the premier, "that a letter to Ireland and the answer back would cost thousands upon thousands of my poor and affectionate countrymen more than a fifth of

their week's wages. If you shut the post-office to
them, which you do now, you shut out warm hearts
and generous affections from home, kindred, and
friends."

The ministry yielded, and on January 10, 1840,
penny postage became the law of the British Empire. As the whole postal service had to be reor-
ganized, the government offered Rowland Hill the
task of introducing the new system, and proposed
to give him five hundred pounds a year for two
years. He spurned the proposal, and offered to
do the work for nothing. He was then offered fifteen hundred pounds a year for two years, and
this he accepted rather than see his plan mismanaged by persons who did not believe in it. After
many difficulties, the new system was set in motion, and was a triumphant success from the first
year.

A Tory ministry coming in, they had the incredible folly to dismiss the reformer, and he retired
from the public service without reward. The English people are not accustomed to have their faithful servants treated in that manner, and there was
a universal burst of indignation. A national testi-
monial was started. A public dinner was given
him, at which he was presented with a check for
sixty-five thousand dollars. He was afterwards
placed in charge of the post-office department, although with a lord over his head as nominal chief.
This lord was a Tory of the old school, and wished

to use the post-office to reward political and personal friends. Rowland Hill said : —

"No, my lord; appointment and promotion for merit only."

They quarreled upon this point, and Rowland Hill resigned. The queen sent a message to the House of Commons asking for twenty thousand pounds as a national gift to Sir Rowland Hill, which was granted, and he was also allowed to retire from office upon his full salary of two thousand pounds a year. That is the way to treat a public benefactor; and nations which treat their servants in that spirit are likely to be well served.

The consequences of this postal reform are marvelous to think of. The year before the new plan was adopted in Great Britain, one hundred and six millions of letters and papers were sent through the post-office. Year before last the number was one thousand four hundred and seventy-eight millions. In other words, the average number of letters per inhabitant has increased from three per annum to thirty-two. The United States, which ought to have taken the lead in this matter, was not slow to follow, and every civilized country has since adopted the system.

A few weeks before Sir Rowland Hill's death, the freedom of the city of London was presented to him in a gold box. He died in August, 1881, full of years and honors.

MARIE–ANTOINE CAREME,

FRENCH COOK.

DOMESTIC servants occupy in France a somewhat more elevated position in the social scale than
is accorded them in other countries. As a class,
too, they are more intelligent, better educated, and
more skillful than servants elsewhere. There are
several works in the French language designed expressly for their instruction, some of the best of
which were written, or professed to have been written, by servants. On the counter of a French bookstore you will sometimes see such works as the following : " The Perfect Coachman," " The Life of
Jasmin, the Good Laquey," " Rules for the Government of Shepherds and Shepherdesses, by the Good
Shepherd," " The Well-Regulated Household,"
"Duties of Servants of both Sexes toward God and
toward their Masters and Mistresses, by a Servant,"
" How to Train a Good Domestic."

Some books of this kind are of considerable an-
tiquity and have assisted in forming several generations of domestic servants. One of them, it is
said, entitled, " The Perfect Coachman," was writ-

ten by a prince of the reigning house of France. In France, as in most old countries, few people expect to change their condition in life. Once a servant, always a servant. It is common for parents in humble life to apprentice their children to some branch of domestic service, satisfied if they become excellent in their vocation, and win at length the distinctions and promotions which belong to it.

Lady Morgan, who visited Paris several years ago, relates an anecdote or two showing how intelligent some French servants are. She was walking along the Quai Voltaire, followed by her French lackey, when he suddenly came to her side and, pointing to a house, said: —

"There, madam, is a house consecrated to genius. There died Voltaire — in that apartment with the shutters closed. There died the first of our great men; perhaps also the last."

On another occasion the same man objected to a note which she had written in the French language.

"Is it not good French, then?" asked the lady.

"Oh, yes, madam," replied he; "the French is very good, but the style is too cold. You begin by saying, You *regret* that you cannot have the pleasure. You should say, I am *in despair*."

"Well, then," said Lady Morgan, "write it yourself."

"You may write it, if you please, my lady, at my dictation, for as to reading and writing, they are branches of my education which were totally neglected."

The lady remarks, however, that Paris servants can usually read very well, and that hackmen, water-carriers, and porters may frequently be seen reading a classical author while waiting for a customer.

A very remarkable case in point is Marie-Antoine Carème, whom a French writer styles, " one of the princes of the culinary art." I suppose that no country in the world but France could produce such a character. Of this, however, the reader can judge when I have briefly told his story.

He was born in a Paris garret, in 1784, one of a family of fifteen children, the offspring of a poor workman. As soon as he was old enough to render a little service, his father placed him as a garçon in a cheap and low restaurant, where he received nothing for his labor except his food.

This was an humble beginning for a " prince." But he improved his disadvantages to such a degree that, at the age of twenty, he entered the kitchen of Talleyrand. Now Prince Talleyrand, besides being himself one of the daintiest men in Europe, had to entertain, as minister of foreign affairs, the diplomatic corps, and a large number of other persons accustomed from their youth up to artistic cookery. Carème proved equal to the situation. Talleyrand's dinners were renowned throughout Europe and America. But this cook of genius, not satisfied with his attainments, took lessons in the art from Guipière, the renowned *chef* of the Emperor Napoleon — he who followed Murat into the wilds of Russia and perished with so many other cooks and heroes.

Carême appears to have succeeded Guipière in the Imperial kitchen, but he did not follow the Emperor to Elba. When the allied kings celebrated their triumph in Paris at a grand banquet, it was Carême who, as the French say, " executed the repast." His brilliant success on this occasion was trumpeted over Europe, and after the final downfall of Napoleon he was invited to take charge of the kitchen of the English Prince Regent. At various times during his career he was cook to the Emperor Alexander of Russia, to the Emperor of Austria, to the Prince of Wurtemberg, and to the head of the house of Rothschild. In the service of these illustrious eaters he gained large sums of money, which, however, he was very far from hoarding.

In the maturity of his powers he devoted himself and his fortune to historical investigations concerning the art of cookery. For several years he was to be daily seen in the Imperial Library, studying the cookery, so renowned, of the ancient Greeks and Romans, desiring especially to know whether they possessed any secrets which had been lost. His conclusion was, that the dishes served upon the tables of Lucullus, Augustus Cæsar, and others, were " utterly bad and atrociously stupid." But he com-

mended the decoration of their tables, the cups and
vases of gold, the beautiful pitchers, the chased silver, the candles of white Spanish wax, the fabrics of
silk whiter than the snow, and the beautiful flowers
with which their tables were covered. He published
the results of his labors in a large octavo volume,
illustrated by a hundred and twenty-eight engrav-
ings. He continued his studious labors, and published at various periods " Ancient and Modern
Cookery Compared," in two volumes, octavo, " The
Paris Cook, or the Art of Cooking in the Nineteenth Century," and others. Toward the close of
his life, he wrote a magazine article upon Napoleon's way of eating at St. Helena.

He dedicated one of his works to his great in-
structor and master in the art of cookery, Guipière.
To give the reader an idea of his way of thinking
and feeling I will translate a few sentences of this
dedication : —

" Rise, illustrious Shade ! Hear the voice of the
man who was your admirer and your pupil ! Your
distinguished talents brought upon you hatred and
persecution. By cabal you were obliged to leave
your beautiful native land, and go into Italy to
serve a prince (Murat) to whose enjoyment you
had once ministered in Paris. You followed your
king into Russia. But alas, by a deplorable fatal-
ity, you perished miserably, your feet and body
frozen by the frightful climate of the north. Arrived at Vilna, your generous prince lavished gold

23

to save you, but in vain. O great Guipière, receive the public homage of a faithful disciple. Regardless of those who envied you, I wish to associate your name with my labors. I bequeath to your memory my most beautiful work. It will convey to future ages a knowledge of the elegance and splendor of the culinary art in the nineteenth century; and if Vatel rendered himself illustrious by a point of honor, dear to every man of merit, your unhappy end, O Guipière, renders you worthy of the same homage! It was that point of honor which made you follow your prince into Russia, when your gray hairs seemed to assure you a happier destiny in Paris. You shared the sad fate of our old veterans, and the honor of our warriors perishing of hunger and cold."

All this, the reader will admit, is very strange and very French. In the same work, Carême chronicles the names of all the celebrated cooks who perished in the retreat from Russia. This prince of the kitchen died in 1833, when he was scarcely fifty years of age. His works are still well known in France, and some of them have passed through more than one edition. It is an odd contradiction, that the name of this prince of the kitchen should be the French word for the time of fasting. Carême means *Lent*.

WONDERFUL WALKER.

I HAVE here a good story for hard times. It is of a clergyman and cotton spinner of the Church of England, who, upon an income of twenty-four pounds a year, lived very comfortably to the age of ninety-four years, reared a family of eight children respectably, gave two of his sons a University education, and left an estate worth two thousand pounds.

Every one will admit that this was a good deal to do upon a salary of one hundred and twenty dollars; and some readers, who find the winter hard to get through, may be interested to know how he did it. To this day, though he has been dead one hundred years, he is spoken of in the region where he lived, as Wonderful Walker. By this epithet, also, he is spoken of by the poet Wordsworth, in the "Excursion:" —

> " And him, the Wonderful,
> Our simple shepherds, speaking from the heart,
> Deservedly have styled "

He lived and died in the lake country of England. near the residence of Wordsworth, who has embalmed him in verse, and described him in prose.   Robert Walker, the youngest of twelve children, the son of a yeoman of small estate, was bred a scholar because he was of a frame too delicate, as his father thought, to earn his livelihood by bodily labor.   He struggled into a competent knowledge of the classics and divinity, gained in strength as he advanced towards manhood, and by the time he was ordained was as vigorous and alert as most men of his age.

After his ordination, he had his choice of two curacies of the same revenue, namely, five pounds a year — twenty-five dollars.   One of these, Seathwaite by name, too insignificant a place to figure upon a map, or even in the " Gazetteer," was situated in his native valley, in the church of which he had gone to school in his childhood.   He chose Seathwaite, but not for that reason.   He was in love ; he wished to marry ; and this parish had a small parsonage attached to it, with a garden of three quarters of an acre.   The person to whom he was engaged was a comely and intelligent domestic servant such as then could frequently be found in the sequestered parts of England.   She had saved, it appears, from her wages the handsome sum of forty pounds.   Thus provided, he married, and entered upon his curacy in his twenty-sixth year, and set up housekeeping in his little parsonage.

Every one knows what kind of families poor cler-

gymen are apt to have. Wonderful Walker had
one of that kind. About every two years, or less, a
child arrived; and heartily welcome they all were,
and deeply the parents mourned the loss of one
that died. In the course of a few years, eight
bouncing girls and boys filled his little house; and
the question recurs with force: How did he support them all? From Queen Anne's bounty, and
other sources, his income was increased to the sum
mentioned above, twenty-four pounds. That for a
beginning. Now for the rest.

In the first place, he was the lawyer of his parish, as well as its notary, conveyancer, appraiser,
and arbitrator. He drew the wills, contracts, and
deeds, charging for such services a moderate fee,
which added to his little store of cash. His labors
of this kind, at the beginning of the year, when
most contracts were made, were often extremely severe, occupying sometimes half the night, or even
all night. Then he made the most of his garden,
which was tilled by his own hands, until his children were old enough to help him. Upon the mountains near by, having a right of pasturage, he kept
two cows and some sheep, which supplied the family with all their milk and butter, nearly all their
meat, and most of their clothes. He also rented
two or three acres of land, upon which he raised
various crops. In sheep-shearing time, he turned
out and helped his neighbors shear their sheep,
a kind of work in which he had eminent skill.

As compensation, each farmer thus assisted gave him a fleece. In haying time, too, he and his boys were in the fields lending a hand, and got some good hay-cocks for their pains.

Besides all this, he was the school-master of the parish. Mr. Wordsworth positively says that, during most of the year, except when farm work was very pressing, he taught school eight hours a day for five days in the week, and four hours on Saturday. The school-room was the church. The master's seat was inside the rails of the altar; he used the communion table for a desk; and there, during the whole day, while the children were learning and saying their lessons, he kept his spinning-wheel in motion. In the evening, when school was over, feeling the need of exercise, he changed the small spinning-wheel at which he had sat all day for a large one, which required the spinner to step to and fro.

There was absolutely no waste and no luxury known in his house. The only indulgence which looked like luxury was that, on a Saturday afternoon, he would read a newspaper or a magazine. The clothes of the whole family were grown, spun, woven, and made by themselves. The fuel of the house, which was peat, was dug, dried, and carried by themselves. They made their own candles. Once a month a sheep was selected from their little flock and killed for the use of the family, and in the fall a cow would be salted and dried for the winter, the hide being tanned for the family shoes. No house was more hospitable, nor any hand more generous, than those of this excellent man. Old parishioners, who walked to church from a distance and wished to remain for the afternoon service, were always welcome to dinner at the parsonage, and sometimes these guests were so numerous that it took the family half the week to eat up the cold broken remains. He had something always to spare to make things decent and becoming. His sister's pew in the chapel he lined neatly with woolen cloth of his own making.

"It is the only pew in the chapel so distinguished," writes the poet, "and I know of no other instance of his conformity to the delicate accommodations of modern times."

Nineteen or twenty years elapsed before this singular and interesting man attracted any public notice. His parishioners, indeed, held him in great esteem, for he was one of those men who are not only virtuous, but who render virtue engaging and attractive. If they revered him as a benevolent, a wise, and a temperate man, they loved him as a cheerful, friendly, and genial soul. He was gay and merry at Christmas, and his goodness was of a kind which allures while it rebukes. But beyond the vale of Seathwaite, he was unknown until the year 1754, when a traveler discovered him, and published an account of his way of life.

"I found him," writes this traveler. "sitting at

the head of a long square table, dressed in a coarse blue frock, trimmed with black horn buttons, a checked shirt, a leathern strap about his neck for a stock, a coarse apron, a pair of great wooden soled shoes, plated with iron to preserve them, with a child upon his knee, eating his breakfast. His wife and the remainder of his children were, some of them, employed in waiting upon each other, the rest in teasing and spinning wool, at which trade he is a great proficient; and, moreover, when it is ready for sale, he will lay it upon his back, sixteen or thirty-two pounds' weight, and carry it on foot to the market, seven or eight miles."

He spoke also of his cheerfulness, and the good humor which prevailed in the family, the simplicity of his doctrine, and the apostolic fervor of his preaching; for, it seems, he was an excellent preacher as well. The publication of this account drew attention to the extreme smallness of his clerical income, and the bishop offered to annex to Seathwaite an adjacent parish, which also yielded a revenue of five pounds a year. By preaching at one church in the morning, and the other in the afternoon, he could serve both parishes, and draw both stipends. Wonderful Walker declined the bishop's offer.

" The annexation," he wrote to the bishop, "would be apt to cause a general discontent among the inhabitants of both places, by either thinking themselves slighted, being only served alternately or neglected in the duty, or attributing it to covetousness; all of which occasions of murmuring I would willingly avoid."

Mr. Wordsworth, to whom we are indebted for this letter, mentions that, in addition to his other gifts and graces, he had a "beautiful handwriting."

This admirable man continued to serve his little parish for nearly sixty-eight years. His children grew up about him. Two of his sons became clergymen of the Church of England; one learned the trade of a tanner; four of his daughters were happily married; and, occasionally, all the children and grandchildren, a great company of healthy and happy people, spent Christmas together, and went to church, and partook of the communion together, this one family filling the whole altar.

The good old wife died first. At her funeral the venerable man, past ninety years of age, had the body borne to the grave by three of her daughters and one granddaughter. When the corpse was lifted, he insisted upon lending a hand, and he felt about (for he was almost blind) until he got hold of a cloth that was fastened to the coffin; and thus, as one of the bearers of the body, he entered the church where she was to be buried.

The old man, who had preached with much vigor and great clearness until then sensibly drooped after the loss of his wife. His voice faltered as he preached; he kept looking at the seat in which she had sat, where he had watched her kind and beautiful face for more than sixty years. He could not pass her grave without tears. But though sad and melancholy when alone, he resumed his cheerfulness and good-humor when friends were about him. One night, in his ninety-fourth year, he tottered upon his daughter's arm, as his custom was, to the door, to look out for a moment upon the sky.

" How clear," said he, " the moon shines tonight."

In the course of that night he passed peacefully away. At six the next morning he was found dead upon the couch where his daughter had left him. Of all the men of whom I have ever read, this man, I think, was the most virtuous and the most fortunate.

SIR CHRISTOPHER WREN.

OF the out-of-door sights of London, none makes
upon the stranger's mind so lasting an impression
as huge St. Paul's, the great black dome of which
often seems to hang over the city poised and still,
like a balloon in a calm, while the rest of the edifice is buried out of sight in the fog and smoke.
The visitor is continually coming in sight of this
dome, standing out in the clearest outline when all
lower objects are obscure or hidden. Insensibly he
forms a kind of attachment to it, at the expression
of which the hardened old Londoner is amused;
for he may have passed the building twice a day
for forty years without ever having had the curiosity to enter its doors, or even to cast a glance up-
wards at its sublime proportions.

It is the verdant American who is penetrated
to the heart by these august triumphs of human
skill and daring. It is we who, on going down
into the crypt of St. Paul's, are so deeply moved
at the inscription upon the tomb of the architect of
the cathedral : —

"Underneath is laid the builder of this church

and city, Christopher Wren, who lived more than ninety years, not for himself, but for the public good. Reader, if you seek his monument, look around ! "

The writer of this inscription, when he used the word *circumspice*, which we translate *look around*, did not intend probably to confine the reader's attention to St. Paul's. Much of the old part of London is adorned by proofs of Wren's skill and taste; for it was he who rebuilt most of the churches and other public buildings which were destroyed by the great fire of London in 1666. He built or rebuilt fifty-five churches in London alone, besides thirty-six halls for the guilds and mechanics' societies. The royal palaces of Hampton Court and Kensington were chiefly his work. He was the architect of Temple Bar, Drury Lane Theatre, the Royal Exchange, and the Monument. It was he who adapted the ancient palace at Greenwich to its present purpose, a retreat for old sailors. The beautiful city of Oxford, too, contains colleges and churches constructed or reconstructed by him. It is doubtful if any other man of his profession ever did so much work as he, and certainly none ever worked more faithfully.

With all this, he was a self-taught architect. He was neither intended by his father to pursue that profession, nor did he ever receive instruction in it from an architect. He came of an old family of high rank in the Church of England, his father, a clergyman richly provided with benefices, and his uncle being that famous Bishop of Ely who was imprisoned in the Tower eighteen years for his adherence to the royal cause in the time of the Commonwealth.

He derived his love of architecture from his father, Dr. Christopher Wren, a mathematician, a musician, a draughtsman, who liked to employ his leisure in repairing and decorating the churches under his charge. Dr. Wren had much mechanical skill, and devised some new methods of supporting the roofs of large buildings. He was the ideal churchman, bland, dignified, scholarly, and ingenious.

His son Christopher, born in 1631 (the year after Boston was founded), inherited his father's propensities, with more than his father's talents. Like many other children destined to enjoy ninety years of happy life, he was of such delicate health as to require constant attention from all his family to prolong his existence. As the years went on, he became sufficiently robust, and passed through Westminster school to Oxford, where he was regarded as a prodigy of learning and ability.

John Evelyn, who visited Oxford when Wren was a student there, speaks of visiting "that miracle of a youth, Mr. Christopher Wren, nephew of the Bishop of Ely." He also mentions calling upon one of the professors, at whose house "that prodigious young scholar, Mr. Christopher Wren," showed him a thermometer, " a monstrous magnet," some dials, and a piece of white marble stained red, and many other curiosities, some of which were the young scholar's own work.

There never had been such an interest before in science and invention. The work of Lord Bacon in which he explained to the scholars of Europe the best way of discovering truth (by experiment, comparison, and observation) was beginning to bear fruit. A number of gentlemen at Oxford were accustomed to meet once a week at one another's houses for the purpose of making and reporting experiments, and thus accumulating the facts leading to the discovery of principles. This little social club, of which Christopher Wren was a most active and zealous member, grew afterwards into the famous Royal Society, of which Sir Isaac Newton was president, and to which he first communicated his most important discoveries.

All subjects seem to have been discussed by the Oxford club except theology and politics, which were becoming a little too exciting for philosophic treatment. Wren was in the fullest sympathy with the new scientific spirit, and during all the contention between king and Parliament he and his friends were quietly developing the science which was to change the face of the world, and finally make such wasteful wars impossible. A mere catalogue of Christopher Wren's conjectures, experiments, and inventions, made while he was an Oxford student, would more than fill the space I have at command.

At the age of twenty-four he was offered a professorship of astronomy at Oxford, which he modestly declined as being above his age, but afterwards accepted. His own astronomy was sadly deficient, for he supposed the circumference of our earth to be 216,000 miles. This, however, was before Sir Isaac Newton had published the true astronomy, or had himself learned it.

After a most honorable career as teacher of science at Oxford, he received from the restored king, Charles II., the appointment of assistant to the Surveyor General of Works, an office which placed him in charge of public buildings in course of construction. It made him, in due time, the architect-general of England, and it was in that capacity that he designed and superintended very many of the long series of works mentioned above. There never was a more economical appointment. The salary which he drew from the king appears to have been two hundred pounds a year, a sum equal perhaps to four thousand of our present dollars. Such was the modest compensation of the great architect who rebuilt London after the great fire.

That catastrophe occurred a few years after his appointment. The fire continued to rage for nearly four days, during which it destroyed eighty-nine churches including St. Paul's, thirteen thousand two hundred houses, and laid waste four hundred streets.

Christopher Wren was then thirty-five years of age. He promptly exhibited to the king a plan for rebuilding the city, which proposed the widening and straightening of the old streets, suggested a broad highway along the bank of the river, an ample space about St. Paul's, and many other improvements which would have saved posterity a world of trouble and expense. The government of the dissolute Charles was neither wise enough nor strong enough to carry out the scheme, and Sir Christopher was obliged to content himself with a sorry compromise.

The rest of his life was spent in rebuilding the public edifices, his chief work being the great cathedral. Upon that vast edifice he labored for thirty-five years. When the first stone of it was laid, his son Christopher was a year old. It was that son, a man of thirty-six, who placed the last stone of the lantern above the dome, in the presence of the architect, the master builder, and a number of masons. This was in the year 1710. Sir Christopher lived thirteen years longer, withdrawn from active life in the country. Once a year, however, it was his custom to visit the city, and sit for a while under the dome of the cathedral. He died peacefully while dozing in his arm-chair after dinner, in 1723, aged ninety-two years, having lived one of the most interesting and victorious lives ever enjoyed by a mortal.

If the people of London are proud of what was

done by Sir Christopher Wren, they lament perhaps still more what he was not permitted to do. They are now attempting to execute some of his plans. Miss Lucy Phillimore, his biographer, says : —

" Wren laid before the king and Parliament a model of the city as he proposed to build it, with full explanations of the details of the design. The street leading up Ludgate Hill, instead of being the confined, winding approach to St. Paul's that it now is, even its crooked picturesqueness marred by the Viaduct that cuts all the lines of the cathedral, gradually widened as it approached St. Paul's, and divided itself into two great streets, ninety feet wide at the least, which ran on either side of the cathedral, leaving a large open space in which it stood. Of the two streets, one ran parallel with the river until it reached the Tower, and the other led to the Exchange, which Wren meant to be the centre of the city, standing in a great piazza, to which ten streets each sixty feet wide converged, and around which were placed the Post-Office, the Mint, the Excise Office, the Goldsmiths' Hall, and the Insurance, forming the outside of the piazza. The smallest streets were to be thirty feet wide, ' excluding all narrow, dark alleys without thoroughfares, and courts.'

" The churches were to occupy commanding positions along the principal thoroughfares, and to be ' designed according to the best forms for capacity

24

and hearing, adorned with useful porticoes and lofty ornamental towers and steeples in the greater parishes. All church yards, gardens, and unnecessary vacuities, and all trades that use great fires or yield noisome smells to be placed out of town.'

" He intended that the church yards should be carefully planted and adorned, and be a sort of girdle round the town, wishing them to be an ornament to the city, and also a check upon its growth. To burials within the walls of the town he strongly objected, and the experience derived from the year of the plague confirmed his judgment. No gardens or squares are mentioned in the plan, for he had provided, as he thought, sufficiently for the healthiness of the town by his wide streets and numerous open spaces for markets. Gardening in towns was an art little considered in his day, and contemporary descriptions show us that ' vacuities ' were speedily filled with heaps of dust and refuse.

" The London bank of the Thames was to be lined with a broad quay along which the halls of the city companies were to be built, with suitable warehouses in between for the merchants' to vary the effect of the edifices. The little stream whose name survives in *Fleet* Street was to be brought to light, cleansed, and made serviceable as a canal one hundred and twenty feet wide, running much in the line of the present Holborn Viaduct."

These were the wise and large thoughts of a great citizen for the metropolis of his country.

But the king was Charles II. ! Our race produces good citizens in great numbers, and great citizens not a few, but the supreme difficulty of civilization is to get a few such where they can direct and control.

SIR JOHN RENNIE,

ENGINEER

———◆———

ONE of the most striking city scenes in the world
is the view of London as you approach London
Bridge in one of the small, low-decked steamers
which ply upon the Thames. London stands where
navigation for sea-going vessels ceases on this famous stream, which is crossed at London, within
a stretch of three or four miles, by about fifteen
bridges, of which seven or eight can be seen at one
view under the middle arch of London Bridge.

Over all these bridges there is a ceaseless tide of
human life, and in the river below, besides long
lines of ships at anchor and unloading, there are as
many steam-vessels, barges, skiffs, and wherries as
can find safe passage. A scene more animated,
picturesque, and grand is nowhere else presented,
especially when the great black dome of St. Paul's
is visible, hanging over it, appearing to be suspended in the foggy atmosphere like a black balloon, the cathedral itself being invisible.

Three of these bridges were built by the engineers, father and son, whose name appears at the

head of this article, and those three are among the
most wonderful structures of their kind. One of
these is London Bridge ; another is called Southwark, and the third, Waterloo. The time may
come when the man who builds bridges will be as
celebrated as the man who batters them down with
cannon ; but, at present, for one person who knows
the name of Sir John Rennie there are a thousand who are familiar with Wellington and Waterloo.

He had, however, a pedigree longer than that of
some lords. His father was a very great engineer
before him, and that father acquired his training
in practical mechanics under a Scotch firm of ma-
chinists and mill-wrights which dates back to the
reign of Charles the Second. It is to be particularly noted that both John Rennie, the elder, and
Sir John, his son, derived an important part of
their education in the work-shop and model-room.
Both of them, indeed, had an ideal education ; for
they enjoyed the best theoretical instruction which
their age and country could furnish, and the best
practical training also. Theory and practice went
hand in hand. While the intellect was nourished,
the body was developed, the hand acquired skill,
and the eyesight, certainty. It is impossible to imagine a better education for a young man than for
him to receive instruction at Edinburgh University under the illustrious Professor Black, and afterwards a training in practical mechanics under

Andrew Meikle, one of the best mechanics then living. This was the fortunate lot of Rennie's father, who wisely determined that his son should have the same advantage.

When the boy had passed through the preparatory schools, the question arose, whether he should be sent to one of the universities, or should go at once into the workshop. His father frequently said that the real foundation of civil engineering is mechanics, theoretical and practical. He did not believe that a young man could become an engineer by sitting in a class-room and hearing lectures; but that he must be placed in contact with realities, with materials, with tools, with men, with difficulties, make mistakes, achieve successes, and thus acquire the blended boldness and caution which mark the great men in this profession. It is a fact that the greatest engineers of the past century, whatever else they may have had or lacked, were thoroughly versed in practical mechanics. Smeaton, Telford, Arkwright, Hargreaves, George Stephenson, Rennie, were all men who, as they used to say, had "an ounce of theory to a pound of practice."

Young Rennie worked eight hours a day in the practical part of his profession, and spent four in the acquisition of science and the modern languages, aided in both by the first men in London in their branches. Four or five years of this training gave him, as he says in his autobiography, the

" *rudiments* " of his profession. His father next determined to give him some experience in bearing responsibility, and placed him as an assistant to the resident-engineer of Waterloo Bridge, then in course of construction. He was but nineteen years of age; but, being the son of the head of the firm, he was naturally deferred to and prepared to take the lead. Soon after, the Southwark Bridge was begun, which the young man superintended daily at every stage of its construction.

English engineers regard this bridge as the *ne plus ultra* of bridge-building. A recent writer speaks of it as " confessedly unrivaled as regards its colossal proportions, its architectural effect, or the general simplicity and massive character of its details." It crosses the river by three arches, of which the central one has a span of two hundred and forty feet, and it is built at a place where the river at high tide is thirty-six feet deep. The cost of this bridge was four millions of dollars, and it required five years to build it. The bridge is of iron, and contains a great many devices originated by the young engineer, and sanctioned by his father. It was he also who first, in recent times, learned how to transport masses of stone of twenty-five tons weight, used for the foundation of bridges.

Having thus become an accomplished engineer, his wise old father sent him on a long tour, which lasted more than two years, in the course of which he inspected all the great works, both of the ancients and moderns, in Europe, and the more accessible parts of Africa and Asia. Returning home, the death of his father suddenly placed upon his shoulders the most extensive and difficult engineering business in Great Britain. But with such a training, under such a father, and inheriting so many traditional methods, he proved equal to the position, continued the great works begun by his father, and carried them on to successful completion.

His father had already convinced the government that the old London Bridge could never be made sufficient for the traffic, or unobstructive to the navigation. A bridge has existed at this spot since the year 928, and some of the timbers of the original structure were still sound in 1824, when work upon the new bridge was begun.

Thirty firms competed for the contract for building the new London Bridge, but it was awarded to the Rennies, under whose superintendence it was built. The bridge is nine hundred and twenty-eight feet in length, and has five arches. In this structure although utility was the first consideration, there in an elegant solidity of design which makes it pleasing and impressive in the highest degree. The rapid stream is as little obstructed as the circumstances admitted, and there does not appear to be in the bridge an atom of superfluous material. London Bridge is, I suppose, the most crowded thoroughfare in the world. Twenty-five thousand vehicles cross it daily, as well as countlesss multitudes of foot-passengers. So great is the throng, that there is a project now on foot to widen it. In 1831, when it was formally opened by King William IV., the great engineer was knighted, and he was in consequence ever after called Sir John Rennie.

During the period of railroad building, Sir John Rennie constructed a great many remarkable works, particularly in Portugal and Sweden. We have lately heard much of the disappointment of young engineers whom the cessation in the construction of railroads has thrown out of business. Perhaps no profession suffered more from the dull times than this. Sir John Rennie explains the matter in his autobiography : —

"In 1844," he tells us, "the demand for engineering surveyors and assistants was very great. Engineering was considered to be the only profession where immense wealth and fame were to be acquired, and consequently everybody became engineers. It was not the question whether they were educated for it, or competent to undertake it, but simply whether any person chose to dub himself engineer ; hence lawyers' clerks, surgeons' apprentices, merchants, tradesmen, officers in the army and navy, private gentlemen, left their professions and became engineers. The consequence was that innumerable blunders were made and vast sums of money were recklessly expended."

It was much the same in the United States; and hence a good many of these gentlemen have been obliged to find their way back to the homelier occupations which they rashly abandoned. But in our modern world a thoroughly trained engineer, like Sir John Rennie, will always be in request; for man's conquest of the earth is still most incomplete; and I do not doubt that the next century will far outdo this in the magnitude of its engineering works, and in the external changes wrought by the happy union of theory and practice in such men as Telford, Stephenson, and Rennie.

Sir John Rennie spent the last years of his life in writing his Memoirs, a most interesting and useful work, recently published in London, which, I hope, will be republished here. It is just the book for a young fellow who has an ambition to gain honor by serving mankind in a skillful and manly way. Sir John Rennie, like his father before him, and like all other great masters of men, was constantly attentive to the interests and feelings of those who assisted him. He was a wise and considerate employer; and the consequence was, that he was generally served with loyal and affectionate fidelity. He died in 1874, aged eighty years.

SIR MOSES MONTEFIORE.

WE still deal strangely with the Jews. While at one end of Europe an Israelite scarcely dares show himself in the streets for fear of being stoned and abused, in other countries of the same continent we see them prime ministers, popular authors, favorite composers of music, capitalists, philanthropists, to whom whole nations pay homage.

Sir Moses Montefiore, though an English baronet, is an Israelite of the Israelites, connected by marriage and business with the Rothschilds, and a sharer in their wonderful accumulations of money. His hundredth birthday was celebrated in 1883 at his country-house on the English coast, and celebrated in such a way as to make the festival one of the most interesting events of the year. The English papers tell us that nearly a hundred telegrams of congratulation and benediction reached the aged man in the course of the day, from America, Africa, Asia, and all parts of Europe, from Christians, Jews, Mahomedans, and men of the world. The telegraph offices, we are told, were clogged during the morning with these messages, some of which were of great length, in foreign languages and in strange alphabets, such as the Arabic and Hebrew. Friends in England sent him addresses in the English manner, several of which were beautifully written upon parchment and superbly mounted. The railroad passing near his house conveyed to him by every train during the day presents of rare fruit and beautiful flowers. The Jews in Spain and Portugal forwarded presents of the cakes prepared by orthodox Jews for the religious festival which occurred on his birthday. Indeed, there has seldom been in Europe such a widespread and cordial recognition of the birthday of any private citizen.

Doubtless, the remarkable longevity of Sir Moses had something to do with emphasizing the celebration. Great wealth, too, attracts the regard of mankind. But there are many rich old Jews in the world whose birthday excites no enthusiasm. The briefest review of the long life of Sir Moses Montefiore will sufficiently explain the almost universal recognition of the recent anniversary.

He was born as long ago as 1784, the second year of American independence, when William Pitt was prime minister of England. He was five years old when the Bastille was stormed, and thirty-one when the battle of Waterloo was fought. He was in middle life before England had become wise enough to make Jew and Christian equal before the law, and thus attract to her shores one of

the most gifted and one of the most virtuous of
races.

The father of Sir Moses lived and died in one
of the narrow old streets near the centre of London
called Philpot Lane, where he became the father
of an old-fashioned family of seventeen children.
This prolific parent was a man of no great wealth,
and consequently his eldest son, Moses, left school
at an early age, and was apprenticed to a London
firm of provision dealers. He was a singularly
handsome young man, of agreeable manners and
most engaging disposition, circumstances which led
to his entering the Stock Exchange. This was at
a time when only twelve Jewish brokers were allowed to carry on business in London, and he was
one of the twelve.

At the age of twenty-eight he had fully entered
upon his career, a broker and a married man, his
wife the daughter of Levy Cohen, a rich and
highly cultivated Jewish merchant. His wife's
sister had married N. M. Rothschild, and one of
his brothers married Rothschild's sister. United
thus by marriage to the great banker, he became
also his partner in business, and this at a time
when the gains of the Rothschilds were greatest
and most rapid.

Most readers remember how the Rothschilds
made their prodigious profits during the last years
of Bonaparte's reign. They had a pigeon express
at Dover, by means of which they obtained the

first correct news from the continent. During the
"Hundred Days," for example, such a panic prevailed in England that government bonds were
greatly depressed. The first rumors from Waterloo were of defeat and disaster, which again reduced consols to a panic price. The Rothschilds,
notified of the victory a few hours sooner than
the government itself, bought largely of securities
which, in twenty-four hours, almost doubled in
value. Moses Montefiore, sharing in these transactions, found himself at forty-five a millionaire.

Instead of slaving away in business to the end
of his life, adding million to million, with the risk
of losing all at last, he took the wise resolution of
retiring from business and devoting the rest of his
life to works of philanthropy.

When Queen Victoria came to the throne in
1837, Moses Montefiore was sheriff of London.
The queen had lived near his country-house, and
had often as a little girl strolled about his park.
She now enjoyed the satisfaction of conferring
upon her neighbor the honor of knighthood, and a
few years later she made him a baronet. Thus he
became Sir Moses, which has an odd sound to us,
but which in England seems natural enough.

During the last fifty years Sir Moses has been,
as it were, a professional philanthropist. Every
good cause has shared his bounty, but he has been
most generous to poor members of his own race
and religion. He has visited seven times the Holy

Land, where the Jews have been for ages impoverished and degraded. He has directed his particular attention to improving the agriculture of Palestine, once so fertile and productive, and inducing the Jews to return to the cultivation of the soil. In that country he himself caused to be planted an immense garden, in which there are nine hundred fruit trees, made productive by irrigation. He has promoted the system of irrigation by building aqueducts, digging wells, and providing improved apparatus. He has also endowed hospitals and almshouses in that country.

In whatever part of the world, during the last fifty years, the Jews have been persecuted or distressed, he has put forth the most efficient exertions for their relief, often going himself to distant countries to convey the requisite assistance. When he was ninety-one years of age he went to Palestine upon an errand of benevolence. He has pleaded the cause of his persecuted brethren before the Emperor of Russia, and pleaded it with success. To all that part of the world known to us chiefly through the Jews he has been a constant and most munificent benefactor during the last half century, while never turning a deaf ear to the cry of want nearer home.

In October he completes his hundredth year. At present (January, 1884), he reads without spectacles, hears well, stands nearly erect, although six feet three in height, and has nothing of the somnolence of old age. He drives out every day, gets up at eleven, and goes to bed at nine. His diet is chiefly milk and old port wine, with occasionally a little soup or bread and butter. He still enjoys the delights of beneficence, which are among the keenest known to mortals, and pleases himself this year by giving checks of ninety-nine pounds to benevolent objects, a pound for each year that he has had the happiness of living.

MARQUIS OF WORCESTER,

INVENTOR OF THE STEAM-ENGINE.

⸺◆⸺

In the English county of Monmouthshire, near Wales, a region of coal mines and iron works, there are the ruins of Raglan Castle, about a mile from a village of the same name. To these ruins let pilgrims repair who delight to visit places where great things began; for here once dwelt the Marquis of Worcester, who first made steam work for men. The same family still owns the site; as indeed it does the greater part of the county; the head of the family being now styled the Duke of Beaufort. The late Lord Raglan, commander of the English forces in the Crimea, belonged to this house, and showed excellent taste in selecting for his title a name so interesting. Perhaps, however, he never thought of the old tower of Raglan Castle, which is still marked and indented where the second Marquis of Worcester set up his steam-engine two hundred and twenty years ago. Very likely he had in mind the time when the first marquis held the castle for Charles I. against the Roundheads, and baffled them for two months, though he was then eighty-five years of age. It was the son of that valiant and tough old warrior who put steam into harness, and defaced his ancestral tower with a ponderous and imperfect engine.

For many centuries before his time something had been known of the power of steam ; and the Egyptians, a century or more before Christ, had even made certain steam toys, which we find described in a manuscript written about 120 B. C., at Alexandria, by a learned compiler and inventor named Hero. One of these was in the form of a man pouring from a cup a libation to the gods. The figure stood upon an altar, and it was connected by a pipe with a kettle of water underneath. On lighting a fire under the kettle, the water was forced up through the figure, and flowed out of the cup upon the altar. Another toy was a revolving copper globe, which was kept in motion by *the escape* of steam from two little pipes bent in the same direction. Of this contrivance the French Professor Arago once wrote : —

" This was, beyond doubt, a machine in which steam engendered motion, and could produce mechanical effects. It was *a veritable steam-engine !* Let us hasten, however, to add that it bears no resemblance, either by its form or in mode of action, to steam-engines now in use."

Other steam devices are described by Hero. By one a horn was blown, and by another figures were made to dance upon an altar. But there is no trace in the ancient world of the application of steam to an important useful purpose. Professor Thurston of Hoboken, in his excellent work upon the " History of the Steam-Engine," has gleaned from the literature of the last seven hundred years several interesting allusions to the nature and power of steam. In 1125 there was, it appears, at Rheims in France, some sort of contrivance for blowing a church organ by the aid of steam. There is an allusion, also, in a French sermon of 1571, to the awful power in volcanic eruptions of a small quantity of confined steam. There are traces of steam being made to turn a spit upon which meat was roasted. An early French writer mentions the experiment of exploding a bomb-shell nearly filled with water by putting it into a fire. In 1630 King Charles the First of England granted to David Ramseye a patent for nine different contrivances, among which were the following : —

" To raise water from low pits by fire. To make any sort of mills to go on standing waters by continual motion without help of wind, water, or horse. To make boats, ships, and barges to go against strong wind and tide. To raise water from mines and coal pits by a way never yet in use."

This was in 1630, which was about the date of the Marquis of Worcester's engine. It is possible, however, that these devices existed only in the imagination of the inventor. The marquis was then twenty-nine years of age, and as he was curious in matters of science, it is highly probable that he was acquainted with this patent, and may have conversed with the inventor.

It is strange how little we know of a man so important as the Marquis of Worcester in our modern industrial development. I believe that not one of the histories of England mentions him, and scarcely anything is known of the circumstances that led to his experimenting with steam. Living in a county of coal and iron mines, and his own property consisting very much in coal lands, his attention must of necessity have been called to the difficulties experienced by the miners in pumping the water from the deep mines. There were mines which employed as many as five hundred horses in pumping out the water, and it was a thing of frequent occurrence for a productive mine to be abandoned because the whole revenue was absorbed in clearing it of water. This inventor was perhaps the man in England who had the greatest interest in the contrivance to which in early life he turned his mind.

He was born in the year 1601, and sprung from a family whose title of nobility dated back to the fourteenth century. He is described by his English biographer as a learned, thoughtful, and studious Roman Catholic; as public - spirited and humane; as a mechanic, patient, skillful, full of resources, and quick to comprehend. He inherited a great estate, not perhaps so very productive in

money, but of enormous intrinsic value. There is
reason to believe that he began to experiment with
steam soon after he came of age. He describes
one of his experiments, probably of early date : —

" I have taken a piece of a whole cannon,
whereof the end was burst, and filled it with water
three quarters full, stopping and screwing up the
broken end, as also the touch-hole, and making a
constant fire under it. Within twenty-four hours
it burst, and made a great crack."

That the engine which he constructed was designed to pump water is shown by the very name
which he gave it, — " the water-commanding engine," — and, indeed, it was never used for any
other purpose. The plan of it was very simple,
and, without improvements, it could have answered
its purposes but imperfectly. It consisted of two
vessels from which the air was driven alternately
by the condensation of steam within them, and into
the vacuum thus created the water rushed from
the bottom of the mine. He probably had his first
machine erected before 1630, when he was still a
young man, and he spent his life in endeavors to
bring his invention into use. In doing this he
expended so large a portion of his fortune, and excited so much ridicule, that he died comparatively
poor and friendless. I think it probable, however,
that his poverty was due rather to the civil wars,
in which his heroic old father and himself were so
unfortunate as to be on the losing side. He at-

tempted to form a company for the introduction of
his machine, and when he died without having succeeded in this, his widow still persisted in the same
object, though without success.   He did, however,
make several steam-engines besides the one at Raglan Castle; engines which did actually answer the
purpose of raising water from considerable depths
in a continuous stream.   He also erected near
London a steam fountain, which he describes.

During the next century several important improvements were made in the steam-engine, but
without rendering it anything like the useful agent
which we now possess.   When James Watt began
to experiment, about the year 1760, in his little
shop near the Glasgow University, the steam-engine
was still used only for pumping water, and he soon
discovered that it wasted three fourths of the steam.
He once related to a friend how the idea of his
great improvement, that of saving the waste by a
condenser, occurred to his mind.   He was then a
poor mechanic living upon fourteen shillings a
week.

" I had gone to take a walk," he said, " on a fine
Sabbath afternoon.   I had entered the Green by
the gate at the foot of Charlotte Street, and had
passed the old washing-house.   I was thinking upon
the engine at the time, and had gone as far as the
herd's house, when the idea came into my mind
that, as steam was an elastic body, it would rush
into a vacuum, and, if a communication were made

between the cylinder and an exhausted vessel, it would rush into it, and might be there condensed without cooling the cylinder."

He had found it! Before he had crossed the Green, he added, "the whole thing was arranged in my mind." Since that memorable day the invention has been ever growing; for, as Professor Thurston well remarks: "Great inventions are never the work of any one mind." From Hero to Corliss is a stretch of nearly twenty centuries; during which, probably, a thousand inventive minds have contributed to make the steam-engine the exquisite thing it is to-day.

AN OLD DRY-GOODS MERCHANT'S RECOLLECTIONS.

OUR great cities have a new wonder of late years. I mean those immense dry-goods stores which we see in Paris, London, New York, Vienna, Boston, Cincinnati, Chicago, in which are displayed under one roof almost all the things worn, or used for domestic purposes, by man, woman, or child.

What a splendid and cheering spectacle the interior presents on a fine, bright day! The counters a tossing sea of brilliant fabrics; crowds of ladies moving in all directions; the clerks, well-dressed and polite, exhibiting their goods; the cash-boys flying about with money in one hand and a bundle in the other; customers streaming in at every door; and customers passing out, with the satisfied air of people who have got what they want. It gives the visitor a cheerful idea of abundance to see such a provision of comfortable and pleasant things brought from every quarter of the globe.

An old dry-goods merchant of London, now nearly ninety, and long ago retired from business with a large fortune, has given his recollections of

business in the good old times. There is a periodical, called the "Draper's Magazine," devoted to
the dry-goods business, and it is in this that some
months ago he told his story.

When he was a few months past thirteen, being
stout and large for his age, he was placed in a London dry-goods store, as boy of all work. No wages
were given him. At that time the clerks in stores
usually boarded with their employer. On the first
night of his service, when it was time to go to bed,
he was shown a low, truckle bedstead, under the
counter, made to pull out and push in. He did
not have even this poor bed to himself, but shared
it with another boy in the store. On getting up in
the morning, instead of washing and dressing for
the day, he was obliged to put on some old clothes,
take down the shutters of the store, — which were
so heavy he could hardly carry them, — then clean
the brass signs and the outside of the shop windows, leaving the inside to be washed by the older
clerks. When he had done this, he was allowed
to go up stairs, wash himself, dress for the day,
and to eat his breakfast. Then he took his place
behind the counter.

We think it wrong for boys under fourteen to
work ten hours a day. But in the stores of the
olden time, both boys and men worked from fourteen to sixteen hours a day, and nothing was
thought of it. This store, for example, was opened
soon after eight in the morning, and the shutters

were not put up till ten in the evening.   There
was much work to do after the store was closed;
and the young men, in fact, were usually released
from labor about a *quarter past eleven.*   On Saturday nights the store closed at twelve o'clock, and
it was not uncommon for the young men to be employed in putting away the goods until between
two and three on Sunday morning.

" There used to be," the old gentleman records,
" a supper of hot beafsteaks and onions, and por-
ter, which we boys used to relish immensely, and
eat and drink a good deal more of both than was
good for us."

After such a week's work one would think the
clerks would have required rest on Sunday.   But
they did not get much.   The store was open from
eight until church time, which was then eleven
o'clock; and this was one of the most profitable
mornings of the week.   The old gentleman explains why it was so.   Almost all factories, shops,
and stores were then kept open very late, and the
last thing done in them was to pay wages, which
was seldom accomplished until after midnight.
Hence the apparent necessity for the Sunday morning's business.

Another great evil mentioned by our chronicler
grew out of this bad system of all work and no
play.   The clerks, released from business towards
midnight, were accustomed to go to a tavern and
spend part of the night in drinking and carousing;

reeling home at a late hour, much the worse for drink, and unfit for business in the morning until they had taken another glass. All day the clerks were in the habit of slipping out without their hats to the nearest tap-room for beer.

Nor was the system very different in New York. An aged book-keeper, to whom I gave an outline of the old gentleman's narrative, informs me that forty years ago the clerks, as a rule, were detained till very late in the evening, and often went from the store straight to a drinking-house.

Now let us see how it fared with the public who depended upon these stores for their dry-goods. From our old gentleman's account it would seem that every transaction was a sort of battle between the buyer and seller to see which should cheat the other. On the first day of his attendance he witnessed a specimen of the mode in which a dexterous clerk could sell an article to a lady which she did not want. An unskillful clerk had displayed too suddenly the entire stock of the goods of which she was in search; upon which she rose to leave, saying that there was nothing she liked. A more experienced salesman then stepped up.

" Walk this way, madam, if you please, and I will show you something entirely different, with which I am sure you will be quite delighted."

He took her to the other end of the store, and then going back to the pile which she had just rejected, snatched up several pieces, and sold her one of them almost immediately. Customers, the old merchant says, were often bullied into buying things they did not want.

"Many a half-frightened girl," he remarks, "have I seen go out of the shop, the tears welling up into her eyes, and saying, 'I am sure I shall never like it:' some shawl or dress having been forced upon her contrary to her taste or judgment."

The new clerk, although by nature a very honest young fellow, soon became expert in all the tricks of the trade. It was the custom then for employers to allow clerks a reward for selling things that were particularly unsalable, or which required some special skill or impudence in the seller. For example, they kept on hand a great supply of what they were pleased to call "remnants," which were supposed to be sold very cheap; and as the public of that day had a passion for remnants, the master of the shop took care to have them made in sufficient numbers. There were heaps of remnants of linen, and it so *happened* that the remnants were exactly long enough for a shirt, or some other garment. Any clerk who could push off one of these remnants upon a customer was allowed a penny or twopence as a reward for his talent; and there were certain costly articles, such as shawls and silks of unsalable patterns, upon which there was a premium of several shillings for selling.

There was one frightfully ugly shawl which had hung fire so long that the master of the shop offered a reward of eight shillings (two dollars) to any one who should sell it at the full price, which was twenty dollars. Our lad covered himself with glory one morning, by selling this horrid old thing. A sailor came in to buy a satin scarf for a present. The boy saw his chance.

"As you want something for a present," said he to the sailor, "would you not like to give something really useful and valuable that would last for years?"

In three minutes the sailor was walking out of the store, happy enough, with the shawl under his arm, and the sharp youth was depositing the price thereof in the money-drawer. Very soon he had an opportunity of assisting to gull the public on a great scale. His employer bought out the stock of an old-fashioned dry-goods store in another part of the town for a small sum; upon which he determined to have a grand "selling off." To this end he filled the old shop with all his old, faded, unsalable goods, besides looking around among the wholesale houses and picking up several cart-loads of cheap lots, more or less damaged.

The whole town was flooded with bills announcing this selling off of the old established store, at which many goods could be obtained at less than half the original cost. As this was then a comparatively new trick the public were deceived by it, and it had the most astonishing success. The selling off lasted several weeks, the supply of goods being kept up by daily purchases.

Our junior clerk was an apt learner in deception
and trickery. Shortly after this experiment upon
the public credulity, a careless boy lighting the
lamps in the window (for this was before the introduction of gas) set some netting on fire, causing
a damage of a few shillings, the fire being almost
instantly extinguished. As business had been a
little dull, the junior clerk conceived the idea of
turning the conflagration to account. Going up
to his employer, and pointing to the singed articles,
he said to him : —

"Why not have a selling off here, and clear out
all the stock damaged by fire?"

The master laughed at the enormity of the joke,
but instantly adopted the suggestion, and in the
course of a day or two, flaming posters announced
the awful disaster and the sale. In preparing for
this event, the clerks applied lighted paper to the
edges of whole stacks of goods, slightly discolored
the tops of stockings, and in fact, they singed to
such an extent as almost to cause a real conflagration. During these night operations a great deal
of beer was consumed, and the whole effect of the
manœuvre was injurious and demoralizing to every
clerk in the store.

This sale also was ridiculously successful. A
mob surrounded the doors before they were opened,
and to keep up the excitement some low-priced
goods were ostentatiously sold much below cost.
Such was the rush of customers that at noon the

young men were exhausted by the labor of selling; the counters were a mere litter of tumbled dry-goods; and the shop had to be closed for a while for rest and putting things in order. To keep up the excitement, the master and his favorite junior clerk rode about London in hackney coaches, in search of any cheap lots that would answer their purpose.

In the course of time, this clerk, who was at heart an honest, well-principled fellow, grew ashamed of all this trickery and fraud, and when at length he set up in business for himself, he adopted the principle of " one price and no abatement." He dealt honorably with all his customers, and thus founded one of the great dry-goods houses of London.

Two things saved him : first, he loathed drinking and debauchery; secondly, he was in the habit of reading.

The building up of the huge establishments, to which some persons object, has nearly put an end to the old system of guzzling, cheating, and lying. The clerks in these great stores go to business at eight o'clock in the morning, and leave at six in the evening, with an interval for dinner. They work all day in a clean and pleasant place, and they are neither required or allowed to lie or cheat. A very large establishment must be conducted honestly, or it cannot long go on. Its very largeness *compels* an adherence to truth and fact.

WHY BUSINESSMEN
NEED A PHILOSOPHY
OF CAPITALISM

BY

ADAM STARCHILD

Capitalism has built the modern world. Although there are some who would dispute that claim, it is clear, at least for those who examine the facts without bias or political intent, that economies based on capitalism are stronger and expand at a faster rate than other economic systems. This fact has been well established throughout history.

At its simplest and purest, capitalism is an economic system in which private individuals and companies produce and exchange goods and services through free markets. Ideally, capitalism is not hindered by governmental controls; in reality, however, there are many shades and nuances of capitalism that result in economic systems that are often described as a *mixed economy*. In some lands, capitalism is restrained by laws and governmental regulations; the degree determined by political and social objectives. Many political leaders hope to influence their people via the economy, they may attempt to protect domestic business from foreign competition, or they may try to increase revenue with tariffs or export duties. That these types of objectives usually only hinder economic activity over the long term is frequently ignored, lost in the rhetoric about social considerations and goals.

Of the many factors that can affect how the capitalist spirit develops in a country, one which is often overlooked is that of entrepreneurship. In lands where capitalism is unfettered by unnecessary regulation and where entrepreneurship is dynamic, impressive economic gains and advancements can be expected. Entrepreneurship is perhaps one of the greatest driving forces of capitalism. Indeed, the two are inseparable.

Capitalism is an economic system in which the means of production and distribution are privately owned and operated, and an entrepreneur is an individual who undertakes to start and conduct a business. Entrepreneurs propel capitalism forward. The bottom line here is quite clear: if a person is restricted in his ownership of a business through governmental regulations or social constraints, why should he or she risk starting any economic enterprise? Conversely, if an individual perceives that his or her efforts will be the overall deciding factor in economic gain or loss, he or she is more likely to risk investment in a business venture.

The world has seen many different economic systems throughout history. With its origins deep in the mists of ancient societies, barter was one of the first economies in which individuals and groups exchanged goods and services, paying for one commodity with another. Rudimentary forms of capitalism were not far behind and their origins are likewise obscure. Capitalism is generally thought to have arisen in various places around the world, gained prominence in old Europe centuries ago where it developed slowly and gradually spread through most of the world, reaching its zenith during the 19th century and remaining dominant until World War I. For a time during the 20th century, communism, a system in which the state plays a major role in economic ownership, regulation, and intervention, challenged capitalism's dominance, particularly in the Eastern Hemisphere, but as the century ended, capitalism, in one form of another, has re-emerged as the world's premier economic system.

The effect of capitalism extends far beyond economics, however, for capitalism is a major factor in the evolution of nations. Virtually every great nation through history has been a potent economic power as well. An excellent example of this in the 20th century is the ascendance of the Soviet Union as a world power after World War II. For a time the Soviet Union, founded on communism, seemed ready to challenge the United States for world military, cultural, and economic supremacy, but their threat was short-lived. While some observers of the world scene argue that it was American President Ronald Reagan's hard-line military stance against the Soviet Union that led to the eventual breakup and dissolution of that communist state, it was American economic power, based on capitalism, that provided Reagan with the foundation on which he could make his stand. Communism could not keep pace with America's economic strength. Reagan's policies also have led to the People's Republic of China slowly but steadily turning to capitalism to enhance their economy. Mainland China's appreciation of capitalism is well illustrated with the reversion of Hong Kong – one of the world's greatest free-market success stories – to Mainland control and the pledge of the Chinese government not to tamper with Hong Kong's economy, a promise the Chinese have honored.

The resurgence of capitalism at the end of the 20th century has been driven by a powerful tide of entrepreneurship in the technology sector, most apparent in the explosive growth of the Internet, and has led to spectacular economic gains. E-commerce (electronic commerce) is without question changing the way the world does business, and it can easily be termed E-capitalism.

We are in a period in which economic opportunity has seldom been greater. As technology and the Internet continue to advance, every business or enterprise that can benefit from them has the opportunity to advance as well. Ten years ago, few of the top Internet companies had even been imagined. Ten years ago, we were only on the verge of the new capitalist economy that, while built on the old principles of capitalism, is immeasurably enhanced by technological know-how. Ten years ago, traditional businesses were still the norm. And now, new ideas are giving rise to new companies every day. The businesses, services, and companies that may dominate the economic landscape ten years from now are still in the formulation stages of their creators. The opportunities for entrepreneurs are perhaps greater than ever.

Certainly we are witnessing the coming of a new economic age in which those individuals and companies that produce the goods and services that satisfy the needs of a modern, fast-paced world will be the most successful. Technology permits customers to buy the items or services they desire with a mere click of a mouse. Individuals who embrace the spirit of the entrepreneur and who are able to ascertain the needs of potential customers stand to benefit handsomely.

After all, entrepreneurs have been creating and running businesses since primitive times. Going back to the earliest societies, farmers, fisherman, and merchants traded their goods and services. Every business that exists today at one time was the dream and ambition of an entrepreneur. The entrepreneur is the visionary, the man or woman with the better idea, the innovator, the doer. It is the entrepreneur who creates the original product, acquires the facilities and materials, obtains the capital, assembles the workforce, and brings the finished product to market. It is also the entrepreneur who reaps the profits of a successful venture. In the case of failure, the entrepreneur stands to take the major loss.

Capitalism and entrepreneurship are closely linked. Capitalism is the economic system most conducive to entrepreneurship, and entrepreneurship provides the innovation and energy of capitalism. Each sustains and gains strength from the other, together forming a solid bedrock for economic activity.

While opportunity for entrepreneurs is present in the most advanced economies, clearly developing economies offer the greatest opportunities because of their nature, which usually includes a rapidly growing middle class with a strong desire for consumer products. As companies attempt to meet the needs of these new consumers, entrepreneurs are likely to find countless opportunities. In advanced nations new products and services are typically brought to market by major corporations that maintain huge staffs, whose primary purpose is the design and creation of new products. In smaller, developing nations, however, niche markets and special needs present an environment that is ripe for innovation. In many of these nations, governments may actively support entrepreneurs through a variety of special programs, including tax incentives, special trade status, and an assortment of grants, to encourage investment and economic activity. The leaders of such governments are aware that entrepreneurs energize capitalism, which in turn leads to economic growth.

As the global economy continues to expand, world trade will undoubtedly increase. At the same time, because of the growing role of technology, boundaries between nations and markets will shrink, providing entrepreneurs will marvelous opportunities, limited only by their own imaginations. The world is entering a rare and wonderful environment for the entrepreneur.

ABOUT THE AUTHOR:

Over the past 25 years, Adam Starchild has been the author of over two dozen books, and hundreds of magazine articles, primarily on business and finance. His articles have appeared in a wide range of publications around the world -- including Business Credit, Euromoney, Finance, The Financial Planner, International Living, Offshore Financial Review, Reason, Tax Planning International, The Bull & Bear, Trust & Estates, and many more.

Now semi-retired, he was the president of an international consulting group specializing in banking, finance and the development of new businesses, and director of a trust company.

Although this formidable testimony to expertise in his field, plus his current preoccupation with other books-in-progress, would not seem to leave time for a well-rounded existence, Starchild has won two Presidential Sports Awards and written several cookbooks, and is currently involved in a number of personal charitable projects.

His personal website is at http://www.adamstarchild.com/